FAITH *without* FEAR

Risky choices facing contemporary Christians

KEITH MASCORD

WIPF & STOCK · Eugene, Oregon

Wipf and Stock Publishers
199 W 8th Ave, Suite 3
Eugene, OR 97401

Faith Without Fear
Risky Choices Facing Contemporary Christians
By Mascord, Keith
Copyright©2016 by Mascord, Keith
ISBN 13: 978-1-4982-9360-0
Publication date 3/2/2016
Previously published by Morning Star Publishing, 2016

FAITH *without* FEAR

Risky choices facing contemporary Christians

This is a powerful and arresting book. It is easy to read, with many poignant human narratives. Keith Mascord shows the dangerous error of adhering blindly to notions of the inerrancy of the Bible, literally understood. Approached in this way, many of its words and stories cannot be reconciled with objective facts, or with contemporary perceptions of universal human dignity for all, including slaves, women and homosexuals. Yet far from destroying the central divine message of Jesus, Mascord demonstrates that the only path to the survival of Christianity in an age of growing atheism is one that accepts the necessity of courage to rethink unscientific, patriarchal and homophobic ways, even at the risk of accelerating the emptying of churches, as congregants yearn for clear, unbending rules. Mascord explains that rationality, truthfulness and the love of God are the ingredients essential to efforts to revive Christianity in countries in steep religious decline, such as Australia. His is a message for all Christians everywhere – but particularly for evangelical Protestants as they approach the 500th anniversary of Martin Luther's fateful Reformation.

The Hon Michael Kirby,
Sydney Anglican and past Justice of the High Court of Australia

A must read for those who struggle with biblical literalism, inerrancy of Scripture, male headship and anti-homosexuality stances within their Christian denomination; and an invaluable resource for those in dialogue with friends or relatives holding such views. After many years teaching within this tradition exemplified by the Sydney Anglicans, but now outside it, Mascord respectfully explains the assumptions, beliefs and concerns, and offers nuanced critiques of how these stances are problematic today. Advocating Jesus' example of love and compassion over outdated doctrines and biblical interpretation, Mascord encourages both humility to admit uncertainty and courage to challenge what needs to change. This invaluable gift is a number one recommendation from me for 2016.

Dr Val Webb
..is an Australian theologian and author of eleven books including 'In Defence of Doubt: an invitation to adventure' and 'Testing Tradition and Liberating Theology: finding your own voice.'

Keith Mascord grew up a conservative evangelical, believing that the Bible's every word had to be taken literally. He lost his literalism, but not his faith, and wrote this warm, wise and accessible book for others on a similar path.

Professor Marion Maddox,
Macquarie University, Sydney

This well written book may provoke disquiet and make the theologically acute reader question her assumptions and long-held theological convictions. But if, like me, you are enthralled by gospel engagement with our mostly secularised world, then *Faith without Fear* is sure to stimulate you to re-think some of the most important and pressing questions facing today's faith communities.

Dr Lindsay Stoddart,
former Archdeacon of Wollongong, Anglican Diocese of Sydney,
former Dean of Hobart, Anglican Diocese of Tasmania

If your faith journey starts in the zone of Reformed Calvinism, as has mine, the path to a confident faith free of addiction to inerrancy, and toward the freedom to live fully in, and to be continuously amazed at, the transformative power of the unconditional love of a God beyond our knowing, takes a path through the issues and questions and challenges raised by this book. The truth that sets us free comes from science, shared experience, and a vital faith in the God to whose love the Bible bears witness. This book takes the reader on such a journey boldly, faithfully, and with the promise of transformation by a gospel set free to do its work.

Professor, the Reverend Gary D Bouma AM;
Monash University and St Johns Anglican Church, East Malvern

A lot of people are disillusioned by the obvious moral failings of today's church and are frustrated with the lack of intellectual integrity evidenced by its leadership. Keith Mascord shares fully in that frustration and disillusionment, and is willing to discuss these matters openly. Those who are looking for simple answers to the church's problems won't find them in this book, but they will find someone there who is willing to struggle with them in attempting to find an honest way forward.

Father Dave Smith,
minister of Holy Trinity Anglican Dulwich Hill

Keith Mascord has written a truly unique book. He has tackled the bogey of biblical literalism as one who was once in its thrall. He knows its power, and the ways in which it is exercised in this country and beyond. From his own experience, he is able to demolish it, with insider knowledge and insight, yet always with the deepest respect and courtesy for its contemporary protagonists. *Faith Without Fear* is a 'must read' for all Australian Anglicans.

Dr Muriel Porter OAM,
author and Anglican laywoman

Contents

This book is dedicated to the memory of
Bishop John McIntyre

A courageous and much loved advocate for
Australia's first peoples, women, gays and those seeking asylum
A much missed friend

Foreword

Perhaps the greatest disadvantage of ageing is that you have endless time to read. Your days can be filled with books and articles and research papers on a dazzling variety of themes. And in the rare moments of pause you wish you had read just a fraction of this material when you were starting your career.

The receipt of Keith's *Faith Without Fear* was one such book. His request that I write its Foreword was a great pleasure, but it also added to my discomfort. From almost the first page, I realised that he had implicitly traced my world of early to mid-life adulthood. I could sense in the play and counter play of ideas hints of my own shortcomings, misgivings, doubts and profound fear that someone would have actually seen the man I would become. That is the disturbing power of this book. I challenge you to read it with that same self-interrogation. You may find yourself there. And you may discover fresh ways of understanding faith and life-values. That was certainly my experience.

Sometimes the book troubled me. I think you will have the same reaction. Your thoughts – and the pattern of your taught faith and life – will rebel against Keith's challenges and accusations. At other times, perhaps as you read the suggestions and 'textual appropriations' of chapter 8, you may even be '*almost* persuaded.' This is not a comfortable Christian bedside book. To quote from one of my recent ageing meanders into disquieting literary territory:

> For those of us who recognise that humankind left Eden long ago – if it ever existed – counterfactuals must be considered one more tool to help us make sense of our chaotic and unordered world, where knowledge sometimes has the effect of accelerating disorder …. An avowedly interdisciplinary book aspires to a multidisciplinary readership, and I believe [this] study has something of interest to say to social scientists, historians and humanists.[1]

I apply every word of this quotation to Keith's book. I add to its reader-categories theologians, community chaplains, and ordinary men and

---

1   Richard Ned Lebow, *Forbidden Fruit: Counterfactuals and International Relations*, Princeton NJ: Princeton University Press, 2010.

women struggling to hold faith in our *chaotic and unordered world*. Keith argues counterfactually: change the conditions, read the text with a different emphasis and explore those possibilities. As soon as you attempt this you start conversing with the text.

This is a dialogue in which there are no clear winners and losers. Keith simply asks you to question your own priorities, prejudices and certainties. When he turns Bible texts on their head, he is always putting you in that dangerous place where you have to ask yourself about what and why you believe. And by the end of the book Keith will have asked you counterfactually about your own ultimate quest for God.

At times the book is highly technical, with a veritable smorgasbord of ancient and contemporary philosophers, scientists and theologians quoted and analysed. Must-read names kept distracting me to explore in fresh areas of human creativity. Almost as if he was measuring these lapses in concentration, his text would suddenly become chatty, friendly, persuasive.

Deep inside I need to know – desperately need to know – if the faith that has motivated my long life remains credible. With armchair, fireplace words, Keith settles me for conversation:

> Perhaps this book could be marketed solely for academics and theological students, for those who need to know what the scholars in their ivory towers are getting up to. Don't trouble the flock. But the fact is: the flock is being troubled. The information in this, and in all of this book's chapters, is in the public domain (Chapter 3).

He has already touched my core. Yes, I am troubled by much of what I read and see around me. I can no longer believe as easily and as clearly as once seemed possible. My own now lengthy counterfactual exploration of life and faith unsettle old certainties. Helpfully at this point, Keith underscores the importance and power of 'inquisitiveness':

> Inquisitiveness is provoked, in theology and science, when cognitive disso- nance occurs. Some piece of data doesn't quite fit one's current theory, which therefore needs to be re-thought (Chapter 7).

Throughout his book, Keith sees inquisitiveness as the basis for counterfactual argument and dissertation. If current debates on same-sex relationship trouble you, or, if at a broader place of theological interest, you need to recast your ideas about St Paul, be sure to spend quality time with Keith's elaborate and counterfactual exploration of Romans chapter 1 in chapter 7 of the book. You may not be convinced, the argument may distress you, but hopefully your inquisitive self will be energised.

But almost from the outset of reading, the book had a strange, out-of-sequence impact on me. I kept hearing echoes from another time. Behind Keith's voice I heard other voices and engaged other long ago controversies.

After twenty pages of reading, I had scribbled some comments to myself. The argument seemed to reflect hints of Reformed philosopher Alvin Plantinga. This was in the way Keith balanced theologically conservative propositions about God with his own counterfactual way of arguing. Only when my review took me to chapter 9 did Keith confirm this guess that Plantinga was a background, though secondary source.

Keith endorsed Plantinga's method of public debate, but then challenged Plantinga's Reformed theological conviction on inerrancy. Keith asks his readers to enter that large international evangelical debate on Bible authority and interpretation. His views on this may have lost him friends, but here, I think more engagingly than Plantinga, he hopes that the debate will remain civil and open to discussion:

> Much or all of what I have just now written is sure to be vigorously denied. And such a reaction is an honourable one, if it is followed by careful and persuasive argumentation in the opposite direction (Chapter 4).

He is saying powerfully, let's explore the counterfactual arguments with charity and hope. Let's re-read the Bible and historical texts through contrary questioning. This is not a book for 'soft' unreflective reading.

As you begin this exploration, you may be unaware that the refrain of a later theme has begun to play. Alvin Plantinga is a measured tune, adequate enough for the tensions of Keith's Reformed audience. But Keith is drawing on the urgencies of a wider more complex audience, for now, unheralded. Paul Ricoeur is pianissimo. The rigorous beat of his ideas will swell to full chorus in Keith's final chapters.

At this point you may want to leave this Foreword and dip into the book's themes before reading the larger text more closely. If you want some racy pugnacious style then the final paragraph of chapter 3 will be a good place to start. This briefest of reading will alert you to the close theological argument that will be ahead. If you want to dip your whole foot into the larger waters then try out chapter 4 in its entirety – but of course don't stop there. Get ready to engage the entire enthralling argument. And let me warn you ahead, until you manage the last three chapters you won't have got to the nub of the matter. At some point you will need to start at the beginning and follow *the method* of argument as closely as you will its content.

Having read the book, I feel I might offer this critique. Maybe a follow-up book or study series could shape questions and group research material. This is especially so in the light of Keith's pressing and persistent comment:

> Pretty much everything about Christianity is being questioned at the moment, and efforts to stifle healthy debate are not only likely to be abusive, they won't help in the process of finding good answers to those questions, (Chapter 7).

This book will take you on a journey across critical biblical studies in a language easy to follow and academically astute. But the text also interested me as a historian. Pause with me a moment while I set a brief fresh scene. Once long ago, I also taught at Moore College and knew Keith there as I also knew others mentioned in his text. In a way, he was reintroducing me to old colleagues. But the debate he raised pointed my historical interests in a fresh direction. In my days at Moore, I do not recall inerrancy being a central topic of much conversation. As someone who trained at Moore in the mid-1950s and still teaching there in the late 1980s, I recall an Evangelicalism still able to embrace difference on this as on many other themes and ideas – yes, even difference on atonement theory and the nature and destiny of the church.

And that brings me directly to the primary question this book began to raise for me. The old Evangelicalism had a passion to convert the world, and it permitted a passion for social justice. Some of us have stayed the course because of the urgencies it awoke. If the world needed saving, to what extent were we also 'men and women of the world' immersed in its life and circumstance? I cannot speak for the current experiences of Anglican clergy but I found Moore a place where my own ideas could expand – and on the few occasions I met with opposition I was simply able to challenge it.

Keith's text is a superb historical survey of contemporary conservative Evangelical thought – and Sydney Anglican preoccupation. It is a breathtaking insight into some of the now closed doors of Evangelical social outreach. It is a must-read for anyone interested in Australian Anglican history and the changing role of religion in Australian society.

Chapter 5 raises thorny issues that need extended discussion. Not least is the debate about the meaning of secularism. This chapter left me unsettled and with too many questions about church and society unresolved. But chapter 6 rushed me back to the centre of the Sydney Anglican camp. For people like me this is a different way of experiencing Anglicanism. Is what we experience simply a historical hiccup or is the denomination on a major downward spiral? Chapters 5 and 6 offer questions for a much more exhaustive study on the sociology of religion.

The long section in chapter 6 on same sex attraction is breathtakingly powerful, as is the critique of the Sydney Doctrine Commission *Report into Human Sexuality*, released in March 2015. If Keith's challenges are correct then the Diocese needs to open its investigations to public and scientific scrutiny.

The energy of this book changes radically with chapters 8 and 9. You begin to see here much more dynamically what motivates Keith's personal theological quest. For the first time in this study, chapter 8 introduces you to Keith's hermeneutical mentor. References to Paul Ricoeur in the first three pages of this chapter tumble over each other reflecting Keith's own insistence that:

> The object of interpretation … is to come to a deeper and more complete understanding of oneself, to come to 'self-understanding by means of understanding others.'

You achieve this by *making [your] own what is initially alien* – or what Ricoeur calls 'appropriation.' Keith is at pains to point out what you now realize has been the fundamental principle of his whole book: 'hermeneutics is the very deciphering of life in the mirror of the text.'[2] Keith's exploration of what he owns as Ricoeur's *hermeneutical arc* begins with *first naïveté*, where we engage story through a mix of belief and prejudice. As we increase in *critical engagement* we bring objectivity to bear on the story. Bible teachers

---

2   Ricoeur, 'Preface to Bultman', *Essays in Biblical Interpretation*, 53.

and theologians will often rest their case here. But this is no more than settling for rationalism.

Critical analysis, no matter how respectful and responsive, will … also create challenges as older ways of understanding the text are shown to be inadequate … To read these stories as narratives of sober fact is, more often than not, to misread them, is to not respect them for what they are, is to read into them prejudices we now need to set aside … The way forward, for Ricoeur, is the way of *appropriation*, which he describes in terms of the need for a 'second naïveté,' a coming back to the text to be challenged and transformed by it.

You reflect on this and wish that the current debates on gender, women in active ministry, and same sex relationships could have been addressed by the Evangelical leadership with more attention to a critical analysis of biblical text and a pastoral care more attuned to social transformation. When we read the Bible, as any text, 'the text's career escapes the finite horizon of its author.'[3] As reader of this book, you already know that you can own this observation immediately. It is the most obvious commentary on every text you have ever written from Facebook note to research essay. Context influences meaning and interpretation.

Here as Foreword writer rather than his reviewer I began to face my own acceptance and 'accommodation' crisis. I add this comment solely to identify with those who will have struggled with other issues raised in this book. I too have to set aside my prejudice and allow the argument to unsettle me. I must open my inquisitiveness and ask fresh questions. Now I also must shape my responses counterfactually.

The deep beauty of what follows in Keith's text is quite overwhelming. You sense here the heart-beat of a man who knows how to translate ideas into relationships. Bible reading, even at its most complex and mind-challenging is, Keith says, 'a love- driven process.'

> We must again become known for love. It is our most reliable guide in every-thing we do and think (Chapter 9).

---

3   Ricoeur, "The Model of the Text: Meaningful Action Considered as Text, *New Literary History*, 5.1, 1973, pp. 93-97.

In many respects the book might have ended here, say with a final generalised summary. Chapter 10 is both revealing and deceptive. There is the anticipated repetition and analysis. In part, we cover old ground. But steadily a theme persistently hinted at in earlier chapters begins to dominate the final pages:

> We will certainly end up with a different form of Christianity than most of us have grown up with.

You will need to read this text very carefully and not miss the threads of doubt now suggested and analysed: 'Suppose we begin to question some of our formerly cherished beliefs.' This is now not the territory of earlier chapters. 'Integrity demands of us that we are honest about what we don't know, and that we honestly pursue even uncomfortable truths … Integrity also requires a willingness to re-configure our belief system if necessary.'

After hours of close reading, here at last was the ultimate theme I had been waiting for:

> God, if God exists, appears hidden, out of sight … No sooner do we see or sense this reality called God than we are again in doubt and wonder whether what we saw was simply the inanimate shadow cast by the trees of the garden; a garden whose existence has no ultimate rhyme or reason.

This is our 21st century issue. This is our debate, captured by a growing literature from philosophy and neuroscience. A moment ago I deliberately described this chapter as 'deceptive.' I used that word not to decry any of the text's themes or inquisitive explorations, simply to say that unless we engage this question as our central concern we will only have been toying with the life and faith changing themes of this significant piece of research. When we ask who God is, we inevitably begin to ask who we are. Faith, ethics and lifestyle will focus in fresh ways.

Bill Lawton

25 July 2015

Christians Under the Pump

Christianity stands at a crossroad. Some have suggested that the challenges currently facing it are so serious and so potentially devastating that nothing short of a reformation or revolution is needed to prevent Christianity from becoming an unsustainable relic of the past. Not that Christianity will dwindle away or disappear. What is more likely is that it will cease to be a credible option for large swathes of contemporary humankind, who will feel, with some justification, that Christianity lacks sufficiently strong intellectual and moral support.

Most of the challenges facing Christianity have been around for as long as it has existed, so they are not new, nor have they been fatal in their impact thus far. Many of the challenges have emerged in the last two to four hundred years, and Christianity has managed to survive and thrive. Nevertheless, there is good reason to think that these more recent challenges, including evolutionary theory, have come to a head in forms that make it increasingly hard for people to continue to embrace Christian faith without intellectual compromise.

Two issues in particular have intensified these more recent challenges. Firstly, research casting further doubt on the Biblical notion that humankind originated with the creation of our first parents, Adam and Eve. Secondly, the hotly debated topic of homosexuality, and, most currently, the issue of same-sex marriage.

Genetic studies are confirming earlier lines of research indicating that humankind did not first exist in the Middle East as described in the Bible, but in Africa, and that our ancestors were not two first-created individuals, but rather multiple ancestors with unbroken lineage to pre-human forms of life. These findings represent an enormous challenge to conservative or traditional forms of Christianity, with wide-ranging implications for how the faith can best be understood.

The second major challenge which is proving to be just as corrosive of conservative Christian faith is homosexuality, with scientific studies increasingly suggesting that homosexuality is a biologically-based variation consistently impacting all human populations, past and present. It is not something people choose, nor is it something for which they can be condemned. Homosexuality was once considered a sin. Such rhetoric is quickly changing with the now common claim that it is homosexual *expression* which is sinful. But even this approach is increasingly being questioned, creating shock waves spreading to almost all forms of Christian faith.

The. challenges are enormous, and how Christians meet them will determine the shape of future Christianity. Throughout the West especially, and certainly here in Australia, people are deserting the faith in large numbers, particularly the young, in an exodus as large as that which occurred in the 1960s and 70s. The big question facing Christians is: can that trend be reversed? This is not just an academic question. It is a practical question facing ageing congregations who struggle to attract new and younger adherents. It is a question facing parents who observe their children voting with their feet and walking away from church, in many cases rejecting Christianity itself.

There is within the hearts of many Christians a growing fear that what they once believed might not be true, or, at least, not true in the way they once thought. Beliefs which were previously held without question are being challenged, and not just by those without Christian faith. I myself have been one of those challengers by telling the story of my own accumulating doubts in the autobiographical *A Restless Faith: Leaving Fundamentalism in a Quest for God* (2012). That book, I know, has shaken the faith of many who have read it. It has also elicited a number of angry rebuttals, mercifully just a few and mostly in private. However, people have rightly asked, 'If what you have written is correct, if those challenges to conservative or fundamentalist Christian belief are hitting the mark as successfully as you suggest, what form of Christian faith do you believe is possible? What will be the shape of your faith?' They are good questions, and, in many ways, have been the impetus for this book.

In this present work, I will attempt two things. Firstly, I will suggest some reasons why Christians, and especially those of a more conservative disposition, are fearful. A major and overarching reason for fear is the prospect of losing what is precious to us. Christians are presently fearful because a great deal of what they consider important is under threat, including long-standing understandings of marriage and gender. Many are also concerned that beliefs considered essential to the protection of the faith, such as the infallibility or inerrancy of the Bible, are being questioned, fuelling fear that the Christian faith itself might crumble. Fear is an extraordinary motivator. It can generate powerful resistance movements. It can embolden those under threat to fight back, creating casualties of themselves and others. Consequences such as these, and the challenges which have generated them, will be explored in chapters one to five.

In the second half of the book, I will attempt to at least begin an answer to the question put to me in the aftermath of writing *A Restless Faith*, 'What form of Christian faith do you see emerging or would you like to see emerge?' This book has been entitled, *Faith without Fear*. I believe that a fearless faith is possible, and that fear can give way to hope. But that can only happen if Christians find the necessary courage to acknowledge the strength of current challenges, and to respond to them with honesty, integrity and love, being humbly willing to embark on the risky process of reconfiguring their faith and lives. This will inevitably involve new explorations of gender, genetics and sexuality, with implications for the place of women and gays within the life of the church, which are major topic areas of this book.

* * *

Before launching into the book proper I would like to share two stories, two very honest and courageous stories. I do so because, as said, the issues discussed in this book are not simply academic. They are also personal and poignant, and, for many, painful and distressing, especially when the issues come close to home. The following two stories are told by a Christian couple who have chosen to remain anonymous, as has their son whose story is told later in the book, along with a postscript from his father. Their personal and theological struggles will hopefully provide a powerful introduction to a discussion of those challenges in the main body of this book.

A mother's story

All of our children are cherished, loved and of course, integral to our identity as parents. This story focuses on our experience of parenting one of those now adult children. It is written with his expressed knowledge and consent. He is our second-born son and he has two siblings.

Our son was born in the early 1980s, almost two years after his brother. His conception was very much planned and desired, the pregnancy went smoothly and his birth was an incredibly positive experience for us. As parents, we adored each other, and still do. When our son was two years old, his dad made a conscious decision to become a Christian. I already was. This was a monumental change for him because until this time, he was an adamant agnostic.

Our son was a soft, gorgeous toddler whose favourite toy was his beloved glow-worm which accompanied him everywhere. Wherever he went, people (especially teenaged girls and women) were drawn to his cheeky smile, and, as a young boy through to adulthood, he was always surrounded by admiring girls his own age. Our son always has been and continues to be creative.

As parents, we prayed for our son, and of course his brother and sister. We prayed for his future as well as his present. We prayed that God would bless him with a beautiful wife. It never occurred to us to pray for his 'partner', because at that stage we just assumed that a wife it would be! We also made a deliberate decision, very early in our parenting journey, that we would love, accept and welcome whoever (friends, acquaintances and life-long partners) our children brought home to us.

When our son was seven, we left the very small outback town where he had been born and moved to a slightly larger rural town where he lived with us until he left home at the age of 17. Our son was a mischievous child with more than a hint of rebellion. His teenage years were traumatic for us all, especially him. When he was 14, instead of going to a friend's sleepover, he 'escaped' and went with some young men to the river bank; there he was involved in a car accident and sustained serious, but not life-threatening injuries. He recovered well physically, but emotionally it was another story. It was around this time that his use of substances became evident – to our knowledge this included marijuana and, to a lesser extent, cigarettes, alcohol and petrol sniffing. For the first time, he was struggling at school academically, and emotionally he was distraught, and so were we as his parents. We intuitively 'knew' that our son was probably homosexual, but his survival at this time took precedence over any thoughts or cares we might have had about his sexual orientation. Self-harm/suicide attempts, admittedly some very half-hearted, were not uncommon, and he often told us he wanted to die. He wanted the pain to stop. He didn't want to be 'him' any more.

One of the most horrific experiences of my life happened around this time. My husband and I were in bed and heard a loud crash coming from our son's bedroom. My first thought was: our son has hanged himself. My second thought, and although it lasted only an instant, will always haunt me: do I go to rescue him or do I allow him to die and be at peace at last? After a few seconds, I did run to his room and found that he had accidentally pulled down a bookshelf, and that was the crash we had heard. The horror comes from the fact that as his mum, for a split second I believed it may be preferable for our son to die and be at peace than to continue living in the anguish he was experiencing. My husband was also going through his own agony at that time. He was experiencing severe depression that lasted for many years. However, as his wife I can honestly say that such was the strength, integrity and determination of this man to be a good dad, that at no time did he allow his depression to intrude on his fathering, to the extent that, as adults, all of our children have told us they were completely unaware of the emotional pain their father was experiencing during their teenage years.

Our son's pain continued, and as a family it was a very difficult time for us. For the sake of our other two children, our son went for a week's 'holiday' to stay with a friend who had been his youth group leader, and who had moved interstate. After a week away, she brought our son home. We were sitting around the dinner table and she asked him, 'What do you want to do in the future?' His response, 'I don't want to do anything! I want to go to sleep and never wake up! I want to stop being me! I just want to die!' She then asked our son what he was prepared to do to stop these thoughts and he replied he would do 'ANYTHING.' To our surprise when she asked him would he prepared to go with her and ask an elderly and very wise couple in our church to pray with him, he immediately said 'Yes.'

A few hours later, our son returned home and informed us that he had made a commitment to become a Christian and that everything would be OK now. Of course we were happy to hear him say this, but we must admit we both also thought, but didn't say, 'We have spent the last seven months in hell with you; an instant miracle may not be that instant!' At this point in our parenting lives, we wanted that miracle as much as our son did.

We believe our son's commitment to Christ was very real. So too, was the pull of his friends, the drugs and his unspoken sexual attraction to men.

When our son was 17, his life was threatened by some 'friends' when they came to our home and told him they were going to cut his tongue out, because he had allegedly stolen some marijuana from them and then 'snitched' on them at school. Our son was petrified and that night he slept on the floor in our bedroom because he felt safer there than anywhere else. He asked us if he could go and stay with his uncle who is a police officer interstate, and this he did. As parents we were distraught and requested the same elderly couple who had prayed with our son on a number of occasions previously to please continue praying for him. This they did and two days later they contacted us and advised us that they believed we should take our son out of his final year of school and send him to the same evangelical Christian organisation they had been to in Hawaii. If it had been anyone else, rather than this wise, elderly couple giving us this advice, we would have ignored it. Our son, of course, was thrilled to leave school and the town he had come to hate so much, and within a week or two he was on the plane en route to Hawaii.

Our son stayed with the Christian evangelical organisation for most of the next decade. As a twenty year old, he brought home his girlfriend to meet us, and we were overjoyed! We thought at first that maybe our parental thoughts that he was homosexual were wrong. Our son informed us that he had rung his girlfriend's Dad overseas and had asked permission to date his daughter with the intention of having a life-long relationship with her. She is a beautiful young woman and their friendship was inspirational. However, it was also obvious that the same physical attraction that was palpable between his older brother and fiancée was not present between our son and his girlfriend. Our son prayed and prayed that God would 'heal' him and make him heterosexual, and he had a multitude of other people, including his parents, agreeing with him in prayer. After a number of months, our son and his girlfriend, by mutual but heartbreaking agreement, decided that while their friendship might become life-long, a sexual relationship would be living a lie and destructive for them both.

During this painful time for her, our son's girlfriend and I spent many hours sharing with one another. For different reasons, this was an extremely painful time for us both, especially for her, but at the same time we were both very thankful to this young man that he had the strength not to persist with the pretence that they would enjoy a sexual relationship. As parents, it was at this stage that we realised that our dream that one day our son would have children (and we grandchildren) was shattered. We were sad for him. We were sad for us, but we also felt relief that our son had the integrity to be honest with himself and others.

For many years, to our knowledge, our son identified as homosexual, but had committed himself to celibacy. As evangelical Christians and parents, we found his celibate lifestyle a very easy one to live with. It fitted nicely with the doctrines we hear regularly in the church we love so much. That is, homosexual activity is a sin, but temptation is not. As long as he was celibate, we felt very comfortable as parents, united in our approach. We were also both very happy for his Dad to remain as an elder in our church.

A few years ago, our son's commitment to celibacy changed and one day he introduced us to his beautiful male partner. As we said earlier, when our children were small we had made the decision to love and accept whoever they bought home to us. Our son's partner is very easy to love and accept, and has become a cherished member of our family.

Reading this makes it all sound so smooth, and in many ways it has been, because we also believe as parents that God holds our adult children responsible for their own actions, and as parents God holds us responsible for our responses to our children. We both believe that unconditional love, the same unconditional love that God our Father has given to us, is at the core of our adult parenting. We are to love, to pray, and to be there to pick up pieces with our adult children, if needed.

Homosexuality in general, and our son's homosexual orientation in particular, is something that I have given a lot of thought and prayer to. Contrary to my church's doctrine, my own belief is that homosexuality per se is not a sin. My journey has taken me on a path very divergent from the path I had previously followed, without too much thought, that homosexual expression is an abomination to God. I no longer believe that, but I have had to question my own motivation for this change of heart. Did my maternal love for our son override what many, but not all Christians believe is straight from God's Word? Did I fear losing our son and his love if I dared disapprove of his homosexuality? Was I deceived by our societal views (or by Satan himself)? Am I manipulating God's Word to suit myself? Was I merely seeking an easy way out? Am I frightened that my mothering may have led to him becoming homosexual, and that is why I am reluctant to come out against homosexuality? It would be very convenient for me if I could answer an emphatic 'No' to each of these questions, but in all honesty, I cannot. My answer is 'No' to each question, but it is a shaky, 'No.' I have been mistaken in the past about what I believe God is sharing with me, and in my older, slightly wiser age I know I need to be open to a change of heart and mind. But as I write this, I can say the most important thing for me, as our son's mum, is that I love him, accept him and his decisions without judgement or condemnation, and thank my God that He has given me the ability and, I believe, the grace, to do this.

A father's story

My wife and I both love our son and his fiancé. They were recently engaged and plan to marry, once Australian law permits. I could not ask for a better male partner for our son. They are both wonderful young men, full of love and care, being compassionate, sensitive and respectful towards others.

I have the utmost respect for each of them, and love them both dearly. And I never want to do anything that could mar or damage my relationship with them. It was for that reason that I recently sought their permission to write my side of this story, and took time to explain to them my position. They have read this story, and have given their permission to have it included in this book, on the condition that our identities remain anonymous.

Our son was less than two years old when I became a Christian. Like many, I soon drifted from grace to become 'righteous' in my own efforts, rather than living in the righteousness of Christ. From that misguided position, I was harsh, even violent - against things, not people, was bigoted, racist and pharisaic. Thankfully, the Holy Spirit and my wife have helped me move to a more Christ-like position on issues such as refugees, racism, forgiveness, and homosexuality. A crucial approach that my wife and I have settled on is our desire to love our children unconditionally, and to also love those whom they love. We recognise that we will not be called to account for the actions of others, but will be called to account for our reactions.

I have read a few articles, and had many a long chat with many and varied people about the issues of homosexuality and gay sex. I can see how others, including my wife, can arrive at their respective positions, and a large part of me wants to be there too, as such a stance appears to be less likely to damage our relationships with our son and his partner. I have come to the position where I believe that a celibate gay relationship is okay, but that gay sex is not what God desires.

Somehow I need to separate these two crucial aspects. I have come to believe that the propensity towards being gay is not wrong. Neither is the propensity towards overeating or pride or greed. It is when we allow this to be fulfilled in our hearts or by our actions that we cross the line and do the wrong thing. Thus, I believe that being gay is not wrong, but participating in gay sex is wrong. An interesting aside is that when I gave this nearly completed story to our son to read and to give his permission before we sent it for inclusion in this book, part of his response read, '*One thing that I found interesting (hilarious) was the amount of times dad used the term "gay sex." Mum and Dad, we have been together for almost 4 years and just like any other couple of 4 years, (gay) sex is not something that we have a lot of. Our relationship is built around love and trust and companionship, sex is not the base.*'

In an attempt to explain how I arrived at my position, I would like to detail a few conflicts through which I have processed.

Humans often look at the wrongdoing of others and grade it according to what is appropriate and suitable punishment, according to its perceived severity. However, I believe that God sees that sin is sin is sin. He puts all wrong doing in one basket and calls it sin, and he has dealt with it all through the shed blood of Jesus his Son. And I believe that he loves us just the way we are, but is not willing to leave us like that. He wants us to move on, not in our own efforts, but through his grace and forgiveness and the power of his Spirit.

At various stages throughout history, Church and State have been identified, or, at least, closely linked. Not so in present-day Australia. It seems likely to me that the State, in our case the Federal and/or State governments, will soon legitimate gay marriages, as we have seen happen in other parts of the world, and, for a very short time, in the Australian Capital Territory (ACT). Some in the Church have already, or may soon follow suit and provide marriage ceremonies for gay couples, and may also ordain practicing gay ministers. Others in the Church will continue to see gay sex as sinful.

Jesus often spoke of how different we are from the world; that we are in, but not of the world. I have concluded that on this issue the Church should not follow the world's view, thus potentially putting itself at odds with the State.

For some time I struggled with the concept of how people who are made in God's likeness and image can have a propensity to sin. It really annoyed me. Then, in discussion with one of my friends, I came to see that it was our fallen nature. That made so much sense. We are made in His likeness and image, but our fallen nature impacts us with sickness, disease, temptation and sin.

I often meet with two other older blokes to pray. We are seeking God for His healing and salvation for many people with whom we are in contact. All of our families are affected by sickness and disease, and two of us have children in gay relationships. My triplet has pondered the end result of our adult children participating in gay relationships. We wondered what would happen to our sons' previous confessed faith in Jesus. Some time ago, when I asked our son about his faith, he said he was an agnostic. More recently, as I prepared to write this story, and was desperately concerned that I would damage his and my relationship, I asked again. This time he replied that he was an atheist. Such a decline in his faith frightened me and had me praying for his salvation.

At another time, one of the blokes in our triplet asked, 'Can your son be un-born?' That was a very interesting question. In our triplet deliberations, we pondered this. The prodigal son never lost his sonship, even when he was in a distant country. And his dad was always eagerly awaiting his return! We came to the conclusion that Christians cannot be 'un-born.' They may swerve away from God's best, even being incredibly far away from God, but they will never lose their sonship. And their Father is always waiting for their return. And we confirmed that gay sex is not the unforgivable sin, even though some in the Church act as if it is. It is, in our minds, just another sin.

I do wonder, though, if being gay and celibate would then mean that people would have to be alone for the rest of their life. Such 'aloneness' does not seem to be congruent with my understanding of God's Kingdom and His Family. This has caused me to ponder again on God's opinion on homosexuality and gay sex. It is in the final re-reading of my story that I now have just come to a sense that a celibate, gay relationship could be acceptable to God.

During our son's teenage years, I spent a lot of time praying for him. Most of it was in the Spirit. My heart's cry was for God to deliver him. For a long part of the time that our son was in the Christian evangelical organisation, I believe that he was also pleading with God to remove his gayness and to heal him. Our son reports that over the years, this seemed to get no better, and was in fact adversely affecting his faith and love for God. He later moved to accepting his gay nature and went back to loving God and not pleading. He also desired to be celibate. I must say that this seemed to me to be a most Christ-like approach. A much higher approach than the one I was in where my propensity to sin (overeating) was frequently fulfilled in my heart and in my actions.

This time of our son's celibacy was a much easier time for me. Maybe I was not so confronted. Maybe it was just easier. But then he changed from being celibate, and this was hard for me. Our son and his fiancé are wonderful young men and I love them dearly. I just do not love the lifestyle.

Having our son and his partner come to our home has always been a great joy, as we really enjoy their company. Sleeping arrangements were another matter. 'Not under my roof' seemed to creep into my thinking. And then there was our concern not to affront our son's grandfather, who lives with us and was fairly homophobic. The boys have been very gracious and not demonstrative nor confronting.

An interesting aside is that I seemed to have had less difficulty with my daughter and her fiancé sleeping in the same bed 'under my roof' prior to their wedding!

It appears clear that having a propensity to homosexuality is in itself not sin. The critical point and hardest aspect of our entire journey, has been to consider God's position on gay sex. Scriptures can be used to explain both sides. In an attempt to determine if gay sex is or is not sin, I developed a table with various indicators of what one would expect if gay sex was best considered as sinful, and, in another column, what one would expect if gay sex should not be considered as sinful. If it is sinful, one could reasonably expect that those who engage in it would, if they were Christian, result in a movement away from God and a decreasing desire to fellowship with other Christians. Alternatively, if it is not sinful, one might expect a movement in the other direction, that one would continue to see evidence of the Spirit's work, and a growing likeness to Christ.

From my limited anecdotal experience, it appears that for most gay people, including gay Christians, the movement is away from, rather than towards God. However, that might well be because many Christians have driven gay people away by their self-righteous, indignant and un-Christlike behaviour!

My struggle is with the aspect of healing. I recall our son's pleading with God to be healed. As yet, we have not seen a physical manifestation of Christ healing him. That makes me wonder – do we need to continue to pray, believing that we have received, and we are just waiting for the answer, or is it that we do not need to pray as there is no sin from which to be healed. I do not have an answer for that one yet. To compound the dilemma are the reports from Christian ministries that indicate few, if any, gay people are healed.

All I know is that our journey with our son has been a bumpy ride. But we would rather have this ride than not to have had our beautiful son! My wife and I are not totally on the same page, but we know without doubt that we love our son and his fiancé unconditionally, that they are always welcome in our home, and when they get married, we will be there, God willing, and we will have their wedding photos up with the rest of our family wedding photos.

CHAPTER ONE

The Lure of Literalism

I grew up believing in the literal truth of almost everything I encountered in the Bible. Not that I wasn't quickly aware of stories and ways of speaking that weren't meant to be taken literally. For example, when I came across references to God having arms or eyes, or of being sighted from behind by Moses, I didn't take those descriptions as literally true. I was quickly schooled to recognize metaphor and parable, poetry and symbolism, and to differentiate them from literal or straightforward descriptions. I learnt to identify figures of speech, and, in later years, the genre being employed by the Biblical writers. I wasn't literalistic in my literalism, in other words. Nevertheless, if something could be taken literally, that's how I took it. In fact, that was the advice my father gave me. His rule of thumb was: accept the literal truth of what you read unless it is obvious that you should take it as metaphor or symbol. Or as someone else has put it, 'read as literally as possible and as figuratively as necessary.'

As a rough guide for reading the Bible, that advice worked, and still works for many people. Large tracts of the Scripture can easily be read as matter-of-factly true. The Bible's stories are beautifully written and plausibly told. They are honest in their warts-and-all depiction of human nature. They are written with a matter-of-fact feel, as good stories are. Almost all the Bible's stories are told in this way, including the stories of Adam and Eve, Cain and Abel, Noah, Abraham, Moses and David. And not only are these stories told matter-of-factly, they are embedded within a storyline that suggests that these stories are meant to be taken as factual. Adam and Eve, Cain, Abel and Noah are included in genealogies that are populated with other ancestors who are indisputably historical, including Jesus, whose lineage is traced all the way back to Adam by the author of the Gospel of Luke.[1]

Reading the Biblical stories as literal descriptions of what actually took place is an understandable reading strategy. But, of course, the Bible consists of more than stories. It also contains laws and statutes, which are written to be obeyed; wisdom and poetry, written to inspire and instruct. Christians have long believed that these instructions, statutes and stories are inspired by the God who stands behind the Bible as its ultimate author. It is not just that Christians *can* take the Bible as straightforwardly true, they believe they *must*.

Making it even harder for Christians to not take the Bible as literally and straightforwardly true is the fact that Jesus, whose disciples we are, appeared to take his Bible, the Hebrew Scriptures, as literally and straightforwardly true. He appears to have believed in Adam and Eve as real people, as, in all likelihood, did St Paul, as did the Apostles and other writers of the New Testament. They appear to have accepted the Bible's stories as factual, and its instructions as binding, because they were God-given. Many Christians believe they have no choice but to follow suit. It is what discipleship entails. It is what being a Christian involves. And so, when those who want to critique Christian faith make fun of the literalism of Christians, it creates an understandably defensive, and often fearful reaction.

The pressure on Christians, especially conservative Christians, is enormous, and that pressure is getting stronger and more insistent. It is not just a few high profile atheists who are savouring the opportunity to ridicule fundamentalists, as conservative Christians are often called, it is people right across the spectrum of scholarship in a host of academic fields. Geology, biology, physics, genetics, archaeology, history and anthropology all appear to be conspiring against a literal reading of the Jewish and Christian Scriptures. Not only are the stories of Adam, Eve and Noah being characterised as non-factual myth or legend, other Biblical stories are rapidly being swept under the same carpet, or, like dominoes, are collapsing, one after the other, into the category of fiction, or, at best, historical fiction. The patriarchs, the Exodus, even descriptions of the glory of David's and Solomon's kingships are being questioned as to their historicity. And the

---

1   Luke 3:23-38

acid of criticism hasn't stopped there. It continues into the New Testament as this or that aspect of the Biblical narrative is questioned.

There seems to be no relief from the criticisms. The conclusions of academic culture trickle down into popular culture, and into endless documentaries and nature programs where the sometimes assured results of scholarship are beamed into the living rooms of populations around the world, where the plain and literal truth of the Bible is constantly being questioned. As one small illustration, when writing this chapter, the block-buster movie *Noah* had just come out. It did well at the box office, but perhaps part of its appeal is that it also seeks to undercut the literalism of Christians, who, for generations, have taken this story as true to fact. One reviewer sums up the movie in these terms:

> Whatever its strengths and weaknesses, *Noah* does make sense of the biblical tale as a powerful piece of myth and legend, and as a portrait of the pitfalls and pay-offs of obsession, as well as a rallying call to make the most of humanity's second chance before the waters rise and eradicate us all.[2]

It is little wonder that Christians, who for all of their lives have taken the story of Noah as true-to-fact, are disturbed by such descriptions and depictions. Fearfulness and even anger is understandable, because what is happening through all these mediums and sources of learning is that their very faith, or, at least, the long-held shape of their faith, is being undermined.

What perhaps makes things even worse is that it isn't just the New Atheists or Hollywood or ivory tower academics who are questioning the literal truth of what the Bible says. It is also some of their fellow Christians who have likewise had trouble accepting the literal truth of many of the Bible's stories, and who have questioned the abiding purchase of at least some of the Bible's prescriptions. This too is an understandable cause of concern.

A question worth considering, in this chapter and in chapters to follow, is: 'Is there no option for Christians other than to be literal in our approach

---

2   From an article by Karl Quinn, entitled 'Darren Aronofsky sails with Noah into myth and madness', included in the *Sydney Morning Herald* on March 30, 2014. Quinn approves of Aronofsky's take on Noah in these terms: 'It's not a literal rendering of the story – how could it be? Can anyone really believe that a pair of every species that ever lived was on that ark? – but a rendering of what he sees as its core meaning. "There are ideas in there that mean things and make it powerful enough to tell the story over and over again," Aronofsky told *The Atlantic*. "The strength is in making it into myth and legend."'

to the Scriptures? Is literalism required of those who consider themselves disciples of Jesus?' I don't believe so, hence this chapter's somewhat provocative title. There are other ways. In order to explore that possibility, it might help to briefly consider the history of literalism.

To begin with, it is worth noting that problems with literalism go all the way back to the beginnings of Biblical interpretation. The book of Genesis, for example, has puzzled interpreters from the time of its composition, with a number of obvious questions raised by its early chapters, including the following:

- Why are humans and animals created twice?
- Who are the other people that Cain is afraid might kill him?
- Who was Cain's wife? Was she his sister?
- How many animals did Noah take into the ark – two of each animal or seven pairs of the clean animals and one pair of unclean animals?
- Did Methuselah drown in the flood?

Puzzles such as these prompted early interpreters to consider other ways of reading and understanding Biblical passages. Over time, they came up with a number of assumptions, assumptions that were shaped by what they found in the Bible.[3] Their first assumption was that the Bible is cryptic. A cryptic text has hidden or coded meanings, and the interpreter's task is to unearth them. The existence of hidden meanings is flagged by obscurities in the text, which become an invitation to look deeper. For example, the puzzling juxtaposition of two contrasting creation stories suggests the presence of figural or symbolic elements.

The second assumption brought to the text by ancient interpreters is that the Bible is relevant, and so even if the literal meaning is obscure or not obviously relevant, its deeper meanings will speak to every present situation.

The third assumption is that the Bible is divine and therefore perfect. Early Jewish interpreters reasoned that because the Torah of God is the Torah *of God*, it is perfect. It won't have internal contradictions, nor will it conflict

---

3   I am indebted for the discussion that follows to Ronald Hendel's excellent treatment in *The Book of Genesis: A Biography*, Princeton: Princeton University Press, 2013. He, in turn, expresses indebtedness to James Kugel, *The Bible as it Was*, Cambridge MA: Harvard University Press, 1986.

with the world beyond the text. Any apparent or superficial contradictions are therefore likely to be an invitation to look for hidden meanings.

Christian interpreters, who came to inherit their own Scriptures, shared these assumptions. They also acquired a key hermeneutical (or interpretive) principle that would guide them in their reading of Biblical texts. That key principle was Christ, made incarnate in the person of Jesus. As Irenaeus, an early Church Father, put it:

> Anyone who reads the Scriptures with attention will find in them a discourse about Christ, and a prefiguration of a new calling. For Christ is the treasure hidden in the field, that is, in this world, for the field is the world, but he is also hidden in the scriptures, since he was signified by types and parables which could not be understood, humanly speaking, before the consummation that was prophesied as coming, that is, the advent of Christ.[4]

It was this conviction that led to a proliferation of allegorical interpretations of Old Testament texts, following the example of St Paul,[5] but also of earlier Jewish interpreters. The first person to use the word allegory (Greek *allegoria*) was the Jewish philosopher Philo of Alexandria (c. 20 BCE – c. 50 CE) who lived at the same time as St Paul and Jesus, though he did not refer to them. For him, as for early Christian interpreters, problems with the literal sense of the Hebrew Scriptures led to the development of allegory. For example, Philo wrote this about Genesis 1 and its description of God creating in six days:

> 'And on the sixth day God finished his work which he made.' It would be a sign of great simplicity to think that the world was created in six days, or indeed all in time ... But ... it would be correctly said that the world was not created in time, but that time had its existence as a consequence of the world ... When, therefore, Moses says, 'God completed his works on the sixth day,' we must understand that he is speaking not of a number of days, but that he takes six as a perfect number.[6]

A theologian deeply influenced by Philo was the third-century Church Father Origen. He too expressed dissatisfaction with the literal sense of at least some Biblical texts. About Genesis 2 and 3, he wrote:

---

4   Irenaeus, *Against Heresies,* 4.26.1

5   Galatians 4:22-26

6   Philo, *Allegories of the Sacred Laws after the Work of the Six Days of Creation,* II. (2) & (3)

> Who is so silly as to believe that God, after the manner of a farmer, 'planted a paradise eastward in Eden,' and set in it a visible and palpable 'tree of life,' of such a sort that anyone who tasted its fruit with his bodily teeth would gain life: and again that one could partake of 'good and evil' by masticating the fruit taken from the tree of that name? And when God is said to 'walk in the paradise in the cool of the day' and Adam to hide himself behind a tree, I do not think anyone will doubt that these are figurative expressions which indicate certain mysteries through a semblance of history and not through actual events.[7]

Origen also questioned the literal truth of some of the Gospel accounts, for example, Satan's leading of Jesus 'into a high mountain' to show him 'all the kingdoms of the earth':

> How could it possibly have happened literally … as if they [all the kingdoms of the earth] were lying close to the foot of a single mountain?[8]

It is worth noting that even Origen did not neglect nor depreciate the literal sense of the Biblical text. He simply saw it as one level of meaning which sometimes needed to be supplemented by a search for a deeper meaning thought to exist within the text. He suggested three levels of meaning, which he identified as body, soul and spirit,[9] corresponding to tripartite division of human nature accepted by early Christians. The 'body' of Scripture is its obvious interpretation, its literal sense. The 'soul' of Scripture is its meaning as discerned by the Christian who has made some progress in the faith. The 'spirit' is its deeper meaning discerned by someone who has been perfected in the faith.[10] By the Middle Ages, Origen's three levels of meaning were expanded to four; the literal, allegorical, moral, and mystical senses.

Not all Christian theologians employed this method of reading, which was characteristic of the Alexandrian school of interpretation. Another school, known as the Antiochian school, concentrated on the literal sense.

---

7   Origin, *On First Principles*, 4.3.1

8   Origen, *On First Principles*, 4.3.1

9   Origen, *On First Principles*, 4.2.4

10   Dale B. Martin, in *Pedagogy of the Bible: An Analysis and Proposal,* 2008, notes that Origen 'was seldom rigorous in using precisely these three terms for three meanings, nor in maintaining three distinct senses, nor even in maintaining three rather than two senses. Origen's practices of interpretation … are remarkably fluid, creative and adapted to the peculiarities of the text in question and the situation of writing,' 50.

Their aim was to discover what the Biblical writers themselves intended to teach, rather than what could be read into their words with the benefit of hindsight.[11] Moreover, Origen's occasional discomfort with the literal sense of the Bible created discomfort for the majority of Christian theologians who continued to privilege literalism as the Bible's primary sense,[12] even as they looked beyond the literal sense of Biblical passages to other, or additional, meanings and senses.

This included Martin Luther who had likewise been schooled to employ allegory in his interpretation of the Bible. However, under influence from the Renaissance and its renewed emphasis on understanding texts in their literary and historical context, Luther became impatient with the essentially uncontrolled nature of allegorical methods of interpretation, becoming the champion of the literal sense of the Bible, arguing that within it alone was 'life, comfort, power, instruction and skill.' Allegory, by contrast, no matter how brilliant the impression it might leave, was 'foolishness.'[13]

Against the church of his day, Luther embraced 'Scripture alone' (*sola scriptura*) as the basis for faith and life, though still retaining a place for reason. In his reply to the accusation of heresy at the Diet of Worms (1521) he contrasts his approach to the fallible approach of the church:

> Since your Imperial Majesty and Lordships demand a simple answer I will do so without horns or teeth as follows: Unless I am convinced by the testimony of Scripture or by clear reason – for I do not trust either in the pope or in councils alone, since it is well known that they have often erred and contradicted themselves – I am bound by the Scriptures I have quoted, and my conscience is captive to the Word of God. I cannot and will not recant.[14]

Luther embraced Scripture and clear reason as the sole guarantors of truth, rejecting tradition. He also became the pioneer of the plain sense (*sensus*

---

11   Karen Armstrong, *The Bible: A Biography,* New York: Grove Press, 2007, 107.

12   Martin notes that '[Even when Christian theologians] believed that typological or allegorical readings of Scripture were proper, they usually taught that those readings should not contradict the literal sense,' *Pedagogy of the Bible*, 43.

13   Martin Luther, *Table Talk*, ed. and trans. Theodore G. Tappert, Luther's Works, 54; Philadelphia: Fortress Press, 1967, 406 (no. 5285).

14   Martin Luther, Career of the Reformer, Vol. 2, trans. George W. Forell, Luther's Works 32: Philadelphia: Fortress Press, 1958, 112.

literalis) approach to reading the Scriptures, in the belief that God would surely make the Bible accessible to every reader, even the most uneducated.[15]

Luther's approach had much to commend it, certainly at the time. Along with his efforts to make the Scriptures more accessible, and in the native tongue of those who could now read it for themselves, it made sense that any and every reader could have immediate access to the Scriptures, and, through them, be addressed by God directly. It was a revolutionary democratization of Bible reading and interpretation.

It was also a vote of confidence in God, that God was a sufficiently skilled communicator to successfully communicate to all those who would encounter the Bible. What's more, it isn't hard to take the Bible literally. Not only has it been the preferred approach by Biblical interpreters from the beginning, not only does it appear to have been the preferred approach of Jesus and his Apostles, it is the usual method employed by most Christians today.

Luther's recommended approach does seem to have much to commend it. But it also has its problems, problems which interpreters have been aware of from the beginning, as we have noted. Luther's decision to rule out figural or allegorical interpretations of Biblical passages, and to not follow early interpreters in looking for hidden meanings, meant that those earlier recognized problems would inevitably resurface.

That Luther was aware of those problems is illustrated in his discussion of the creation of Eve from the rib of Adam:

> What, I ask you, could sound more like a fairy tale if you were to follow your reason? This is extravagant fiction and the silliest kind of nonsense if you set aside the authority of Scripture and follow the judgement of reason.
>
> Although it sounds like a fairy tale to reason, it is the most certain truth. It is revealed in the word of God, which alone impacts true information.[16]

Luther maintained that the Garden of Eden was a real place, and that the four rivers of paradise were real rivers, not allegorical symbols. All of these

---

15   In his words, 'I prefer what is simplest and can be understood by those with little education,' *Lectures on Genesis* 1.10.

16   *Lectures on Genesis* 1.123

details he described as 'historical facts.'[17] While admitting that some of the details of the Eden story appear dubious and fictional, he felt obliged to simply submit to the authority of the plain sense of Scripture:

> The more it seems to conflict with all experience and reason, the more carefully it must be noted and the more surely believed.[18]

Luther couldn't have been clearer. Although he acknowledged the indispensable role of human reason in coming to understand the Scriptures, he counselled Christians to adopt and to submit to a literal and plain sense understanding of the Scriptures, regardless of whether that understanding contradicts other Scripturally-independent deliverances of human reason. Human reason and the Scriptures were thus effectively pitted against each other in a way that would have massive implications in the years which followed, right up until the present.

Almost immediately, the tensions created by this approach became obvious. Through adhering to the plain sense of Scripture, Luther and the other Reformers were quick to dismiss Copernicus, because, as they rightly saw, a heliocentric universe conflicts with a literal reading of the Bible.[19] The Roman Catholic Church followed suit in 1616, officially condemning Copernicus' theory as 'false [and] altogether contrary to Scripture.'[20] They were, of course, right in noticing the differences between Copernican and ancient understandings of the cosmos which are implicit and often explicit within the pages of the Bible. The ancient and Biblical understanding of the universe was decidedly geocentric, with the heavenly bodies understood to be set in the solid dome of heaven, revolving in their celestial paths around the earth. This understanding of the universe had been articulated most thoroughly by Ptolemy (ca. CE 90–168), and had been accepted by Christians, including Luther and the other Reformers, as

---

17   *Lectures on Genesis* 1.93

18   *Lectures on Genesis* 1.123

19   Melanchthon described Copernicus's theory as 'pernicious', and added, 'It is a part of a good mind to accept the truth as revealed by God and to acquiesce in it', *Initia Doctrinae Physicae*, quoted in Kent Sparks, 'The Sun Also Rises: Accommodation in Inscripturation and Interpretation', in V. Bacote, L. C. Miguelez and D. L. Okholm, *Evangelicals and Scripture: Tradition, Authority and Hermeneutics*, Downers Grove: InterVarsity Press, 2004, 114.

20   Maurice Finocchiaro, ed. and trans., *The Essential Galileo*, Indianapolis, IND: Hackett Publishing, 2008, 177.

an accurate description of God's creation. They could do so because Biblical descriptions match that understanding, including the account of the sun being halted in its course by God, in Joshua 10:12-14.

Luther accepted the literal truth of Biblical descriptions of a fixed and solid firmament, and of waters kept in storage above the heavens, as well as below the earth. In his *Lectures on Genesis*, for example, Luther wrote the following regarding the sun and stars:

> Indeed, it is more likely that the bodies of the stars, like that of the sun, are round, and that they are fastened to the firmament like globes of fire, to shed light at night, each according to its endowment and its creation.[21]

And this about the waters above the firmament:

> We Christians must be different from the philosophers in the way we think about the causes of these things. And if some are beyond our comprehension (like those before us concerning the waters above the heavens), we must believe them and admit our lack of knowledge rather than either wickedly deny them or presumptuously interpret them in conformity with our understanding.[22]

Luther was consistent in his literalism. But with that consistency came the inevitability of challenge as accepted understandings of cosmology increasingly came under question. Copernicus, and later Galileo, were proved right in their theories, to the embarrassment of many Christians, certainly those who followed Luther in his consistent literalism.

But this was only the first of a succession of challenges, which continue to this day. In early modern times, Genesis' account of the early history of the world began to be called into question. The discovery of the New World changed people's understanding of the antiquity and spread of human civilisation, creating insurmountable problems for those trying to harmonize those discoveries with the literal sense of the Bible. Not only is the world much older than a plain reading might suggest, so also are human civilisations. Up to that point, Genesis had been the standard model of world history, with the Table of Nations in Genesis 10 taken to be the canonical list of the world's peoples. But with the discovery of the

---

21   Lectures on Genesis - Martin Luther, *Luther's Works. Vol 1. Lectures on Genesis*, ed. Jaroslav Pelikan, St. Louis: Concordia Publishing House, 1958, 42.

22   *Lectures on Genesis*, 30; *Luther's Works, Vol. 1*, 30.

New World, it became clear that there were peoples and lands the writers of Genesis did not know about. All sorts of creative efforts were made to harmonise Genesis with these new discoveries, but without success, as it became increasingly obvious that the genealogies of Genesis did not correspond to factual reality.[23]

The age of the earth also appeared to be getting older and older, as from the 1700s geologists became aware of what is now called 'deep time.' Genesis places the origin of the universe at approximately 6,000 years ago, spawning efforts to postulate a 'gap' between Genesis 1:1 and 1:2, as well as continuing doomed efforts to hold out for a young earth. It is this apparent conspiracy of scientific enterprise which is creating widespread anxiety amongst conservative Christians who are increasingly depicted as ignorant and obscurantist.

Other Christians are not so disturbed, however. While reading this chapter, you may have been thinking, 'Surely there are some obvious and sensible answers to these puzzles you have raised. Yes, Luther was a consistent literalist, and yes that level of literalism was bound to get him into trouble, but you haven't mentioned two obvious strategies to defuse those challenges, the first being genre, the second being accommodation.' That is true.

The issue of genre is hugely important, and almost certainly is the key to unravelling these problems. St Augustine is a helpful guide on this topic. He was aware of the importance of genre in reading passages like Genesis 1-11. His rule of thumb was that if the literal sense of a text of Scripture was in obvious conflict with the reasonably held conclusions of science, the Biblical text should be reinterpreted in figural or metaphorical terms. He was thereby open to a non-literal reading of the early chapters of Genesis. He strongly counselled against interpreting the Biblical text literally if it contradicts what can be known from science and our God-given reason.[24]

St Augustine's advice seems sensible. But it does create problems. If one does decide, sensibly, to leave literalism behind at this point, and to go looking for comparable examples of the type of literature used in Genesis 1-11, then myth and/or legend certainly commend themselves as the most likely genres employed within these narratives. These chapters certainly have the

---

23   For a fuller discussion, see Ronald Hendel, *The Book of Genesis: A Biography*, 176f.

24   See, for example, 'The Literal Interpretation of Genesis' 1:19-20; 2:9.

feel of myth or legend. They are similar in form to any number of Ancient Near Eastern (ANE) myths and legends current at the time the Hebrew Scriptures were written. For reasons such as these, most critical scholars have come to the conclusion that the early stories of Genesis are, most probably, a mixture of myth and legend (*Sage*),[25] albeit with a historical feel.

The best suggestion I have come across to describe the genre of Genesis 1-11, and of Genesis as a whole, is elaborated by John Van Seters in his *Prologue to History: The Yahwist as Historian in Genesis* (1992).[26] Van Seters argues that the book of Genesis is a work of ancient history, an *archaeologia*, designed to serve as a 'prologue' to the national history of Israel. It has a number of significant similarities with other ancient histories, including the works of Herodotus, Dionysius, Livy and Pausanias, each of whom included myth and legend within their histories, particularly the earlier (pre-historical) parts.

Van Seters notes two possible processes at work in the formation of Genesis 1-11; firstly, the historicisation of myth, and, secondly, the mythologization of history. The historicisation of myth he describes as 'a process of rationalization of myths or mythical elements by the use of historical categories of arrangement or explanation, such as the imposition of genealogical or chronological succession on myths and legends.'[27] The mythologization of history is 'the imposition of mythical motifs and elements onto historical materials and traditions.'[28] Given the essentially pre-historical nature of Genesis 1-11, one would be inclined to see historicization of myth as predominating.

---

25 John Van Seters defines a myth as 'a traditional story about events in which the god or gods are the primary actors, and the action takes place outside of historical time. In addition, myth contains some structure of meaning that is concerned with the deep problems of life and offers explanations for the way things are'. He defines legends as stories about heroes and eponymic forefathers, which, because they are usually about godlike figures and set in a time that is essentially a-historical or pre-historical, are more similar to myth than history, *Prologue to History: The Yahwist as Historian in Genesis,* Westminster: John Knox Press, 1992, 25.

26 Van Seters's suggestions are also included in my earlier book, *A Restless Faith* (2012), 116, 117, more or less word for word.

27 *Prologue to History,* 25.

28 *Prologue to History,* 25.

If Van Seters is right that the content of Genesis 1-11 is largely mythical –
myth[29] in the service of national self-understanding - then we misread these
chapters if we take them as literal fact. We misread and misuse them if we
appeal to them to work out the age or shape of the earth, or to guide us in
our geological or archaeological digs, or if they send us on a search for the
Garden of Eden or Noah's ark, or the remains of the Tower of Babel.[30] To use
the texts in those ways is to misunderstand them – it is to misunderstand
their genre.

However, as said, if one does opt to take many or all of the details of these
early chapters as myth or legend, one will encounter other difficulties,
which, for many Christians, are insurmountable. Most decisively, Jesus
and those who wrote the New Testament don't appear to have understood
these chapters as mythical or legendary, or, if they did, they haven't left
any indication of that. Their use of these chapters suggests a very literal
and straight-forward understanding. Moreover, the details of these stories
are used in the development of theology, both within and beyond the New
Testament, so much so that many Christians are loathe to surrender their
non-mythical understanding of these early chapters, sending them back
in the direction of literalism, and back to all the problems associated with
literalism.

This was recently illustrated for me when a conservative friend of mine
encouraged me to have a read of what turned out to be a very good
commentary on Genesis by John H. Walton, Professor of Old Testament at
Wheaton College Graduate School in the US. Walton, who shows himself
to be fully aware of the many myths and legends current at the time Genesis
was written, and who is also well aware of how similar those myths and
legends are to what we find in Genesis, nevertheless feels he must resist the

---

29   Or, perhaps, anti-myth, which, in my opinion, amounts to the same thing. It has long
been recognized that the writers of Genesis were skilfully engaged in critiquing Ancient
Near Eastern myths. They would employ the storylines and the language of such myths,
while stripping them of unacceptable elements, all in the service of theological correction.
But the upshot of such critique was the production of alternative myths, albeit theologically
corrected alternative myths.

30   On this way of seeing things, the stories of Genesis 1-11, although deliberately set
within, or at the beginnings of, history tell us more about historical existence than they
do about historical or pre-historical events, such as the fall, a flood or the confusion of
languages.

highly sensible conclusion that Genesis 1-11 is mythical. Like Luther before him, he reverts to literalism. Discussing the talking snake of Genesis 3, he writes:

> [Unless] one if willing to consider the whole of Genesis 1-11 as myth (which I am not), the face value of the text suggests that the author wants us to believe that this event really happened. Moreover, the reality of the Fall is an essential foundation to Pauline theology, and the New Testament consistently shows it considers the events of Genesis 3 to be true, as historical realities. Thus, as students of genre and considering its source, we must discount the unnatural behaviour attributed to the serpent and accept the story at face value.[31]

Walton is forced to engage in mental gymnastics; all because he is aware that an appeal to genre, though sensible, doesn't solve the problems of Biblical literalism.

Another promising way to circumvent those problems is to appeal to a suggestion originally made by St Augustine and later developed by Swiss Reformer John Calvin (1509 - 1564),[32] and that is the idea of divine accommodation, which is the idea that God accommodated himself to the understandably limited and culture-bound understandings of those who wrote and would read the Bible. Calvin cautioned against using the early chapters of Genesis for the purposes of astronomy or science, whilst suggesting that at least some of its details reflected cosmological understandings no longer reasonably held. For example, unlike Luther, he questioned whether the heavens were a solid vault, above which water was stored. As he put it:

> For, to my mind, this is a certain principle: that nothing is treated here except the visible form of the world. Whoever wishes to learn astronomy and other esoteric arts, let him go elsewhere ... Therefore, the things which [Moses] relates serve as decorative objects from that theatre which [God] places before

---

31   NIV Application Commentary on Genesis, Grand Rapids: Zondervan, 2001, 212.

32   For a discussion of Calvin's use of the accommodation principle, see Kent Sparks, 'The Sun Also Rises: Accommodation in Inscripturation and Interpretation,' in V. Bacote, L. C. Miguelez and D. L. Okholm, *Evangelicals and Scripture: Tradition, Authority and Hermeneutics*, Downers Grove: InterVarsity Press, 2004, 114-118. See also, Stephen D. Benin, *The Footprints of God: Divine Accommodation in Jewish and Christian Thought*, NY: State University of New York Press, 1993. See also, Jon Balserak, 'The Accommodating Act Par Excellence?' An Inquiry into the Incarnation and Calvin's Understanding of Accommodation,' Scottish Journal of Theology 55 (2002), 408-23.

our eyes. From this, I conclude that the waters intended here are such as the crude and unlearned may perceive.[33]

Calvin's and Augustine's suggestion has promise because it allows interpreters to acknowledge what often seems so patently obvious to contemporary readers, and that is that those who wrote the Bible shared with their contemporaries all sorts of assumptions and beliefs which we no longer share, for example that the earth is flat and surrounded on all sides by water.

Some form of the doctrine of accommodation seems necessary. However, once again, Christians have found it difficult, even impossible, to go down this path, because a disturbing implication of this approach is that the Bible does contain errors of fact and belief. The Bible is not completely true in all that it teaches or touches upon. To go all the way back to the early Jewish interpreters, the Bible is not perfect, or, at least not perfect in the sense of being straightforwardly true. For many, this is not a possibility they dare to countenance. To even consider it creates anxiety, which observation is a good introduction to our next chapter.

---

33   Calvin, *Commentaries on the First Book of Moses called Genesis*, 79-80.

CHAPTER TWO

The Error of Inerrancy

About ten years ago, I attended a School of Theology at Moore Theological College, the intellectual power-house of the Anglican Diocese of Sydney. The then Archbishop of Sydney, Peter Jensen, was one of the speakers, his topic: 'The humanity of the Word of God.' My memory of the lecture's content has now faded, but what I do still remember is a question posed during question time. Peter was asked, 'Don't you think it is time we gave up on the doctrine of inerrancy?'

It was, I think, a brave question. Moore College is known for its conservatism, some would say ultra-conservatism. Archbishop Peter is a conservative, some would say an ultra-conservative. Prior to becoming Sydney's Anglican Archbishop in 2001, he had lectured at Moore College for 25 years, mostly as Principal, and primarily in the area of doctrine. He himself is an avowed inerrantist. In a book published just two years prior to this lecture, Peter had outlined his understanding of inerrancy in the following terms:

> Those wishing to assert inerrancy (as I do) use the word 'inerrant' to signify 'the quality of being free from all falsehood and mistake,' and hence assert that 'Holy Scripture is entirely free from all falsehood in all its assertions.' This includes all matters historical and scientific in its scope.[1]

Peter's reply to the question he was asked is revealing. He said, 'No, we must not give up on inerrancy, because of what it safeguards.' In other words, if I have understood him correctly, inerrancy is like a dam wall, which, if it was removed, would allow the dam's precious water to escape. The dam's water, in this case, are important Christian doctrines which might be lost,

---

1   *The Revelation of God,* Nottingham: Inter-Varsity Press, 2002,199.

or may need to be rethought. In his then recently published book, Peter had expressed his preference for inerrancy over infallibility which he considered to be a weaker and less protective doctrine. As he expressed it:

> Infallibility makes the lesser claim that the Bible is trustworthy in matters of salvation or faith, though not necessarily in matters of science or history.[2]

Given Peter's very public, and no doubt influential advocacy of inerrancy, the similarly very public question is all the more remarkable. I have long pondered this interchange, wondering about its significance. One thing is fairly clear. Both the question and Peter's answer suggest significant uneasiness with the doctrine of inerrancy. It was as if this person was naming a very large and obvious elephant in the room that day, which others were not so game to draw attention to, but this person was, to his credit.

Peter's answer is similarly revealing. From memory, he did not deny that inerrancy has problems. Instead, he drew attention to what might be lost if inerrancy is discarded. On reflection, I think Peter was right. Inerrancy is like a dam wall, to use my own analogy. Things *are* likely to be lost if inerrancy is dispensed with, things which are understandably precious to those who hold on to them. Just to give a few examples, if it is true that Holy Scripture is 'entirely free from all falsehood in all of its assertions,' then:

- In reading the Scriptures, one can relax and feel confident that what one is reading, on whatever matter, is true and reliable. Inerrancy is a very effective safeguard to Biblical authority.[3]

- One is saved from the need to be critical of the text, from the need to ask, 'Do I believe this?' or 'Is this a reasonable belief to hold?' It will be both reasonable and true because each and every text of the Bible expresses inerrant truth.

---

2   *The Revelation of God*, 199.

3   Donald Bloesch, a renowned evangelical scholar, has argued along similar lines to Peter Jensen, that the Bible's authority and truthfulness is safeguarded by inerrancy. Although Bloesch expresses dissatisfaction with inerrancy because of its acknowledged weaknesses and limitations, he nevertheless argues that inerrancy 'should not be abandoned for it preserves the nuance of truthfulness and is necessary for a high view of Holy Scripture,' Donald G. Bloesch, *Holy Scripture, Revelation and Interpretation*, Downers Grove, Ill.: InterVarsity, 1994, 116.

- One can more readily take a devotional approach to reading the Bible on the assumption that the words of the Bible are God's inerrant words, through which the reader is addressed by God, and in response to which the reader can be trustingly obedient.

- One can confidently go about collecting the Bible's statements, on whatever topic, to create doctrines or conclusions which have a good chance of being reliable because their building blocks are true and reliable Biblical statements.

- If one wants to know about heaven or hell or homosexuality or hope or hubris, one simply has to go looking for relevant Biblical statements, put them into reasonable context, and out will come reliable conclusions upon which one can base one's life.

Without inerrancy, the task becomes decidedly more complex. The precious cargo of doctrinal and ethical conclusions, which have been arrived at over centuries, instantly become less certain because their building blocks are not necessarily true. They could be erroneous. I think Peter is right in thinking that infallibility, as he defines it, supplies significantly less protection for the historic doctrines of the church. If the Bible's statements are not to be relied upon when they touch on areas of history or science, then on what reasonable grounds can one argue that matters of faith and salvation are quarantined from error?

Inerrancy does appear to be needed. No other dam wall is built of sufficiently strong material to prevent precious Christian doctrines from leaking away from the dam, or, more alarmingly, of creating a flood capable of destroying historic Christian belief. It was fear of this possibility that fuelled the creation of a doctrine of inerrancy.

A brief history of inerrancy

As we saw in chapter one, the earliest of Biblical interpreters affirmed the divinity and therefore perfection of Scripture. Ever since those early days, the Bible has been consistently affirmed as trustworthy and true, although not necessarily in all of its details. Luther, for example, was unconcerned by occasional errors of detail or fact, arguing that the Bible's major doctrines were clear. As he put it, 'The Holy Ghost has an eye only to the substance and is not bound by words.'[4] The conviction that the Bible is true in all of

---

4   Quoted in Roland H. Bainton, 'The Bible in the Reformation,' in *The Cambridge History*

its details has been insisted on most strongly in the modern era chiefly to arrest the erosion of confidence in the Bible created by wave after wave of Biblical criticism. During the 18th and 19th centuries, the literal truthfulness of a number of the Bible's stories came under question, particularly the early chapters of the Bible. Jewish and Christian interpreters tried valiantly to reconcile those early stories, taken literally, with emerging theories about the age of the earth, and with what was increasingly known about the origins and spread of human civilisation. Their task became even more challenging with the publication in 1859 of Charles Darwin's *On the Origin of Species*. Darwin's theory of evolution became the mother of all challenges to conservative Christian belief and it elicited fierce criticism. Bishop Samuel Wilberforce of Oxford wrote a scathing review of Darwin's book:

> Man's derived supremacy over the earth ... man's fall and redemption; the incarnation of the Eternal Son; the indwelling of the Eternal Spirit – all are equally and utterly irreconcilable with the degrading notion of the brute origin of him who was created in the image of God.[5]

Almost as challenging to conservative Christian belief was the fact that Christian scholars were also beginning to question the literal truth of Biblical stories. Four months after the appearance of *On the Origin of Species*, another book, *Essays and Reviews*, appeared, written by seven Oxford scholars to up-date ordinary church-going Christians with developments occurring in Biblical scholarship, much of it emerging out of Germany.[6] The authors argued that the Bible cannot be accepted as scientifically accurate, but that it was, nevertheless, still powerfully relevant because of the moral and spiritual lessons it contained and continued to convey.

The impact of this book dwarfed the initial reaction to Darwin's book. *Essays and Reviews* sold over 20,000 copies in two years, more than Darwin's *Origin* sold in twenty years.[7] The twin threats of critical biblical scholarship and evolution gave rise to the articulated doctrine of inerrancy.

---

of the Bible, Vol. 3: The West from the Reformation to the Present Day, ed. S. L. Greenslade, Cambridge: Cambridge University Press, 1963, 12.

5   Quoted in Ronald Hendel, *The Book of Genesis: A Biography*, 183.

6   See further Victor Shea and William Whitla, (eds.), *Essays and Reviews: The 1860 Text and Its Reading*, Charlottesville: University Press of Virginia, 2000.

7   So incensed was Samuel Wilberforce by *Essays and Reviews* that he called for the expulsion of the authors from the Church of England, *The Book of Genesis*, 185.

Not long after Darwin published the even more controversial sequel to *On the Origin of Species*, *The Descent of Man, and Selection in Relation to Sex* (1871), a group of Protestant Evangelicals produced a fourteen-point creed in response to what they perceived to be a departure from the faith and a giving in to seductive spirits. The first point of what became known as the Niagara Creed affirmed the inspiration of every detail of Scripture:

> We believe … that the Holy Ghost gave the very words of the sacred writings to holy men of old; and that his Divine inspiration is not in different degrees, but extends equally and fully to all parts of these writings, historical, poetical, doctrinal and prophetical, and to the smallest word, and inflection of a word.[8]

In 1881, Archibald A. Hodge and B. B. Warfield published a defence of the literal truth of the Bible, which became a classic. They affirmed that the Bible was without error and absolutely true to fact in all of its claims.[9] Their articulation of the doctrine of inerrancy became standard amongst evangelicals and fundamentalists until it was further refined in the 1970s. Not all evangelicals were comfortable with inerrancy so defined, and alternatives were proposed and developed, including infallibility. None of these suggested alternatives seemed satisfactory, however, with many, probably most, evangelicals holding on to inerrancy as the only sure protection for doctrines and beliefs they considered non-negotiable.

In the 1970s, an International Council on Biblical Inerrancy was established in the United States dedicated to establishing inerrancy as the defining evangelical doctrine.[10] In 1978, they produced and adopted the Chicago Statement on Biblical Inerrancy. It was unambiguous in its rejection of alternatives:

---

8   Quoted in Hendel, *The Book of Genesis,* 187.

9   In their words, 'All the affirmations of Scripture of all kinds whether of spiritual doctrine or duty, or of physical or historical fact, or of psychological or philosophical principle, are without any error, when the *ipsis-sima verba* of the original autographs are ascertained and interpreted in their natural and intended sense,' A. A. Hodge and Benjamin B. Warfield, 'Inspiration,' *Presbyterian Review 2* (1881), 238.

10   As some indication of the Council's success in making inerrancy a defining characteristic of evangelical belief, the US based Evangelical Theological Society includes inerrancy, and very little else, in its 43-sentence-long statement of faith: 'The Bible alone, and the Bible in its entirety, is the Word of God written and is therefore inerrant in the autographs.' http://www.etsjets.org/about

Being wholly and verbally God-given, Scripture is without error or fault in all its teaching, no less in what it states about God's acts in creation, about the events of world history, and about its own literary origins under God, than in its witness to God's saving grace in individual lives.[11]

The Statement's preface goes on to warn:

To stray from Scripture in faith or conduct is disloyalty to our Master. Recognition of the total truth and trustworthiness of Holy Scripture is essential to a full grasp and adequate confession of its authority.[12]

Later in the Statement, the doctrine's indispensability is driven home again in these terms:

The authority of Scripture is inescapably impaired if this total divine inerrancy is in any way limited or disregarded …[13]

The stakes were high, the battle-lines clear. There was no alternative to inerrancy if the dam wall preventing the loss of the historic Christian faith was to remain solid. It alone provided adequate protection.

The International Council on Biblical Inerrancy may have been right in understanding the risks. Peter Jensen may also have been right to insist on the protective importance of inerrancy. But the problem is that the Bible is not, at least obviously, or in ways that are easy to defend, inerrant. Even the most devoted advocate of inerrancy will acknowledge that inerrancy is hard to maintain in the face of mounting evidence against its reasonableness. This can be illustrated by way of reference to two important Biblical characters, the second more important than the first from a theological and interpretive point of view. The first is Noah. The second is Adam.

Noah

In my previous book, *A Restless Faith*, I discussed the Noah story at some length, because it seemed to me then that this story is a significant

---

11   From the preface to *Forever Settled: Various Documents of the International Council on Biblical Inerrancy*, Philadelphia: International Council on Biblical Inerrancy, 1979, 22.

12   *Forever Settled*, 193.

13   From a section entitled 'A Short Statement, quoted in A. Albert Mohler Jr. 'When the Bible Speaks God Speaks: The Classical Doctrine of Biblical Inerrancy', in J. Merrick, Stephen M. Garrett (eds.) *Five Views on Biblical Inerrancy*, Grand Rapids: Zondervan, 2013, 36.

hermeneutical (or interpretative) test case, for all sorts of reasons. For one, it is a story that continues to be taken literally by large numbers of Christians around the world, by many, probably most, evangelical Protestants, for example, but also by people of Roman Catholic and Orthodox persuasion. Muslims mostly accept this story (or at least their version of it) as literally true, which probably means that a large proportion of the world's population believes in Noah, and in a great flood that engulfed the earth not that long ago.

Jesus appears to have believed in the literal truth of Noah and the flood,[14] as did those who wrote the New Testament. The writer of Hebrews includes Noah in his list of heroes of faith, along with other characters mentioned in Genesis 1-11. That he accepted the story as straightforwardly factual is suggested by his description of Noah:

> By faith Noah, warned by God about events as yet unseen, respected the warning and built an ark to save his household; by this he condemned the world and became an heir to the righteousness that is in accordance with faith.[15]

What makes the Noah story such a good test case for issues of interpretation is that it describes an event which, if it was true to fact, would most certainly have left abundant evidence of its occurrence. The doctrine of inerrancy, as consistently articulated by Hodge and Warfield, by the Chicago Statement, and by Peter Jensen, insists that the Scriptures are without error in 'all matters historical and scientific.' The facticity (or otherwise) of Noah's great flood is certainly a matter about which science and history can speak. The big question is: did it happen as described in the Bible?

As I have read and re-read the Noah story, I have become convinced that it is unambiguously a description of a universal or worldwide flood. The whole point of the Noah narrative is that after creating human beings, God regretted that decision (Genesis 6:6). God's reason for regret was because 'all the people on earth had corrupted their ways,' (6:12). God therefore decided to obliterate human and animal life, and did so by means of a gigantic flood, the waters of which rose until 'all the high mountains under the entire heavens' were covered to a depth of at least seven metres, (7:12,

---

14   Matthew 24:37-38; Luke 17:26-27.

15   Hebrews 11:7 NRSV

20) wiping out '*every living thing* on the face of the earth' (7:23), except for Noah and those with him on the ark.

It isn't easy, though some have tried, to exegete these verses as describing anything other than a universal or world-wide flood. Anything less wouldn't sustain the theological points being made by the story teller. Rev. Dr Mark Thompson, the current Principal of Moore Theological College, has said he believes in a worldwide flood as described in Genesis 6 to 9. I agree with him that this is what is being described in these chapters. However, I don't agree with him that such a flood happened or is factual. The scientific evidence, which you would expect to be there in bucket-loads, simply isn't there, not even in cupfuls. In *A Restless Faith*, I itemized some reasons for thinking that Noah's flood was not worldwide. To those, I will add some additional reasons mentioned by John H. Walton in his commentary on Genesis. Walton is an inerrantist, and so his comments are likely to be of special interest.

With respect to the evidence or lack of evidence for a world-wide flood, the following questions serve to highlight some of the difficulties:

- Where did all the water come from? 4.4 billion cubic kilometres of water would have had to be added to the oceans for Mt. Everest and other large mountain ranges to be covered.

- Where did all the water go after the flood, and in so short a time?

- How did the world's plants survive being submerged for between five months and a year?

- How did the world's fresh-water fish survive their marine environment being swamped by salt water - or vice versa if the water was fresh?

- How did Noah and his tiny family keep the animals alive – many with highly specialized dietary requirements? How, for example, were the carnivores fed and kept apart?

- How did Noah manage to keep so many species alive? We now know that there are between 50,000 and 75,000 species of birds and animals and about 30 million modern and extinct species of organisms, which raises the problem of how they would all fit on the ark. Even if we assume that there were only two of each animal, rather than 2 plus 7 of some, it has been estimated that each of these animals would have needed to squash into the volume of a milk carton just to fit into the ark.[16]

• How did the animals manage to return to their specialized environments – many across un-crossable seas (e.g. Tasmania's tiger; animals from North and South America)? How did the sloth, who doesn't walk on land, manage to get all the way back to South America?

• Where is the evidence of this massive destruction in places like Australia?[17]

Questions such as these have mostly emerged in the last two to three hundred years, post-Copernicus, post the emergence of contemporary science, with its inter-related fields of physics, geology, biology, zoology; post the study of plate tectonics. However, it is worth noting that the Noah story would have appeared credible to ancient and even pre-modern readers of this story. Those who first told and then wrote down the story are likely to have believed in a flat earth, above which was a firmament, above which were store houses of water able to be released in the form of rain. They would have believed that the earth rested on water, and was surrounded by water.[18] This understanding makes highly credible the possibility of a universal flood. That the waters above and below and around the earth could flood the earth to a depth greater than the earth's highest mountains would have seemed

---

16   See further Ian Plimer, *Telling Lies for God*, Sydney: Random House, 1994, 110. See also G. R. Morton, 'The Mediterranean Flood,' *Perspectives on Science and Christian Faith*, 49.4 (1997). Morton notes that, 'Assuming that the 21,000 species of amphibian, reptile, bird, and mammal had to be represented on the ark, it would require around 42,000 individuals. Assuming that each of the eight people on the ark had to take care of their share of animals, each person would have 2,637 cages to visit each day for feeding and cleaning. If each person worked a 12 hour shift, then each cage would only get three and two-thirds minutes of attention per day …' 242.

17   Flood stories do exist in the folklore of Australia's Indigenous peoples. So that is at least some evidence. They are also widespread in the Americas and in the islands of the Pacific. However, they are almost entirely lacking in Africa, occur only occasionally in Europe, and are absent in many parts of Asia.

18   See, for example, Nahum Sarna's *Understanding Genesis: The Heritage of Biblical Israel*, (New York: Schocken Books, 1966), 5, for a diagrammatic representation of Biblical cosmology. See also P. Seely, 'The Geographical Meaning of "Earth" and "Seas" in Genesis 1:10', *Westminster Theological Journal*, 59 (1997): 231-55, and John H. Walton's NIV Application Commentary on Genesis, 327.

very possible. That the earth's entire population of humans and animals could be wiped out by such a flood, that an ark could be built to house the world's animals, and that these animals were within walking distance of the ark, would have been plausible. The story is credible given ancient assumptions. However, we no longer share those assumptions.[19] As a result, the Noah story, as it stands, faces formidable challenges to be accepted as credible today, that is, as a literal account of what actually happened in the not too distant past.

John H. Walton, Professor of Old Testament at Wheaton College in the United States, notes four possible ways of understanding the extent of Noah's flood: that it was (a) global, (b) restricted to the known world, (c) regional or (d) local. Against the possibility of a global flood, Walton offers the following information, an elaboration of a point made above:

> If the local sea level rose to the 16,946 foot peak of "Mount Ararat" for 150 days, the sea would have had to rise approximately 16,946 feet all over the planet earth. That would require about 630 million cubic miles of additional water weighing 3,000,000,000,000,000,000 tons, or three quintillion tons. That is an enormous volume of water. The oceans would have to triple in volume in only 150 days and then quickly shrink back to normal. Where would the 630 million cubic miles go to? There is nowhere an ocean can drain to, because the oceans already fill the lowest places. There is no geological evidence that the ocean basins that now exist formed in only 150 days.[20]

Against the possibility that Noah's flood was local, regional or simply covering the known world, Walton offers two critiques, firstly from the text, secondly from geology. Walton notes that ever since the literal truth of Noah's apparently world-wide flood was called into question by emerging scientific evidence, efforts have been made to read the text as asserting no more than a limited flood. One such effort is linguistic. Various words and

19 One interesting assumption shared by ancient peoples, which may help to illuminate the story of Noah, is that the Ararat range to the north of Mesopotamia and the Zagros range to the east were the 'pillars of heaven'. Thus when the ark comes to rest 'on the mountains of Ararat' (8:4) what may well be envisaged is the ark coming to rest on the side of a mountain range reaching up to heaven, with the tops of smaller mountains nearby becoming exposed to the air as the flood waters recede. This makes sense of the text and of ancient assumptions. But, once again, we don't share those assumptions.

20 The acknowledged source of this information is R.M. Best, *Noah's Ark and the Ziusudra Epic*, Fort Myers, Fla: Enlil, 1999, 39-40. Walton points out that the mountains of Ararat are located in the Lake Van region of eastern Turkey, *Genesis*, 314.

expressions used within the narrative could be taken as indicating a local or regional flood. One such word is the word for 'covering' in the description of the world's mountain tops being 'covered'. That word can mean 'to drench.' However, the idea of being drenched to a depth of fifteen cubits doesn't seem all that sensible, nor is drenching a particularly effective way of drowning people. Walton looks at other expressions used in the flood narrative noting that each of them can be read as implying no more than a local or regional flood. However, his sticking point is Genesis 8:3-5, where the flood waters are described as gradually receding until the tops of the mountains appeared. This certainly suggests a global rather than a local or regional flood.[21]

Walton's second criticism is scientific. He notes that levels identified as flood deposits have been found at several Mesopotamian sites including Ur, Uruk, Shuruppak, Nineveh, Lagash and Kish. However, and significantly, the levels at Ur and Nineveh date to the fourth millennium while the others date to the third millennium.[22] Moreover, other cities in the region show no such evidence. It may well be, therefore, that there have been some large floods in and around Mesopotamia, but none large enough to cover nearby mountains, and none requiring a vessel as large as Noah's ark. None of them are likely to have been the cause of widespread drowning. This is a long, long way shy of what the text of Genesis 6-9 describes.

Walton concludes his discussion of the Noah story, by, in effect, admitting he is stumped. None of the four possible ways of reading this story is satisfactory, at least so long as one is of the opinion that the story is meant to be taken literally as a factual account of what happened, and that the Bible is without error. The best that Walton can come up with is:

> While there is no view that I am yet comfortable with, I am committed to the text first (handled with hermeneutical propriety).[23]

A more sensible and less tortured conclusion would be that the Noah Flood story, as described in Genesis 6-9, and as believed in by most Jewish, Christian and Islamic interpreters down through the centuries,[24] and even

---

21   *Genesis*, 326.

22   *Genesis*, 320.

23   *Genesis*, 329.

24   Davis A. Young, professor of geology at Calvin College in Grand Rapids notes that

today, did not occur as described. The Bible is not without error in 'all matters historical and scientific.'

Adam

Whether or not Noah existed and whether or not the gigantic flood described in Genesis occurred (in whatever exact form) are matters of some importance for conservative or Bible-believing Christians, as I have sought to show. However, the importance of Noah's story pales into relative insignificance compared with the significance of another and earlier character described in Genesis 1-11. Whether Adam, Noah's earliest ancestor, existed, and whether the story of his creation and subsequent disobedience to God occurred as described (however symbolically) in Genesis 2 and 3, is a matter of extreme importance for Christians around the world, and, in this instance, it is not just the doctrine of inerrancy that would need to be jettisoned or modified. If Adam was not a discrete individual who, along with Eve, fell from grace, there would be a whole raft of doctrines that would need to be re-thought and re-configured.

Ever since Charles Darwin suggested that animal species had not been created by God on a single day of creation in about 4004 BCE, but had evolved over much longer periods by what he called 'natural selection,' a fierce battle has been waged which continues to this day, with Christians quite reasonably arguing that if Adam was not the first human ancestor, then the whole superstructure of Christian belief threatens to come crumbling down.

Once, when I was teaching at Moore Theological College in Sydney, I had a short conversation with a colleague. I asked him whether he believed that Adam was a discreet and actual person, and not simply a figurative representative of humankind. I had for some years believed the latter. His reply surprised me. He said, 'I don't think we have any choice other than to accept that Adam was a real person,' his reason, 'because St Paul clearly believed that Adam was a real person.' On reflection, I think my colleague

---

ancient Jewish writers 'unhesitatingly assumed that the Old Testament story [of Noah] was literal history.' Young notes that 'only Philo remotely suggested a limited flood, one that "almost" went out beyond the Pillars of Hercules, but for him that was tantamount to being universal,' *The Biblical Flood: A Case Study of the Church's Response to Extrabiblical Evidence*, Carisle: Paternoster Press, 1995, 12. Christian interpreters have understood the story similarly up until recently. I don't think they were misguided.

was right in saying that St Paul believed in a literal and actual Adam. It is hard to interpret the following passages in any other way:

> Therefore, just as sin came into the world through one man, and death came through sin, and so death spread to all because all have sinned – sin was indeed in the world before the law, but sin is not reckoned when there is no law. Yet death exercised dominion from Adam to Moses, Romans 5:12-14.

> But the free gift is not like the trespass. For if the many died through the one man's trespass, much more surely have the grace of God and the free gift in the grace of the one man, Jesus Christ, abounded for the many, Romans 5:15.

While teaching at Moore College, I did not feel under any pressure to believe or teach that Adam was a real person rather than a figurative representative of humankind. However, that is not the case in many conservative theological colleges. Faculty at Wheaton College, for example, where John H. Walton teaches, are required to sign faith statements declaring that God directly created Adam and Eve, the 'historical parents of the entire human race.' I think I understand why. If St Paul was mistaken in believing that Adam was our first human ancestor, then he might also be mistaken on other matters, including his understanding of homosexuality. Surrendering the historicity of Adam and Eve clearly has consequences. Carl Trueman, Professor of Historical Theology and Church History at Westminster Theological Seminary, sees the issue of Adam as arguably the most important issue facing evangelicalism at the moment:

> [If] homosexuality is the clear point of challenge in the area of ethics, then my guess is that the historicity and individuality of Adam will become the clear point of challenge to scriptural authority. For Adam is crucial: Speaking in terms of my own tradition, if there were no historical Adam and no fall, the entire system of doctrine outlined in the Westminster Standards would collapse. More importantly – and beyond the confines of Reformed theology – Paul's statements about Adam in Romans 5 and 1 Corinthians 15 are crucial to interpreting Pauline theology and the gospel itself. The doctrine of all Christians, not just Presbyterians, is vitally connected to Adam.[25]

Trueman is right to think that the historicity and individuality of Adam is a matter of great importance, certainly for evangelical Christians within the Protestant tradition. Yet the existence of Adam, as described in Genesis 2

---

25   Carl Trueman, *The Real Scandal of the Evangelical Mind*, Chicago: Moody Publishers, 2011, 34.

and 3, and referred to elsewhere in the Bible, has increasingly come under question, so much so that an increasingly live option among evangelicals is that Adam and Eve were not the 'historical parents of the entire human race.'

In a recently published book, *Four Views on the Historical Adam*, (2013), four evangelical scholars go head to head on this issue. What makes this book so relevant is that it is a discussion amongst evangelicals, not between evangelicals and others. The book's first contributor, Denis O. Lamoureux, an Associate Professor of Science and Religion at St Joseph's College in the University of Alberta, identifies himself as 'a thoroughly committed and unapologetic evangelical theologian.' He also, relevantly, holds to a version of inerrancy, and yet he believes 'Adam never existed.'[26] A large part of his reason for not believing in an historical Adam is that he is convinced by at least the broad outlines of the picture of human origins emerging from evolutionary science. Lamoureux is himself a convinced evolutionist. As he puts it:

> I find that the evidence for evolution is overwhelming. Every science that deals with human origins fits tightly together and comes to only one conclusion: the universe and life evolved. [As an evolutionary biologist] I have experienced the fruitfulness and predictability of the theory of evolution. Every time a new fossil is discovered, it always fits exactly where it should. I have yet to see evidence that falsifies biological evolution.[27]

On the broad picture emerging from evolutionary science, he writes:

> The fossil record and evolutionary genetics reveal that we share with chimpanzees a last common ancestor that lived about six million years ago. Along the evolutionary branch to humans, there are approximately 6,000 transitional fossil individuals. Scientists have also discovered that about 99 percent of the DNA sequences in our genes are similar to chimpanzees, including defective genes (pseudogenes). This is like our own families in that we share with relatives genetic similarities, both good and bad. In addition, the archaeological

---

26   Denis O. Lamoureux, 'No Historical Adam: Evolutionary Creation View,' in Matthew Barrett, Ardel B. Caneday, (eds.) *Four Views On The Historical Adam*, Grand Rapids: Zondervan, 2013, 38.

27   Lamoureux goes on to point out that 'evolution is the easiest theory to disprove. Find just one human tooth near the bottom of the geological record and you could destroy evolutionary science. That's no exaggeration, but I wouldn't hold my breath waiting for it to happen.' *No Historical Adam: Evolutionary Creation View*, 40.

record discloses that humans who behaved like us (creating art, sophisticated tools, and intentional burials) appeared roughly 50,000 years ago. Burying the dead with items assumed to be needed for the afterlife signifies religious belief. Finally, science has found that the genetic variability among all people today is quite small and indicates that we descended from a group of about 10,000 individuals.[28]

This picture is nothing like what we read in Genesis 1-11. The chronology is different. Human beings have been around a lot longer than the Genesis account suggests, as has death. Lamoureux doesn't mention it, but the geography is also different. Current understandings are that modern humans emerged out of Africa, not Mesopotamia. The arithmetic is also different: 10,000 individuals, rather than two. These are massive differences suggesting that efforts to harmonize the scientific and Biblical pictures will be challenging, to say the least. Lamoureux believes they cannot be harmonized convincingly. He mentions evolutionary genetics. Genetic science has taken quantum leaps in recent years, further enhancing our understanding of human origins. Recent genetic research, associated with the human genome project, appears to have ruled out the possibility that modern humans have descended from a single pair of individuals.[29] Studies have, however, identified a genetic 'Adam' and 'Eve' by projecting back from information currently stored in the genes of contemporary humans. The problem is that genetic Adam and genetic Eve are unlikely to have known each other. Moreover, they were surrounded by thousands of other humans whose many ancestors were more ancient than them.

I am no scientist, but it has been explained to me that the Y chromosome is passed down almost identically from father to son, with slight variations caused by genetic mutations. Evidently, these mutations create the wherewithal for geneticists to trace the male line all the way back to the father of all contemporary males. This capacity has created something of a mad scramble to locate and date Y-chromosomal Adam, as he has been named. A succession of studies have variously calculated that Y-chromosomal Adam lived somewhere between 120,000 and 338,000 years ago.

---

28   *No Historical Adam: Evolutionary Creation View*, 64.

29   Studies of the DNA of contemporary humans appear to imply that current genetic diversity among humans cannot be accounted for if humanity began with just two individuals.

Corresponding to Y-chromosomal Adam is Mitochondrial Eve, the woman from whom all contemporary humans are descended matrilineally. Taking account of the fact that DNA from the mitochondria is carried inside the egg, so that only women pass it on to their children, geneticists have been able trace the maternal line to Mitochondrial Eve, the maternal ancestor of all contemporary humans, with estimates of her antiquity currently ranging between 99,000 and 200,000 years ago.

These studies, still in their infancy,[30] are simply adding to, or filling out, a story of human origins which at almost every point contradicts a literal reading of the Adam and Eve story found in the Bible. This is creating something of a crisis for conservative Christians, which is reflected in the recently published *Four Views on the Historical Adam*. What was fascinating for me as I read *Four Views on the Historical Adam* is that only one of the four authors questions or seeks to contradict the scientific conclusions highlighted by the book's first author, Denis O. Lamoureux. It is only William D. Barrick, a six-day, young-earth creationist, who questions the science, and even he does not offer an alternative scientific case. He simply articulates and defends a literal and straightforward reading of the Biblical text. He opts for the Genesis account as over and against the contradictory scientific account.

What is especially relevant for our purposes is that each of the four authors is an avowed inerrantist. That is surprising. One would have thought it would be impossible to go on affirming the Bible's historical and scientific reliability if, as Lamoureux argues, 'Adam never existed.'

Unravelling this dilemma, will, I think, provide further reasons for thinking that inerrancy ought to be discarded. Note that Lamoureux not only believes that Adam never existed, he also accepts that St Paul believed Adam did exist. According to Lamoureux, not only did St Paul believe that Adam was a real person, he also believed, erroneously, that death post-dated the creation of Adam, and that the natural world was changed as a result of Adam's and Eve's disobedience, subjecting the created order to decay (Rom. 8:20-22). None of these beliefs lines up with contemporary understandings of the natural and human time-line, as accepted by Lamoureux. How, one might ask, could he be an inerrantist?

---

30   For more information on this subject, see the web-site of the BioLogos Foundation – biologos.org – associated with Francis Collins, director of the Human Genome Project.

The fairly simple, but revealing answer is that inerrancy is not monochrome. It comes in a number of versions, which, in itself, is reason to reconsider using the term. Some that I have come across are: absolute inerrancy,[31] critical inerrancy,[32] limited inerrancy,[33] functional inerrancy,[34] well-versed inerrancy[35] and genre inerrancy.[36] The very existence of these many versions is a tacit acknowledgement that inerrancy has problems, or, to make the point slightly differently, the doctrine needs to be refined and re-defined in the face of mounting difficulties and obstacles.

As an illustration of this, and by way of slight digression, the Roman Catholic Church has, over time, had to modify its understanding of inerrancy. In 1893, Pope Leo XIII issued an encyclical 'On the Study of the Holy Scripture' (*Provientissimus Deus*) in which he affirmed that the Bible, in all of its parts, and down to the most insignificant of items, was inspired and errorless. He was responding, in much the same way as Protestants had, to the challenge of Darwinism and critical Biblical scholarship. The encyclical resisted the notion that only some aspects of Scripture are inerrant, whereas others are fallible.

---

31   According to which the Bible is accurate and true in all matters, a view associated with Harold Lindsell.

32   According to which the Scriptures are completely true in all that the Scriptures affirm, to the degree of precision intended by the original author, a view associated with Roger Nicole, J. Ramsey Michaels, D. A. Carson, John Woodbridge.

33   According to which the Bible is inerrant in all matters of salvation and ethics, faith and practice, a view associated with I. Howard Marshall and Donald G. Bloesch.

34   According to which the Bible is inerrant in its purpose or function; in its power to bring people to salvation and growth in Christian life, a view associated with G. C. Berkouwer, Jack Rogers and Donald McKim.

35   This view, which is similar to, and perhaps an instance of, critical inerrancy, is recommended by Kevin J. Vanhoozer, Research Professor of Systematic Theology at Trinity Evangelical Divinity School. For inerrancy to be 'well-versed' it needs to take sufficient account of the complexities, purposes and limitations of language.

36   Genre inerrantists, sensibly in my view, appeal to the genre of Biblical passages to avoid what could otherwise be construed as errors. For example, passages of Scripture which could be described as historical are labelled theological-history, a kind of history which employs literary conventions recognizable to ancient audiences, such as exaggeration and deliberate alterations of detail. These exaggerations and altered details cannot be described as 'errors' because the writers were not simply recounting 'what really happened.' They did not intend to deceive or mislead. Names to associate with this approach are R. Gundry, M. Silva, V. Long, and T. Longman.

However, under the cumulative impact of scientific and historical studies, the Roman Catholic Church modified its understanding of inerrancy in the direction of some of the versions of inerrancy mentioned above, a process which culminated with Article II of Second Vatican Council's *Dei Verbum*, promulgated on 18 November 1965.

> The books of the Scripture firmly, faithfully and without error teach that truth which God for the sake of our salvation wished to see confided to the sacred Scriptures (*Dei Verbum* 11).

This articulation of inerrancy, focusing as it does on truths about salvation, deliberately leaves room for the possibility that the Bible contains scientific and/or historical error, which brings us back to the question of how someone like Lamoureux can be considered an inerrantist.

Returning to the discussion of the various forms of inerrancy, it seems to me that they can be lined up along a number of spectrums. At either end of one spectrum, doctrines of inerrancy divide into those which assert that there are no errors of any sort in the Bible, and those which admit that there are errors, but of an inconsequential kind. There are a number of ways to allow for the existence of error, while continuing to espouse inerrancy. For example, Kevin J. Vanhoozer suggests that the Bible is inerrant only 'in what it affirms.'[37] Others suggest that the Bible is inerrant only in terms of its function or larger purposes, of evoking faith and bringing salvation, a view often associated with the notion that the Bible is infallible. Many of those who acknowledge the existence of errors in the Bible appeal to the notion of accommodation, articulated variously by St Augustine and John Calvin, and according to which God accommodated himself to the sometimes erroneous beliefs of those who wrote the Bible. Lamoureux is one of those. He suggests that 'when the Holy Spirit inspired the Biblical authors, He allowed them to use some of their ancient ideas about nature … in order to communicate inerrant, life-changing spiritual truths.'[38] For him, ancient science is the 'incidental vehicle' used to convey those truths.[39] Lamoureux thus restricts inerrancy to 'spiritual' matters.

---

37   Kevin J. Vanhoozer, 'Augustinian Inerrancy: Literary Meaning, Literal Truth, and Literate Interpretation in the Economy of Biblical Discourse', in *Five Views of Biblical Inerrancy*, 207.

38   *No Historical Adam: Evolutionary Creation View*, 41.

39   *No Historical Adam: Evolutionary Creation View*, 62, 63.

An elephant in the room of all of such efforts to restrict the meaning of inerrancy is that what you end up with is inerrancy with errors. With this way of thinking, the Bible does have errors, though not big or significant ones. The problem with this, as was articulated by Peter Jensen, is that once you admit the existence of errors, in the areas of science or history, for example, then how will you prevent the acids of doubt eating away at larger and more important truths? If the Bible can be wrong in some areas, what good reason is there to think that what it says on other matters is true? Jensen thus prefers an errorless form of inerrancy to prevent errors of any sort creeping in. The problem with his view is that it appears blind to the fact that the Biblical writers do espouse and assume views we no longer reasonably accept.

Another helpful way to differentiate between the various understandings of inerrancy is in terms of how they attempt to reconcile contemporary scientific understandings of the world with what appears to be the worldview expressed and assumed by the Biblical writers. At one end of the spectrum are those who think they can be reconciled. At the other end are those who think they cannot.

Included among those who believe the two accounts cannot be reconciled are two unlikely bed-fellows. One of those is young earth creationism. Creationists typically argue, convincingly I think, that contemporary and evolutionary understandings of human and planetary life are significantly and seriously at odds with a literal and straightforward reading of the Bible. The two accounts cannot be reconciled, and, according to creationist understandings, it is contemporary scientific views which are in error, not the Bible. The second unlikely bed-fellow is someone like Denis O. Lamoureux who argues that because Biblical 'science' is ancient science it contains errors. The cosmology and anthropology of the Biblical authors is pervasively shaped by ancient assumptions, many of which we no longer accept. Because Lamoureux restricts the Bible's inerrancy to 'spiritual' truths, he is willing and able to accept the sufficiently well evidenced conclusions of contemporary science, including evolution.

At the other end of this spectrum are those who believe that what the Bible says and implies about human and planetary origins *can* be reconciled with the well-evidenced conclusions of contemporary science. This view is known as 'concordism. Concordists typically believe that the Biblical and scientific pictures will converge, even if, at times, or temporarily, they may appear to be in tension. Since all truth is God's truth, the Book of Nature and the Book of Scripture, each properly understood, cannot contradict each other.

My own somewhat educated hunch is that Lamoureux and the creationists are right in thinking that Biblical and scientific understandings cannot be reconciled. They do contradict each other, though not necessarily at every point. What keeps persuading me of this is that attempts to reconcile or bring the two accounts into closer harmony seem so unconvincing. We have seen this already with Noah and the account of his gigantic flood. The same applies to recent discussions about the existence of Adam. Concordists typically believe that science and the Bible need to be brought sufficiently into line to allow for the retention of important doctrines such as the doctrine of The Fall. And so, John H. Walton, in his contribution to *Four Views On The Historical Adam*, argues that Adam did exist, as Jesus and the New Testament writers clearly believed, but Walton also suggests, with one eye to contemporary science, that at some stage in the evolutionary process God 'undertook a special act of creation' to give the entire human population the image of God. Because Walton also accepts that human death both preceded and followed this endowment, he further suggests that at some point after being endowed with the divine image, possibly tens of thousands of years later, God designated Adam and Eve 'as representative priests in sacred space,' who, because of their unique and influential fall into sin, were 'doomed to their inherent mortality' and 'lost the chance to become immortal.'[40]

This is a valiant attempt, I must admit, to bring the two apparently contradictory pictures into at least partial alignment. However, it also leaves me with the impression that Walton is trying to mix oil and water; ancient cosmology and contemporary understandings. Such a proposal certainly takes us a long way away from a simple and straightforward reading of the text, as Luther and the other Reformers encouraged us to read it.

---

40   John H. Walton, 'A Historical Adam: Archetypal Creation View,' in *Four Views on the Historical Adam*, 109. Walton tries hard to reconcile contemporary science and Biblical teaching. For example, while acknowledging that the NT teaches that there was 'a historical point in time when sin and death became human realities,' it doesn't necessarily teach that Adam and Eve were the first humans or that contemporary humans are all biologically related to Adam and Eve, 107.

Inerrancy appears to be dying the death of a thousand qualifications. Even in its early days, the qualifications had begun. According to Warfield and Hodge, and the Chicago Statement, inerrancy only applies to the original autographs,[41] which no longer exist; nor should we expect of the text modern standards of precision and accuracy. To these and other possibly reasonable qualifications others have needed to be added as it has become increasingly obvious that a literal reading of the text does not deliver a true picture of what happened, and is, in fact, misleading, sending people in the direction of increasingly improbable conclusions. Maybe Noah's gigantic flood wasn't as gigantic as the text seems to imply. Maybe it didn't wipe out all the peoples of the world. Maybe it wasn't big enough even to cover the whole of Mesopotamia. Maybe Adam and Eve did not exist, or, if they did, it wasn't their disobedience that introduced death into human experience, and so on and so on.

Fuelling these seemingly endless modifications to a doctrine, which should be jettisoned I think, is a similarly unending series of challenges coming from contemporary Biblical and scientific studies, with the battleground continually spreading beyond the early chapters of Genesis to the rest of the Bible. Significant and increasingly difficult-to-counter doubts are being raised about the historical accuracy of the Exodus story, with the category of fictionalised history now being sensibly suggested to describe this and other Biblical stories. No part of the Bible, not even the story of Jesus, has been immune from sustained critical scrutiny, as a result of which doctrines of inerrancy appear to be in retreat, or, alternatively, are digging in and becoming more belligerent and combative, as almost always happens when people are backed into a corner.

This is creating anxiety amongst Christians around the world. It has also thrown up a number of related ethical challenges. What should Christians do in the face of the above elaborated challenges to Biblical inerrancy? What should their leaders do? Should they be up-front about the strength of those challenges, or is it better to keep quiet and soft-peddle the difficulties to protect their constituencies from the anxiety they themselves feel, which raises important issues of leadership and intellectual integrity?

When is the right time to put up the white flag and admit defeat; or, at the very least, let the troops know that you and they are in trouble? It is

---

41   The original Biblical texts, not to copies into which errors have crept.

worth reflecting again on Peter Jensen's suggestion that inerrancy ought to be kept because of what it protects. Implied by the suggestion is a degree of intellectual fragility, an acknowledgment that inerrancy does have the sorts of problems to which his son was alluding. Peter's suggestion can therefore be construed as an argument against inerrancy. Let me explain.

It is true that we do sometimes choose to retain things because of what they protect. We might, for example, invest in a home alarm system which we know isn't fool proof, but which provides at least some protection for our belongings. However, not everything we keep in order to protect something else is so easily justified. For example, nations of the world often enter into alliances with other nations to safeguard their security and way of life. An ethical dilemma is created when some of those allies are manifestly and seriously unjust in the treatment of their citizens. Allies are then faced with some hard choices, such as breaking off alliances or publically rebuking an ally, choices which will be made even harder if one's security and way of life are likely to be significantly jeopardized if they were to do this.

The issue is whether we can justify, on intellectual or ethical grounds, the thing we are relying on to protect the things we value. This is certainly relevant to the issue of inerrancy. If one thought that the case for inerrancy was a weak one, and that the case against inerrancy was becoming stronger, then the ethical thing would be to not rely upon it so strongly. The ethical thing would be to acknowledge this and not to hide it. Even though precious Christian doctrines might appear to depend on inerrancy for their protection, this, in itself, is not reason enough to retain inerrancy. In fact, because the emotional cost involved in jettisoning inerrancy is so high, one ought to be even more vigilant in one's scholarship around the issues. To adopt inerrancy simply or largely because of what it protects makes one highly susceptible to intellectual and therefore moral compromise. You are more likely to make excuses, to rationalize, and to look the other way in the face of legitimate challenges.

To illustrate, imagine your son has become a suspect in an organized crime investigation - God forbid. You are at first staggered by this. You can't believe that your son, the son you raised from infancy, and delighted in as he grew into adulthood, would be capable of such underhand and socially damaging behavior. Let's imagine that it is trade in illicit drugs that he has been accused of. You are shocked by the accusation. You have spent his lifetime educating him to internalize values you and your husband hold dear, and you had believed he had done that. And you have some evidence of this from his high school days when he was given various awards, including a good citizen award. Your son has brought you credit; is well regarded by his cousins and friends. How could he possibly be guilty? How could he possibly bring shame to the family? You certainly have much to lose if your son is found guilty of being involved in a criminal syndicate. The cost would be enormous. And so, you would have every good (personal) reason to keep believing in your son. You would have every good reason to interpret the facts, even the most uncomfortable ones, as supporting your belief that your son is innocent and that a terrible mistake is unfolding.

Being loyal and believing the best isn't a bad thing when it comes to human relationships. It can even be the right thing when the evidence is ambiguous. Your son might be innocent after all. But in this case, and in the case of the church and its teachings, the stakes are high. The potential impact upon others is huge. At some point in the investigation, if you find that the facts don't comfortably line up with the conclusion that your son is innocent, and increasingly do line up with the proposition that he is up to his armpits in a trade wreaking havoc in the lives of countless individuals and families, you will have an ethical obligation, however difficult to fulfill, to cooperate with authorities to see your son arrested and brought to justice.

And just as you will need to face the truth about your son, should the evidence point that way, it is imperative that the church, regardless of the cost, be scrupulous and honest; not just believing something because of what it protects, but only keeping on believing because we think the evidence is sufficiently strong.

I have argued in this chapter that the evidence is not sufficiently strong. Inerrancy in its stronger forms is unsustainable in the face of contrary and accumulating evidence. In its softer more nuanced forms, it appears to have already died the death of a thousand qualifications. The issue for Christian leaders, including those involved in training Christian leaders, is: will they be honest and courageous enough to admit the error of inerrancy, or, at the very least, to admit its serious and increasingly obvious deficiencies?

CHAPTER THREE

The Puzzle of Pseudepigraphy

A response of many Christians, in the face of multiple and mounting challenges to their faith, is to say, 'I will go with what the Bible says. I am a Bible-believing Christian. If the Bible says or implies that Adam existed, or that Noah was a real person, and that his gigantic flood happened, I will submit to what the Bible says or implies. The Bible is God's Word, and, because of that, it is far more reliable than human reason, whose doubtful conclusions I will happily disregard.'

A problem with this admirably trusting approach is that the situation is not quite that simple, even for Bible-believing Christians, because the doubtful conclusions of human reason are not so easily avoided, even for those taking this trustful approach. And that is because human reason needs to be employed even to come to the conclusion that the Bible is God's Word, and therefore can be trusted. Bible-believing Christians will almost always have their reasons for trusting the Bible. They may believe, for example, that the Bible is self-authenticating. It commends itself as true in a direct and convincing way when it is read. They may, alternatively, have concluded that the Bible's reliability is attested to by adequately strong evidence; or they may have chosen to trust those who have told them this. Or they have had a sense of God speaking to them through the Scriptures, which gives them reason to trust what they read. They may also have been persuaded by deductive arguments of the form: God has inspired the Scriptures. God is truthful and reliable. Therefore, the Scriptures are truthful and reliable. Once again, human reason is involved. One cannot escape the need for, or our reliance upon, human reason. This is as much the case for Bible-believing Christians as it is for anyone.

But reliance upon human reason goes even further than that. We say that we rely on the Bible, and trust in the Bible, but what exactly is the Bible? It is a collection of books and/or letters that have been accepted by Christians as authoritative, with human reason integrally involved in that process. A technical term which has come to be used to describe this collection of acceptable books and letters is the 'canon' of Scripture. The word canon comes from a Greek word meaning 'rule' or 'measuring stick.' Deciding which books and letters to include within the canon of Scripture has been a long and strenuous process for Christians. Debates as to what should be included and what should be excluded from the canon reach all the way back to the second century CE. They were still happening at the time of the Protestant Reformation and the Roman Catholic Counter Reformation, with a succession of conferences and confessions opting for this or that collection.

A critical and early stage of the process happened when Marcion, in the early second century, proposed a quite restrictive early Christian canon, which included ten epistles believed to be written by St Paul, as well as a version of the Gospel of Luke. Marcion sought to expunge Jewish elements from the Christian Scriptures. In doing so, he began a centuries' long debate among Christians about what to include and what to exclude from their authoritative Scriptures. In partial and understandable reaction to Marcion, Christians extended the net more broadly to include expressions of the faith that fully embraced its Jewish foundations, including James, Hebrews and the Gospel of Matthew. In extending the net, various criteria of acceptability - human reason again - were suggested, not all of them as 'reasonable' as others. For example, Irenaeus, a second century Church Father, suggested the following as a reason to embrace the four Gospels, Matthew, Mark, Luke and John:

> It is not possible that the gospels can be either more or fewer in number than they are. For, since there are four-quarters of the earth in which we live, and four universal winds, while the church is scattered throughout all the world, and the 'pillar and ground' of the church is the gospel and the spirit of life, it is fitting that she should have four pillars breathing out immortality on every side, and vivifying men afresh ... Therefore the gospels are in accord with these things ... For the living creatures are quadriform and the gospel is quadriform ... These things being so, all who destroy the form of the gospel are vain, unlearned, and also audacious; those [I mean] who represent the

aspects of the gospel as being either more in number than as aforesaid, or, on the other hand, fewer.[1]

Complicating disputes about what to include and what to exclude from the canon of Scripture was the fact that the earliest Christians appeared to accept the Greek-language collection of Jewish writings, the Septuagint, as authoritative. Not all of its books have subsequently been accepted by Jews or Christians as canonical. Moreover, some of the books that have now come to be accepted as canonical or Scriptural, including Hebrews, James, 2 Peter, 2 and 3 John and Revelation, took time to be accepted, and often weren't accepted. For example, Martin Luther (1483-1546) sought to remove Hebrews, James, Jude and Revelation from the canon, believing them to contradict the Protestant doctrines of *sola scriptura* and *sola fide*.

Clearly, human reason needed to be employed in what would always run the danger of being a circular process of deciding what was authoritative and what was not. And not everyone was going to agree. The three major divisions of the Christian faith, Orthodox, Roman Catholic and Protestant all came to slightly different conclusions. Protestants came up with something like the following fourfold criteria of canonicity:

1. Apostolic Origin: attributed to and based upon the preaching/ teaching of the first-generation apostles or their close companions.

2. Universal Acceptance: acknowledged by all major Christian communities in the ancient world by the end of the 4th century, as well as being the accepted canon among Jewish authorities in the case of the Hebrew Scriptures.

3. Liturgical Use: read publicly when early Christian communities gathered for the Lord's Supper.

4. Consistent Message: containing a theological outlook similar to or complementary to other accepted Christian writings.

Whether or not these criteria are sensible or effective, or any longer useful in determining what ought to be considered Scriptural is clearly going to be affected by the discussions of chapters one and two of this book. However, what is clear is that even those who have decided that they will go with what the Bible says, because the Bible is God's Word, cannot, at least in principle, avoid the need to employ human reason in making that very

---

1   *Against Heresies* 3.11.8.

decision. Moreover, the need to activate human reason is again required of Christians because of the challenges mentioned in chapters one and two, and also because some very reasonable doubt has been raised about whether some of the books currently accepted as authoritative by Christians ought to have been so accepted.

One of the fruits of on-going Biblical scholarship is that we have become more and more aware of the history that lies behind the Bible, including the history of its composition. When what became known as the New Testament began to be written, there was a larger number of letters and books in circulation than ended up being accepted as Scriptural. These included documents purporting to be written by Jesus' immediate disciples, including Peter, Paul, Phillip, Mary and Thomas, and his brother James.

For various reasons, these documents were not accepted by the church as authoritative, in part because their teachings were not considered orthodox, but also because of reasonable doubts about their authorship. It wasn't uncommon in the ancient world for people to write things in the name of someone else, usually some esteemed person (like Peter, Mary and Paul) who was more likely to be taken notice of than the actual author. The name given to these sorts of writings is pseudepigraphy, which literally means 'false writing'.[2] It is, more precisely, false ascription, with works being inaccurately, and, in some cases, fraudulently, ascribed to someone other than the actual author or authors, normally with the purpose of bolstering credibility.

There is a fascinating instance of claimed pseudepigraphy in the New Testament. The writer of the second letter to the Thessalonians, supposedly Paul, warns his readers 'not to be deceived' by a 'letter from us' claiming that the return of Christ is imminent or has already arrived (2:2-3), which is at least similar to what is claimed in 1 Thessalonians. It is possible, and many scholars now think it likely, that Paul's first letter to the Thessalonians is genuine, written by the real St Paul, whereas 2 Thessalonians, with its claim that an earlier letter is pseudepigraphical, is itself an instance of pseudepigraphy.

If that is true, this is a disturbing fact, especially for Christians like myself who have grown up believing that the Bible we now have is the Bible

---

2   They are also referred to as pseudepigraphon or 'written under an assumed name.'

God intended for the benefit of humankind. One would have hoped that issues of canonicity would have been resolved by now, but maybe not. If 2 Thessalonians was not written by St Paul, while claiming that it was written by St Paul, then it surely must be excluded from the canon of Scripture. The letter is deceptive, and gallingly so, because a genuine letter of St Paul's has been tarred with the brush of pseudepigraphy.

It might be worth teasing away a little more at the concept of pseudepigraphy, before looking at some even more disturbing possible instances. Bart D. Ehrman, in his recent book on the subject,[3] notes that the term 'pseudepigraphy' includes authentic works which are anonymous, but which have been falsely attributed to some well-known early Christian figure to give the work greater status. The four Gospels, Matthew, Mark, Luke and John, are in that category. We don't know for sure who wrote them, although there are arguments in favor of the long-standing ascriptions. Ehrman differentiates between four possibilities when it comes to ascribing authorship to a book:

1. Orthonymous: rightly named.

2. Homonymous: same named. For example, someone by the name of John wrote the book of Revelation. The book has been ascribed to John the son of Zebedee, and for that reason was included in the canon. However, there is no suggestion of dishonest ascription.

3. Anonymous: having no name. For example, the Gospels, Acts, 1, 2 and 3 John, and Hebrews.

4. Pseudonymous: falsely named. Ehrman notes acceptable instances where an author uses a pen name, falsely ascribed documents such as Matthew's Gospel, and works that claim to be written by someone which were not written by the named author, which he describes as forgery.

In Old Testament biblical studies, the word pseudepigrapha refers to a collection of Jewish religious works written in the period *c* 300 BCE to 300 CE not all of which are literally pseudepigraphical. Some that are generally accepted as pseudonymous are the books of *Enoch*, the *Assumption of Moses*, the *Wisdom of Solomon*, and the *Psalms of Solomon*. Included in

---

3   Bart D. Ehrman, *Forged: Writing in the Name of God – Why the Biblical authors are not who we think they are*, New York: HarperOne, 2011.

the category of Christian pseudepigraphy are the *Gospel of Thomas* and the *Letter of Peter to James* (found in the *Pseudo-Clementine Homilies*).

Another form of literature, common and influential at the time of the New Testament, is apocalypse, from the Greek word meaning to 'unveil' or 'reveal'.[4] These works, including the Old Testament book of Daniel, were written to inspire hope in situations of hopelessness and possible despair. What is 'revealed' in these works is a heavenly perspective on the dire events occurring on earth, conveying the comforting message that God is in control. Apocalypses are almost always written pseudonymously in the name of some revered figure of the past (for example, Daniel, Abraham, Enoch and Adam). It has often been claimed that these works cannot be considered as forgeries because writing in the name of some figure of the distant past was an accepted part of the genre. Maybe so. However, over time, people did come to believe that these works were written by the named author. For example, Tertullian felt the need to argue a case for Enoch's book surviving Noah's flood,[5] and today many, probably most, Christians believe that Daniel was the author of the book by his name.

Possible New Testament Instances of Pseudepigraphy

It is possible that quite a number of the letters of the New Testament are pseudonymous, not certainly, but possibly. Or, to put it slightly differently, there is good reason to question the ascribed authorship of a number of New Testament letters. For example, 2 Peter is widely considered pseudonymous,[6] as are James and Jude. Six of the thirteen letters attributed to St Paul are considered pseudonymous, not amongst Christians in general,

---

4   Apocalypses reveal divine secrets. There is common misconception that apocalypses are eschatological in their focus. Daniel is about the end times, but, for example, 1 Enoch 72-82, and 2 Enoch reveal heavenly secrets.

5   *Forged: Writing in the Name of God,* 270. Questions of deliberate deception are raised by the book of Daniel. For example, chapter 8, verse 26 speaks of events in the 'distant future'; certainly distant from the time of Daniel. However, if, as many Biblical scholars now believe, the book of Daniel was written in the 3rd or 2nd centuries BCE, this verse does give a false impression.

6   1 Peter is also considered to be pseudonymous by many. L. Michael White, Director of the Institute for the Study of Antiquity and Christian Origins at the University of Texas, makes the perhaps overbold claim that the authenticity of 1 Peter is 'now doubted by almost all modern scholars', *From Jesus to Christianity,* San Francisco: Harper San Francisco, 2004, 272.

who are often not informed of these questionings, but certainly amongst New Testament scholars.[7]

That it is even possible that some, or even one, of the New Testament letters are pseudonymous is likely to be very unsettling for Christians who, like me, have grown up putting a great deal of weight on the information these letters convey. The Bible has seemed so fixed and secure, bound as it often is between leather covers, giving the impression of permanence and reliability.

As I have written this chapter, more so than the earlier ones, I have had to ask myself, 'Why should you unsettle people with what surely must be uncertain scholarly conjecture? Why not leave Christians to believe as they always have that Daniel was written by Daniel, that 2 Peter was written by Peter, that St Paul wrote Ephesians, Colossians, 2 Thessalonians and the Pastoral Epistles? Why unsettle people? Surely they and their now even-more-fragile faith can be left alone!'

Those are very good questions. Perhaps this book could be marketed solely for academics and theological students, for those who need to know what the scholars in their ivory towers are getting up to. Don't trouble the flock. But the fact is: the flock *is* being troubled. The information in this, and in all of this book's chapters, is in the public domain. It is out there already, and although most church goers may never come across the works of academic theologians and Biblical scholars, their pastors will have, hopefully, as will those who have taught their pastors. Moreover, they themselves are increasingly likely to come across this information in the form of efforts to discredit or destroy Christian faith – available on-line or in any secular book store. Bart Ehrman's very accessible book is provocatively entitled, *Forged: Writing in the Name of God – Why the Biblical authors are not who we think they are.* A whole raft of new books is being churned out whose sole aim is to expose the perceived weaknesses of the Christian faith. A chapter of one recently published book, dealing specifically with this subject, is provocatively entitled 'Inerrant Forgeries.' The book's title is, *The Christian Delusion: Why Faith Fails.*[8]

---

7   Almost all scholars accept that the following letters are legitimately Pauline: Romans, 1 & 2 Corinthians, Galatians, Philippians, 1 Thessalonians and Philemon.

8   John W. Loftus (ed.), *The Christian Delusion: Why Faith Fails*, New York: Prometheus Books, 2010.

My point is that these are issues which do need to be wrestled with, not swept under the carpet in ultimately misguided attempts to protect the flock. They need to be faced and worked through. Moreover, as we have seen, we simply have no choice but to use our God-given human reason to assess, and, if necessary, keep on assessing the reasons for including or excluding documents from the canon of Scripture. Perhaps the very notion of canon needs to be rethought. I think it does.

Leaving those thoughts aside for a moment, it might be useful to restrict ourselves to just three New Testament letters which are now widely regarded as pseudonymous, 1 Timothy, 2 Timothy and Titus, known as the Pastoral Epistles. Doubts about Pauline authorship of the Pastoral Epistles date back to the early 19th century when the great German theologian Friedrich Schleiermacher argued that various words and ideas used in these letters were at odds with those used in other letters ascribed to St Paul. Over time, other scholars followed Schleiermacher's lead, so much so that New Testament scholars are now mostly agreed that St Paul was not the author of these letters, and that, in all likelihood, they were written, or brought to their final form, by a later church leader seeking to invoke the legacy of St Paul for the needs of his own time. Some argue that 2 Timothy (or at least parts of it) are Pauline, but the others are not.

The reasons for questioning Pauline authorship are as follows:[9]

1. *Attestation:* the Pastoral Epistles are not attested to in early Christian writings, unlike the other ten purportedly Pauline letters.[10] They were not cited by Ignatius of Antioch in his surviving letters (c 110 CE). The earliest unambiguous attestation of any of the Pastoral Epistles occurs in Athenagoras and Theophilus who wrote in about 180 CE.[11] Irenaeus, who also wrote about the same time, cites all three of the Pastoral Epistles and attributes them to St

---

9   I am indebted, in what follows, to a paper written by Mark Harding which brings up to date his own doctoral studies on the subject of the Pauline or non-Pauline authorship of the Pastoral Epistles: Mark Harding, 'The Pastoral Epistles,' in Alanna Nobbs & Mark Harding (eds.), *All Things to All Cultures: Paul among Jews, Greeks and Romans*, Grand Rapids: Eerdmans, 2013, 328-352.

10   A ten letter collection of Pauline letters was in circulation c 100 CE.

11   By way of contrast, I Corinthians is quoted as early as 95 AD by Clement (1 Clement 47).

Paul. However, prior to that, there appears to have been some doubt about the authorship of the Pastorals. For example, Tertullian, writing at around 200 CE notes that Marcion (dc 160 CE)[12] rejected the Pastoral Epistles.[13] Jerome notes that Basilidies (fl. CE 125-150)[14] rejected the Pastorals and that Tatian (fl. 120-180 CE) regarded some letters of St Paul as spurious, though he accepted Titus.

2. *Chronology:* The Pastoral Epistles narrate missionary excursions to Macedonia (1 Timothy 1:3) and to Crete (Titus 1:5) which are not mentioned in Acts. This doesn't comfortably fit into the chronology of St Paul's missionary journeys as recorded in Acts and St Paul's other letters.

3. *Vocabulary and Writing Style:* In 1921, a subsequently influential study by P. N. Harrison drew attention to significant differences in vocabulary and writing style between the Pastoral Epistles and other New Testament letters attributed to St Paul. He suggested that the 'sober didactic, static, conscientious, domesticated' style of the Pastoral Epistles sharply contrasted with the 'Pauline impetus, the drive and surge of mighty thoughts never spoken before.'[15]

Harrison also drew attention to the contrasting vocabulary used by the author of the Pastoral Epistles. He noted that of the 848 words used in the Pastoral Epistles, discounting proper names, 306 of them, or just over a third, are not used in the ten-letter Pauline corpus. Moreover, there are 175 words used in the Pastoral Epistles which are not found anywhere else in the New Testament. Of those, 61 appear in the apostolic fathers, and a further 32 in the apologists of the second century. The remaining 82 appear in contemporary non-Christian writers writing in the years following 100 AD.

Harrison also drew attention to the use of stereotypical phrases and technical terms which do not appear at all in the ten-letter Pauline

---

12 Marcion was excommunicated for heresy in 144 CE.

13 It is possible that Marcion was not even aware of their existence. It could even be that they weren't yet written when he produced his truncated and very Pauline canon.

14 Note the abbreviation fl. is of the Latin *floruit* meaning to flourish, referring to the active years of the person referred to.

15 P. N. Harrison, *The Problem of the Pastoral Epistles*, Oxford: Oxford University Press, 1921, 42.

corpus. He notes the absence of 112 particles, enclitics, prepositions and pronouns which are used in the ten-letter corpus. Of the 77 of these language forms used by the author of the Pastoral Epistles and found in the ten-letter corpus, all of them, Harrison notes, occur in the Apostolic Fathers, the Apologists and in the majority of the other books of the New Testament. These occurrences and non-occurrences are not easily accounted for on the assumption that St Paul was the author of the Pastoral Epistles.

Harrison, while arguing that the words and literary style of the Pastoral Epistles are significantly divergent from those found in the other more clearly Pauline letters, also suggests that parts of the Pastoral Epistles may well have been penned by the Apostle. He suggests that their author had in his possession personal notes, *personalia*, written by the apostle to Timothy (2 Timothy 4:6-22) and Titus (Titus 3:12-15), around which the letters were written. The vocabulary and style of the *personalia* are consistent with Pauline usage in the ten-letter corpus.

4. *Theological Differences:* Scholars have also drawn attention to sometimes subtle theological differences in the text of the Pastoral Epistles. A number of themes which are central to the undisputed Pauline letters are absent in the Pastoral Epistles, such as the cross, faith, righteousness, and the important Pauline notion of being 'in Christ.' Faith is referred to in the Pastorals, but not in the sense of trust or confidence in the promises of God, but in the sense of 'the faith' or the acceptable body of Christian teachings (Titus 1:13).

The Pastorals also appear to differ from St Paul on other matters, including the law. The law is described as good and useful for godly living in 1 Timothy 1:8; without the salvation-historical freight that is carried in St Paul's treatment of the law in Galatians and Romans.

The author of the Pastoral Epistles employs the language of Hellenistic ethical discourse, with the term *eusebeia* (religion or godliness) especially common. This word and its cognates are foreign to the ten-letter Pauline corpus. They appear elsewhere in the New Testament only in Acts and 2 Peter, but are common in broadly contemporary Hellenistic literature (e.g., Philo and Josephus and in *1 and 2 Clement*). The author also appears to differ from St Paul on the issue of marriage and, possibly, on the status or role of women.

5. *Historical Context:* The historical situation presumed by the Pastoral Epistles appears to be significantly different from the situation pertaining when St Paul was alive. There appears to be a change of attitude towards the end of history and the re-appearance of Christ, which St Paul, in the undisputed Pauline letters, considered imminent.[16] In the Pastorals, we observe 'Paul' making provision for the death of *his* followers to pass on his teachings, suggesting the possibility of a long haul ahead.[17] The importance of being well-thought-of by outsiders also suggests that thoughts of an imminent apocalypse had faded. The value of being married is emphasized, rather than celibacy which was recommended in the undisputed Pauline texts. There appears to be a greater emphasis on church order, and less emphasis upon spiritual gifts. Church order appears more settled and hierarchical in the Pastoral Epistles, with paid and formally appointed offices of bishops, presbyters and deacons, and possibly an order of widows.

Although it is not clear which teachings are being resisted by the author or authors of the Pastoral Epistles, there are references to people wanting to be 'teachers of the law,'[18] and a fixation on 'myths and endless genealogies,'[19] and Jewish 'myths,'[20] along with advocacy of some form of asceticism[21] and special knowledge.[22] It is hard to know exactly what is being countered, but Mark Harding suggests that the 'best guess of many scholars is that the opponents are Jewish Christians, with emancipist ideals with respect to women and slaves, who stand at the formative stage of the second century obsession with *gnosis* and its power to enlighten and thus to save.'[23]

---

16   See, for example, 1 Corinthians 7:29f; 1 Thessalonians 4:15-17.

17   2 Timothy 2:1-14.

18   1 Timothy 1:7; Titus 1:10

19   1 Timothy 1:4

20   Titus 1:14

21   1 Timothy 4:3

22   1 Timothy 6:10

23   Mark Harding, *The Pastoral Epistles*, 343.

Regardless of the accuracy of this suggestion, the Pastoral Epistles do appear to imply an historical situation somewhat removed from the one within which St Paul was writing.

6. *Persuasional Approach:* Scholars have also noticed a different style of argumentation adopted by the author or authors of the Pastoral Epistles. In the undisputed letters of St Paul, the argument style tends to be dialogical, with St Paul directly engaging what he considers are false ideas. He takes on the arguments of his opponents.[24] However, in the Pastoral Epistles, unacceptable ideas are rarely countered directly by way of argument.[25] Instead, the false teachers themselves are castigated in what are known as vice lists, using a rhetorical technique designed to create antipathy towards one's opponents in what is essentially an *ad hominem* (to the person) argument. This is not, at least obviously, in the spirit of the real St Paul.[26]

All of the above reasons for concluding that the Pastoral Epistles were not written by St Paul constitute a cumulatively strong case. It is not surprising that the great majority of New Testament scholars are persuaded, and have been for many years, that these letters are pseudonymous. As to exactly when they were written, no one is sure. Suggestions vary from within a few years of the death of St Paul up until the early to mid-second century. We may never know.

If these letters were not written by St Paul, the implications are enormous and, for many, enormously unsettling. For a start, this would mean that what we have here is a Biblical error of massive proportions. What the Bible asserts to be the case is not the case. Moreover, if the real author or authors of the Pastorals were deliberately misleading (they certainly have misled), then what we have is as serious an error as one could imagine, an error of honesty. In my work as a parole officer, I am often working with people who have assumed false identities for financial or other advantage, and many of them have gone to jail for it. They are guilty of fraud, and in some cases, forgery. It is not a trivial matter to mislead people. If the Pastorals were not written by St Paul, then Christians have been misled for most of Christian

---

24   See, for example, 1 Corinthians 6:1-20; 7:1-7; 8:10.

25   With the notable exception of 1 Timothy 4:3-5.

26   See further Mark Harding, *The Pastoral Epistles*, 342.

history. They would not have accepted the Pastorals as Scripture had they believed St Paul was not the author.

Bart Ehrman notes the presence of keen discussion among early Christians about whether or not particular documents were written by the claimed author. They were well aware of the presence and unacceptability of forgery,[27] as were their fellow ancients. As Ehrman puts it:

> [Ancient] writers *did* see this kind of activity as fraudulent, they recognised it as deceitful, they called it lying (and other even nastier things), and they often punished those who were caught doing it.[28]

What should Christians do if they conclude that the author or authors of the Pastoral Epistles have deliberately misled their readers, including us? One could decide, and integrity may demand this, that the Pastoral Epistles should be jettisoned from the canon of Scripture. This has been proposed and enacted with other letters, and maybe that is what needs to happen again. The New Testament would then be reduced in size from 27 books and letters to 24, and, quite possibly, even further to as few as 17 if other of the New Testament books and letters are found to be pseudonymous. This would be a very scary prospect for most Christians, understandably.

But there is another option, and that is to argue that although the author or authors of the Pastoral Epistles did knowingly mislead, and should have been more upfront about their identity and purpose in writing, what they have written nevertheless retains value as an expression of what was clearly an evolving tradition. The Pastorals have also proved to be of immense personal value to Christians down through the years. They have been important to me; at (and after) my ordination to the diaconate and priesthood, for example. For many Christians, they have been extremely precious and inspirational, though not without some downsides.[29] For reasons such as these, Christians might sensibly decide not to do violence to the long-accepted canon of their Scriptures and retain the Pastorals in their Bibles.

---

27 Ehrman draws together his discussion of this reality in these terms: 'In short, there were long, protracted, and often heated debates in the early church over forged documents,' *Forged: Writing in the Name of God*, 22.

28 *Forged: Writing in the Name of God*, 25.

29 The tendency to vilify opponents rather than engaging their ideas through careful argument is one which we would do well not to imitate.

An entirely different option, in the face of the admittedly strong case against Pauline authorship, is to argue that these letters were written by St Paul, as they claim to be. This too is an honourable option. Although it is true that the majority of New Testament scholars, with relevant expertise, have long concluded that St Paul was not the author of the Pastoral Epistles, there has been some recent rear-guard resistance to this broad consensus. A number of well-credentialed scholars have swum against the tide to argue either that it was St Paul who wrote the Pastorals or, at least, it was he who commissioned and oversaw their writing. Notable among these scholars are Luke Timothy Johnson, William Mounce and Ben Witherington III. In the 1990's a group was formed in the Society of Biblical Literature to carefully scrutinize the case against Pauline authorship, with some promising results for those wanting to hold out for Pauline authorship. To mention just a few of the points they have been able to make:

- Although it is true that Irenaeus, Bishop of Lyons and a disciple of Polycarp, is the earliest writer to cite the Pastoral Epistles using St Paul's name, there are earlier instances of the Pastorals being quoted or alluded to by writers from at least the mid-2nd century; with some possible instances of citations in the works of Polycarp himself from earlier in the 2nd century.

- What evidence we have suggests that the Pastoral Epistles were widely accepted as authoritative, with no explicit early questioning of Pauline authorship. That Marcion does not include the Pastorals in his list of acceptable (to him) Pauline letters may suggest that the Pastorals didn't have the same widespread acceptance as other of St Paul's letters, or even that they did not exist when Marcion was writing. However, there were themes in the Pastorals that Marcion is likely to have been uncomfortable with, including that the law is good,[30] the denial of asceticism,[31] and the high value placed on the Hebrew Scriptures,[32] which were rejected by Marcion.

- The argument that the Pastorals don't line up neatly with Acts is no great surprise. There are lots of gaps in the Acts narrative which could easily be filled. It is quite possible, for example, that St Paul

---

30   1 Timothy 1:8.

31   1 Timothy 4:3

32   2 Timothy 3:16

was released from house arrest in Rome (Acts 28:30-31) and, at some later stage, journeyed back to Macedonia and Crete, instead of, or in addition to, journeying on to Spain, as was his express intention.

- The argument that the Pastorals reflect a more ordered and settled church administration can be overstated. According to Acts 14:23, Paul and Barnabas appointed elders (presbyters) on their first missionary journey. The actual structure of authority reflected in the Pastorals resembles that in the Jewish synagogues of the Diaspora, which is what one might expect of a rabbi-trained missionary like St Paul. The structure also resembles those found in Greco-Roman assemblies called *collegia*, as well as in the Qumran community, which existed up to CE 68. St Paul speaks of bishops and deacons in Philippians 1:1, with bishops appearing to have a function similar to what we find in the Pastorals. Romans 16:1 has reference to a woman deacon, and also a reference to a female apostle. Moreover, the gift of prophecy played an important role in the ordination of Timothy.

- Differences in style and vocabulary can be accounted for in terms of different audiences. The Pastorals were, arguably, more personal, even though clearly meant to be 'overheard' by churches.[33] Differences in style can be overstated. Evidently, St Paul made extensive use of diatribe[34] in some of his undisputed letters, but not so much in others.[35] The significance of contrasting style and vocabulary is not as significant as is normally made out. For example, computer analysis of the words, grammatical constructions, and style of Kierkegaard's writing has concluded that his works were written by different authors, whereas it is widely accepted that Kierkegaard wrote them all.[36]

---

33   The personal nature of the Pastorals can be overstated given that the farewell greetings are all plural. They are not solely personal letters.

34   That is, debate with an imaginary opponent.

35   Although this style is noticeable in Galatians, Romans and 1 Corinthians, it is less obvious in 1 Thessalonians, Philippians and Philemon.

36   See Alastair McKinnon, *The Kierkegaard Indices*, Leiden: Brill, 1970-73.

- Differences in style, vocabulary and even theological emphasis can also be accounted for if the Pastorals were written using a secretary or co-author. As Robert W. Walls points out, '[every] Pauline letter is linguistically, theologically, and sociologically inconsistent with every other Pauline letter due to variations of secretary/editors/co-authors, audience, occasion, and Paul's own developing theological understanding.'[37]

This latter point seems to be the one where most emphasis is placed by those seeking to re-assert Pauline authorship. Luke Timothy Johnson, for example, believes it likely that St Paul's letters were frequently co-sponsored or dictated.[38] Gordon D. Fee suggests that the Pastorals were written by a follower of St Paul, but under his authority, and suggests as a possible dating sometime in the 50's or 60's CE. Some have drawn attention to similarities of vocabulary and style between the writings of Luke, St Paul's frequent companion and sole companion at the time 2 Timothy was written, and the vocabulary and style of the Pastorals,[39] pointing out the possibility that St Paul gave to the educated Gentile some freedom in expressing and elaborating on his thinking. This may help to account for discernible differences in style and content between the Pastorals and other of St Paul's letters. These are all reasonable suggestions.

And that is what they are: suggestions and possibilities. It isn't sure, by any means, who wrote the Pastoral Epistles. It may have been St Paul, or it may have been that St Paul wrote just one or some of them, or only some parts of them. We simply do not know. And the Bible doesn't help us here. We can't rely on the Bible, or appeal to the Bible, because the issue being decided here is whether these letters should even be in the Bible. We only have our God-given reason, and the help of relevant experts and carefully considered evidence. Moreover, we must be careful in our reasoning. What we would like to be the case shouldn't guide us, because it will prejudice us against conclusion we don't like.

We need to at least try to be even-handed. And if we are, the most sensible conclusion, at this point in time, is that we simply don't know. What we

---

37   Robert W. Wall, in *1 & 2 Timothy and Titus*, 2012, 6.

38   Luke Timothy Johnson, *Letters to Paul's Delegates*, Valley Forge: Trinity Press International, 1996, 6.

39   2 Timothy 4:11

do know is that there is strong evidence against Pauline authorship. The very best we can say is that he probably did or didn't write these letters. As to the relative probabilities of the cases for and against, that will be a matter of individual judgement. But the bottom line is that we can't be sure, and we need to acknowledge this. To their credit, those mounting the case in favour of Pauline authorship generally do acknowledge this. George T. Montague, for example, in the introduction to his commentary on 1 and 2 Timothy, qualifies his acceptance of Pauline authorship in these terms:

> The disproportionate attention I have given to the defence of authenticity should not be taken as incontrovertible proof. The bottom line is that absolute certainty is not available on either side.[40]

Luke Timothy Johnson, also expresses appropriate epistemic humility:

> I don't think it is possible to *demonstrate* that the Pastoral letters are authentic, but I do think a legitimate case can be made to read them within the context of Paul's own lifetime and ministry.[41]

James W. Aageson, in his study, *Paul, the Pastoral Epistles, and the Early Church*, leans towards the majority view, and, after noting similarities between 2 Timothy and Philippians, offers the following tentative conclusion:

> [There] is a relatively low probability that Paul wrote all three of the Pastorals, a somewhat higher probability that Paul wrote 2 Timothy but not 1 Timothy and Titus, and a slightly higher probability still that Paul did not write any of the Pastorals; rather 2 Timothy was written by one author, and 1 Timothy and Titus were written by yet another.[42]

The situation is clearly complicated, and that needs to be fully acknowledged in whatever is said about the Pastorals, even when, at some point, people will come down on one side or the other of this on-going debate. Let's assume, for the sake of argument, that, after carefully weighing up the evidence, you decide that the probabilities come down on the side of the conclusion that the Pastorals were not written, commissioned or co-written by St Paul,

---

40   George T. Montague, SM, *First and Second Timothy, Titus,* Grand Rapids, Baker Academic, 2008, 23.

41   Luke Timothy Johnson, *Letters to Paul's Delegates,* 26.

42   James W. Aageson, *Paul, the Pastoral Epistles, and the Early Church,* Peabody, Massachusetts: Hendrickson, 2008, 87.

but were instead written by another author or authors at some point after his death. It wouldn't be an unreasonable conclusion, and it would line up with the majority position of New Testament scholars. If that is what you conclude, with due epistemic humility and generous recognition of the strength of alternative points of view, then the implications are likely to be significant.

Biblical authority

The Pastorals are not only precious for many, they also contain crucial building blocks of some equally precious doctrines, including doctrines of Biblical authority. 2 Timothy contains the following oft-quoted description:

> All Scripture is inspired by God, and is useful for teaching, for reproof, for correction, and for training in righteousness, so that everyone who belongs to God may be proficient, equipped for every good work. (2 Timothy 3:16, 17)

If 2 Timothy was not written, commissioned or co-authored by St Paul, then, as mentioned above, the letter is misleading and deceptive. The Bible is not inerrant, or trustworthy, at this point. We'd have good reason to disregard what the letter says, including its statements about Biblical inspiration. We'd have good reason to jettison the letter from the canon of Scripture. Or, if we decide to keep it, we would be more inclined to relativise its teachings and appropriate them more cautiously. We'd also be more inclined to go elsewhere to develop a theology of Biblical authority, although we'd still be able to see the above verses as reflecting the beliefs of not-so-early Christians, while also, possibly, being an accurate reflection of what the real St Paul believed and taught.

Homosexuality

The Pastorals also contain one of just seven Biblical passages considered directly relevant to the hot topic of homosexuality, that is, 1 Timothy 1:8-11.

> Now we know that the law is good, if one uses it legitimately. This means understanding that the law is laid down not for the innocent but for the lawless and disobedient, for the godless and sinful, for the unholy and profane, for those who kill their father or mother, for murderers, fornicators, sodomites, slave traders, liars, perjurers, and whatever else is contrary to the sound teaching that conforms to the glorious gospel of the blessed God, which he entrusted to me. NRSV

This is an important verse for those who argue that homosexuality is sinful, or that sex with someone else of the same gender is sinful. The author of these words assembles a list of very serious misdemeanours, or, rather, of miscreants, with sodomites included along with parent killers, slave traders, murderers and perjurers.

It is possible to raise reasonable questions about whether the writer of these words was speaking directly to what we now understand to be the nature of homosexual orientation, and, for that reason, we might set this verse aside as only relevant to clearly iniquitous same-sex activities. The word translated 'sodomites' in the *New Revised Standard Version* is translated as 'perverts' in the *New International Version*, as 'homosexuals' in the *New Jerusalem Bible*, and as 'them that defile themselves with mankind' in the *King James Bible* of 1611, indicating some uncertainty about the meaning and application of the relevant Greek word, *arsenokoites*.[43] The word literally means 'man-bedders.' James Brownson suggests, drawing on earlier studies, that *arsenokoites* is surrounded in the above vice list by two other words which can be interpreted as referring to particular sorts of people involved in the practice and promotion of same-sex erotic behaviour. The word *pornoi*, translated in the NRSV as fornicators, is also used to refer to male prostitutes. The word *andropodistai,* meaning slave traders or kidnappers, could well refer to slave traders acting as 'pimps' for their captured and castrated boys (the *pornai*), who, in turn, are forced into the service of *arsenokoites*, man-bedders, so that what is being referred to here is the widespread ancient practice of pederasty.[44] Such a translation makes good sense in context, and it again raises the question of whether what is referred

---

43 David P. Gushee devotes a chapter of his book, *Changing our Mind: a call from America's leading evangelical ethics scholar for full acceptance of LGBT Christians in the Church,* Canton: Read the Spirit Books, 2015, to the meaning of the two key Greek words, including *arsenokoitai,* which are used in the vice lists of 1 Timothy 1 and 1 Corinthians 6. Though it is most likely that *arsenokoites* is a Pauline neologism (a new word coined by St Paul), which draws on two Greek words used in the Greek (LXX) translation of Leviticus 18:22 and Leviticus 20:13, Gushee points out that there remains reasonable uncertainty about what this word means and implies.

44 James V. Brownson, *Bible, Gender and Sexuality: Reframing the Church's Debate on Same-Sex Relationships*, Grand Rapids: Eerdmans, 2013, 274. Pederasty is a usually erotic relationship between an adult male and a pubescent or adolescent male. The word pederasty derives from Greek *paiderastia* 'love of boys,' a compound derived from pais, child, boy, and erastēs, lover.

to in these verses has any direct relevance to the issue of sexual orientation, a notion which is unattested in early Jewish and Christian discussions of same-sex behaviour.[45]

Regardless of the exact meaning of these verses, if one concludes that they were not written, commissioned or co-written by St Paul, they are likely to lose at least some of their authority for Bible-believing Christians. They could, of course, retain some residual interest as an expression of what the not-so-early church believed about same-gender sex, so they won't entirely lack relevance, especially given that St Paul, in one of his undisputed letters, includes *arsenokoites* among those who will not inherit the kingdom of God (1 Corinthians 6:9-10), which, of course, raises its own problem, particularly if this word is taken to refer to 'homosexuals' as the NIV translates it. Are all those who are sexually attracted to people of their own gender likely to miss out on the kingdom of God? A tough call, given that even conservative scholars acknowledge that sexual orientation, however it comes about, is not normally able to be reversed. That the apostle did not have in mind homosexuality as an orientation is evidenced by his statement, 'and such were some of you,' (1 Cor. 6:11). Generally speaking, people don't stop being gay, even after hearing and responding favourably to the gospel, nor do they choose to be gay in the first place.

The leadership of women

If the Pastoral Epistles were not written, commissioned or co-authored by St Paul, then another equally serious (for some) casualty is the case against the ordination of women to all positions of leadership within the church. 1 Timothy 2:8-15 is considered by many to be the linchpin of that case.

One of the major reasons that this passage is appealed to so crucially by those who oppose the ordination of women to all levels of leadership in the church is that it appears to be explicit in preventing women from teaching and/or exercising authority over men, and to ground those prohibitions in the Adam and Eve story. This suggests to some that what is on view here are creational imperatives. But if the Pastorals were not written, commissioned or co-authored by St Paul, and this primary reason for including them in the canon of Scripture is removed, then the case against ordination of women

---

45   Although, as Brownson points out, awareness of a natural orientation toward same-sex relations is attested in some Greek and Roman sources, *Bible, Gender and Sexuality*, 229.

to all levels of leadership in the church either collapses or is significantly diminished in strength.

And so the stakes are exceedingly high for both opponents and exponents of equality of leadership for women. In my own context, within the Sydney Anglican Diocese, opposition to the ordination of women to the priesthood and episcopate has become a defining characteristic of the form of Anglicanism which has come to dominance in this city. It is a, or perhaps *the,* key boundary marker used to determine who is 'in' and who is 'out' within the Diocese.

Once again, as with the issue of inerrancy, there are all sorts of powerful reasons, or, better still, motivations, for resisting the evidence against Pauline authorship. The earlier-discussed argument that something needs to be retained in order to safeguard what it protects, rears its head again. Pauline authorship needs to be retained so that the leadership of women in the church can be resisted, so that the currently accepted canon of Scripture is not disturbed, so that the faith of the faithful is not shaken, and so on. None of these are reasons that can legitimately be used in a case either for or against the Pauline authorship of the Pastorals, but they do provide powerful motivation for those involved in sifting through the evidence both for and against. And they ought to caution against dishonesty or manipulation of the evidence to suit desired outcomes.

As a postscript to this now somewhat lengthy discussion, suppose that, after carefully weighing up the evidence, you decide, along with scholars like George T. Montague and Luke Timothy Johnson, that the probabilities favour (however slightly) the conclusion that St Paul did write, commission or co-author the Pastoral Epistles. You wouldn't thereby be morally or intellectually negligent. It would be reasonable conclusion to come to. However, what the above discussion ought to have made clear is that you would not be morally or intellectually justified in going on to vilify, or marginalize, or treat with disrespect, those who, in good conscience, conclude otherwise. You would not be justified in discouraging others from carefully and courageously researching this topic, simply because it might unsettle beliefs you are hoping people will not discard. You would not be justified in restricting the flow of information on this and other topics, simply because adverse conclusions might undercut pet projects such as retaining patriarchy or preventing women from becoming priests or bishops. If you did any of these things, you would have become morally and intellectually compromised. You will have failed to live a life worthy of the gospel you perhaps thought you were defending.

CHAPTER FOUR

Inevitable Pushback

Conservatism, by definition, is about wanting to conserve something, whether that be a way of life, or a way of understanding life. Christian conservatism is characterized by efforts to conserve the Christian faith, usually in some previous or ancient form. The real problem for Christian conservatism at the moment is that past understandings of the faith have come under enormous and sustained pressure, with no likely let up in the foreseeable future. Literalism, which reaches all the way back into the Biblical era, appears to be on its last legs, intellectually at least. Inerrancy also appears to be dying or is dead, a conclusion made all the more certain if a number of the Bible's books were not written by their claimed authors.

For many Christians, this is a grim situation, so grim that much or all of what I have just now written is sure to be vigorously denied. And such a reaction is an honourable one, if it is followed by careful and persuasive argumentation in the opposite direction. It is a good thing to argue back and to not just accept something because it is written in a book like this one. That is something my father taught me. Don't simply acquiesce in the face of what some supposed expert says or writes. It was good advice, but the problem is that Christians have been arguing back, on all of these fronts, for a long time now, with decreasing success. The tide of scholarly, and even of Christian scholarly, opinion is rapidly moving away from traditional understandings.

Which raises the obvious question of what to do. What should Christians do in the face of the sorts of challenges spelled out in chapters one to three of this book? Argue back, certainly, but if that doesn't work, if, in the process of arguing back, one becomes persuaded of the opposite point of view, what then? In the second half of this book, I will make a few suggestions about what one might do in such a situation, but in this chapter I'd like to explore some not-so-good responses.

One of those not-so-good responses is to 'put one's head in the sand.' It is an approach taken by many Christians, often for the understandable reason that they don't feel able or qualified to meet the sort of critical challenges currently facing the church. Billy Graham, the great Christian evangelist, whose worldwide ministry spanned six decades and more, came to a point, very early in his ministry, when he decided he did not have the wherewithal to meet those challenges. A fellow evangelist and good friend of his, Charles Templeton, had gone off to Oxford to enrol in a graduate school to gain a better and deeper understanding of the faith he was so skilfully commending, but while he was there he came to see that his former very literal approach to the Bible faced formidable challenges.

On his return from graduate school, he and Billy engaged in long discussions as they both sought to resolve some of the doubts Templeton's studies had raised. This created a crisis of faith for Graham which came to a head in the summer of 1945, four years shy of his first major crusade. Graham was out walking in a forest during a conference at which he and Templeton were speaking. He decided that somehow he had to put his doubts aside, and, placing his Bible on a stump, he prayed these words, 'Oh God, I cannot prove certain things. I cannot answer some of the questions Chuck Templeton is raising, some of the other people are raising, but I accept this book by faith as the Word of God.'[1]

That is certainly one response to the challenges discussed in this book, and, one might argue, it was a very good response given the ministry Billy Graham went on to complete. For many Christians, it is an understandable and even a rationally defensible response. If the pastors of the churches we attend indicate that these challenges either don't exist, or are not considered worth talking about or are easily met, then maybe one can reasonably keep on trusting in the literal truth of the Bible's stories and teachings. These pastors have been to theological college. They hold bachelors or master's degrees in theology. Some have doctorates. If they have dismissed these challenges, or don't even raise them, then surely the sensible and rational

---

1   P. Pollock, *Billy Graham: the Authorised Biography,* New York: McGraw-Hill, 1966, 53.

thing to do is to trust their judgement, and, like Billy Graham, keep on submitting to the supreme authority of the Scriptures in all matters.

This is to some degree understandable, but it also hides the reality that many of these well-trained religious professionals are not themselves fully aware of the challenges, nor of their strength. Or, more disturbingly still, they are aware, but are unsure how they can be met, and so, like Billy Graham, they keep on preaching and teaching as they've always done, and as their congregations expect them to do, while the watching world becomes increasingly puzzled by the oddness of Christian beliefs. They too become guilty of ostrich-like faith.

Another response, in the face of incessant and mounting challenges, is to argue or fight back - as mentioned above - not giving in to the pressure, but mounting a strong and determined counter attack. When threatened, this is a common human reaction. It was, essentially, the approach of the early fundamentalist movement. Fundamentalism had its origins as a term and as a movement in the United States in the early 1900s at a time when the teachings of Charles Darwin (1823-1913) were becoming increasingly popular. Two wealthy brothers, Lyman and Milton Stewart, bankrolled the production and dissemination of twelve booklets, entitled, *The Fundamentals: A testimony to the Truth*. The booklets represent an effort to resist the inroads of liberal scholarship, which was not only accepting of Darwinian evolutionism, but also of historical-critical scholarship which was calling into question the historicity of many of the Bible's stories.

Another more recent example of fighting back occurred within the Roman Catholic Church shortly after the Second Vatican Council, convened by Pope John XXIII in 1962, and closed under Pope Paul VI in 1965. The Council was called with the optimistic intention of renewing the church in its life and teachings. Robert Crotty, an Australian Catholic academic, describes the pre-Vatican 2 Roman Catholic Church of Australia as very much in need of such renewal, certainly from an academic point of view. In his words:

> The Catholic Church that I knew as a boy in the 1940s and 1950s had been led by priests educated in [a fundamentalist and negative-to-scholarship] thought-world. These priests were too often limited and fearful men whose academic training had been poor. Their biblical knowledge was literalist and

unsophisticated.[2]

By the time of the Second Vatican Council, Crotty had begun to study theology and would soon be teaching Biblical studies, happily taking full account of bourgeoning information in this area. He, like many others, held high hopes that the Roman Catholic Church would open itself up to this new information and its implications. He and they were, however, to be disappointed as the forces of conservatism within the Roman Catholic Church fought back with rapid success. Within a decade, windows and doors that appeared to be opening to new ways of seeing things were all but nailed shut.

The forces of conservatism, in all areas of life, are strong; amazingly strong at times. In my own experience, I have become aware of another two likely-to-become strong movements of reaction.

The Gospel Coalition

The first example involves the creation of a movement dubbed *The Gospel Coalition*. The movement began in the United States in 2004 with some informal conversations between two prominent evangelicals: D. A. Carson and Tim Keller. They wondered how they might re-create a robust and intellectually responsible evangelicalism which would avoid the pitfalls of head-in-the-sand obscurantism on the one hand and theological liberalism on the other.[3] A movement emerged which was committed to conserving and protecting what were considered essential Christian beliefs. A Confessional Statement was forged which was uncompromising in affirming as true what I've suggested is doubtful in chapters one to three of this book. Under the heading of 'Revelation' the Confessional Statement affirms:

> God is a speaking God who by his Spirit has graciously disclosed himself in human words: we believe that God has inspired the words preserved in the Scriptures, the sixty-six books of the Old and New Testaments, which are both record and means of his saving work in the world. These writings alone constitute the verbally inspired Word of God, which is utterly authoritative and without error in the original writings, complete in its revelation of his will for salvation, sufficient for all that God requires us to believe and do, and final in

---

2   Robert Crotty, *Three Revolution. Three Drastic Changes in Interpreting the Bible, Adelaide*, ATF Theology, 2012, 36.

3   http://twincities.thegospelcoalition.org/what-is-the-gospel-coalition

its authority over every domain of knowledge to which it speaks.[4]

Under the heading of 'Creation of Humanity' the Confessional Statement appears to accept the existence of Adam and Eve as historic characters, whilst also making it absolutely clear that the innovation of same-sex marriage is entirely ruled out by the Scriptures, as is the leadership of women over men within the church.

> We believe that God created human beings, male and female, in his own image. Adam and Eve belonged to the created order that God himself declared to be very good, serving as God's agents to care for, manage, and govern creation, living in holy and devoted fellowship with their Maker. Men and women, equally made in the image of God, enjoy equal access to God by faith in Christ Jesus and are both called to move beyond passive self-indulgence to significant private and public engagement in family, church, and civic life. Adam and Eve were made to complement each other in a one-flesh union that establishes the only normative pattern of sexual relations for men and women, such that marriage ultimately serves as a type of the union between Christ and his church. In God's wise purposes, men and women are not simply interchangeable, but rather they complement each other in mutually enriching ways. God ordains that they assume distinctive roles which reflect the loving relationship between Christ and the church, the husband exercising headship in a way that displays the caring, sacrificial love of Christ, and the wife submitting to her husband in a way that models the love of the church for her Lord. In the ministry of the church, both men and women are encouraged to serve Christ and to be developed to their full potential in the manifold ministries of the people of God. The distinctive leadership role within the church given to qualified men is grounded in creation, fall, and redemption and must not be sidelined by appeals to cultural developments.

Under the heading of 'The Fall,' the Confessional Statement appears to accept the historicity of The Fall.

> We believe that Adam, made in the image of God, distorted that image and forfeited his original blessedness—for himself and all his progeny—by falling into sin through Satan's temptation. As a result, all human beings are alienated from God, corrupted in every aspect of their being (e.g., physically, mentally, volitionally, emotionally, spiritually) and condemned finally and irrevocably to death—apart from God's own gracious intervention.

---

4   http://www.thegospelcoalition.org/about/foundation-documents

What is clear about these various statements is that the Gospel Coalition is committed to conserving and protecting the Christian message as it has been understood from at least as far back as the Protestant Reformation. This is, without doubt, a resistance movement, a movement born of challenge, as is obvious from the website's preamble, some of which I'll include here:

> We are a fellowship of evangelical churches in the Reformed tradition deeply committed to renewing our faith in the gospel of Christ and to reforming our ministry practices to conform fully to the Scriptures. We have become deeply concerned about some movements within traditional evangelicalism that seem to be diminishing the church's life and leading us away from our historic beliefs and practices.
>
> These movements have led to the easy abandonment of both biblical truth and the transformed living mandated by our historic faith.
>
> We want to generate a unified effort among all peoples—an effort that is zealous to honor Christ and multiply his disciples, joining in a true coalition for Jesus. Such a biblically grounded and united mission is the only enduring future for the church.[5]

The Global Fellowship of Confessing Anglicans

A second example of an essentially reactive approach also involves the conviction that the 'only enduring future' for the church involves the preservation of historic Christian beliefs. In the latter stages of writing this book, I learnt of a conference being held in Melbourne, Australia, an *Anglican Futures Conference,* which ran for three days in March 2015. One of its aims was to set up a chapter of the Global Fellowship of Confessing Anglicans (GFCA), which it did. GFCA came into being in 2008 at a conference (GAFCON) which was held in Jerusalem and which involved more than a thousand Primates, Archbishops, Bishops, clergy and lay leaders from throughout the Anglican Communion. The Conference was arranged because of widespread alarm that certain sections of the Anglican Communion had become, in the opinion of those who attended GAFCON, guilty of moral and doctrinal error, so much so that a reform movement like GFCA was required. Of special concern was that some North American Episcopal Dioceses had begun to ordain practicing gay and lesbian clergy, including the openly non-celibate gay Bishop Gene Robinson. It was deep

---

5   http://www.thegospelcoalition.org/about/foundation-documents

concern about these developments which led to the creation of GFCA. As the organisation's web-site explains it:

> The GAFCON journey began in 2008 when moral compromise, doctrinal error and the collapse of biblical witness in parts of the Anglican Communion had reached such a level that the leaders of the majority of the world's Anglicans felt it was necessary to take a united stand for truth.[6]

The Melbourne conference aimed to draw evangelical or conservative Anglicans from around Australia to join 'confessing Anglicans' from around the world in the cause of protecting and promoting the Christian gospel, considered to be under threat. Conference attendees were encouraged to sign up to the *Jerusalem Declaration*, a statement of faith forged and agreed upon at the original GAFCON conference. The inaugural chairman of the Australian Chapter of the Fellowship of Confessing Anglicans, Archdeacon Richard Condie, described the Declaration as 'a statement of contemporary orthodox Anglicanism.'[7] Following are some of its relevant contents:

The Jerusalem Declaration

> In the name of God the Father, God the Son and God the Holy Spirit ... we agree to chart a way forward together that promotes and protects the biblical gospel and mission to the world, solemnly declaring the following tenets of orthodoxy which underpin our Anglican identity.

Declaration 2, on the authority of the Scriptures:

> We believe the Holy Scriptures of the Old and New Testaments to be the Word of God written and to contain all things necessary for salvation. The Bible is to be translated, read, preached, taught and obeyed in its plain and canonical sense, respectful of the church's historic and consensual reading.

Declaration 7 on the creation of males and females in the image of God

> We acknowledge God's creation of humankind as male and female and the unchangeable standard of Christian marriage between one man and one woman as the proper place for sexual intimacy and the basis of the family. We repent of our failures to maintain this standard and call for a renewed commitment to lifelong fidelity in marriage and abstinence for those who are not married.

---

6   http://fca.net/about

7   As reported by http://sydneyanglicans.net/news/whole-church-movement-gathers-momentum

Declaration 12 on churches which have deviated from orthodoxy.

> We reject the authority of those churches and leaders who have denied the orthodox faith in word or deed. We pray for them and call on them to repent and return to the Lord.

Some things to notice

One of the things that struck me as I became aware of these two movements is that they bear striking resemblance to the early fundamentalist movement. Fundamentalism was, and still is in its many contemporary forms, religion under threat, and *feeling* under threat. The Gospel Coalition and the Fellowship of Confessing Anglicans have essentially the same spirit and concerns as the early Christian fundamentalist movement. Encountering these movements gives one the feeling of déjà vu. Very little seems to have changed within conservative Christianity as represented by these movements.

A second thing to note is that some things have changed. The challenges to traditional or conservative Christianity have intensified. Evolutionary theory is now widely accepted, even amongst conservative Christians, though its implications have not, as yet, been fully thought through. Doubts about the historicity of the Biblical storyline have grown. Moreover, there are new challenges, new fronts opening up, including the gender front. Conservative Christians are engaged in a struggle that hasn't become easier. It has, in fact, become more challenging.

A third thing to notice is that these two movements are focussed on gospel protection. It is believed that the gospel, as it previously has been understood, is under threat, and so each of the two founding documents articulates what are believed to be historic and Biblically-based understandings of the gospel.

The Final Statement of the 2008 GAFCON Conference expresses these concerns succinctly and unambiguously:

> The Global Anglican Future Conference (GAFCON), which was held in Jerusalem from 22-29 June 2008, is a spiritual movement to preserve and promote the truth and power of the gospel of salvation in Jesus Christ as we Anglicans have received it.
>
> [GAFCON has come about, in part, because of] the acceptance and promo-

tion within the provinces of the Anglican Communion of a different 'gospel' (cf. Galatians 1:6-8) which is contrary to the apostolic gospel. This false gospel undermines the authority of God's Word written and the uniqueness of Jesus Christ as the author of salvation from sin, death and judgement. It promotes a variety of sexual preferences and immoral behaviour as a universal human right. It claims God's blessing for same-sex unions over against the biblical teaching on holy matrimony. In 2003 this false gospel led to the consecration of a bishop living in a homosexual relationship.[8]

A fourth thing to notice about these two movements is that they both turn disputed matters into articles of faith. To join these movements, people are expected to sign up to *The Confession* and/or to *The Jerusalem Declaration*, both of which are detailed statements of faith. Included among these disputed matters are the authenticity and canonicity of all sixty six books of the Bible, the existence of Adam and Eve as initially devout and then fallen human beings, an errorless and fully authoritative Bible, the permanent unacceptability of marriage between people of the same gender, and, in the case of the Gospel Coalition, the timeless prohibition of women exercising authority over men within Christian congregations.

What these movements have done is to draw lines in the sand declaring that they will not budge on these issues. As was the case with the early fundamentalists, the positions are not up for discussion. They are considered crucial for gospel defence, and therefore must be resolutely protected against any efforts to dislodge them.

As I have thought about the above four characteristics, it has seemed to me that those who align themselves with these movements will almost inevitably find themselves caught up in a certain sort of culture; and the sort of culture most likely to develop is a warlike culture.

Conservative Christianity is like an army that has already been fighting for some considerable time to protect its spiritual and ideological home: its nation's capital (the gospel). The army has dug itself in on the outskirts of the capital; protecting a number of strategic vantage points, which, if they were to fall, would render the city vulnerable to more direct attack, or so its commanders believe. The battle is fierce, and has got fiercer, as the enemy appears to be gaining in strength, with its attacks more damaging.

---

8   Interestingly, GAFCON avoids the issue of women in ministry, no doubt because many of its participants are comfortable with an egalitarian reading of relevant Biblical texts.

In the face of such sustained assault, the resolve of at least some of the troops appears to be wavering, with insidious doubts beginning to be expressed about whether the army's current course of action is sustainable or necessary. There are other options, including the option of pulling back and re-grouping; surrendering the old city to find a better location, with better defences, and perhaps better leadership.

In a situation like this, it is all but inevitable that those committed to the protection of the city will not only call for renewed efforts to resist the inroads of invading forces, they will also do what is necessary to unify the troops and to stand firm against all efforts to dislodge them.

This analogy of a war helps to make sense of some of the observed characteristics of movements like the Gospel Coalition and the Fellowship of Confessing Anglicans. Such movements are likely, but not certain, to have the following characteristics:

1. Militant

Defensive movements need to be militant or combative to have any chance of success. Militancy is built into the ethos and is reflected in the rhetoric of such movements. It is not accidental that the Gospel Coalition is a 'coalition,' reminiscent of George Bush's 'coalition of the willing' marshalled to invade Iraq in 2003. GAFCON located its first conference in Christianity's heartland, Jerusalem. This was a clearly strategic move, designed to emphasize this new movement's bona fides reaching all the way back to origins of the Christian movement. At its first conference in Melbourne in March 2015, participants were encouraged to join a movement of gospel 'defence.' The person chosen to be the chairman of the Australian Chapter of the movement, Archdeacon Richard Condie, observed that Australia had been well served, thus far, by its Anglican Bishops, who 'have kept to orthodox teaching and have protected our church from doctrinal and moral evil,' despite on-going pressure to 'cave in as key teaching gives way to all kinds of error.'[9]

This is battle language. According to reports, not long after Archdeacon Condie uttered these well-accepted words, one of the creeds was recited eliciting a spontaneous outburst of emotion with participants breaking out into song. Without a doubt, those present were committing themselves to

---

9   http://sydneyanglicans.net/news/fca-underway

a fight, one that many of them had been engaged in for some time already. One of the speakers at the conference noted how many grey-haired men there were in the audience.[10] This was not just a call to war. It was a call to keep fighting.

In thinking about these movements as militant or warlike, it is worth noting that these movements have themselves been influenced by cultures which already display this characteristic. One of those cultures, of which I have some knowledge, is the culture of the Sydney Anglican Diocese. Sydney Anglicanism has become famous, and, in some quarters, infamous, for its stubborn efforts to protect the gospel from perceived threats to it. The Diocese of Sydney has always been predominantly evangelical. Moreover, from the early 1900s, roughly coinciding with the early fundamentalist movement, an organisation emerged within the Diocese whose very reason for existence was the protection of the Diocese's evangelical heritage. The Anglican Church League (ACL), as it was called, became increasingly conservative over the years, and also increasingly influential as highly effective political means were employed to populate and dominate Diocesan committees, while also determining who was acceptable and who was not when it came to recruitment, appointments and promotion within the Diocese. The organisation continues to have extraordinary power.

But the ACL has not been the only influential body within the Sydney Diocese. Back in the 1990s, a movement known as REPA,[11] dubbed by some as the 'grim REPA,' was formed in response to the growing success of moves to ordain women as priests in Anglican dioceses across Australia.[12] REPA began as a call to 'revolution' by Peter Jensen's younger brother, Phillip, who, at that time, was Anglican Chaplain to the University of New South Wales. Phillip enlisted a small band of trusted clergymen to join him in resisting liberalising trends within the church, and in creating a new movement of evangelism and church growth. Phillip's co-combatants dubbed themselves 'colonels' in symbolic preparation for a battle to reverse the flagging

---

10   Alan Nichols noted in a report published in *The Melbourne Anglican* (April 2015), p 5, that of the 460 attendees at the conference, only 20 were women.

11   The Reformed Evangelical Protestant Association, formed in 1992.

12   Anglicans from Sydney had previously attempted, unsuccessfully, to thwart efforts by other Dioceses to ordain women as priests, even to the point of taking legal action. Those enlisted to join REPA began talk of secession from the national church.

fortunes of Anglican churches around Australia. Their ambitious aim was to create a grassroots movement able to change the character and priorities of Australian Anglicanism.

REPA didn't last long, only for a couple of years. However its ghost has lived on in the relentless mainstreaming of what came to be described as 'hard' evangelicalism. Its abiding presence continues to be felt in the spread of this form of evangelicalism around Australia and beyond, through university ministries patterned on the ministry of Phillip Jensen, and through the success of Moore College trained graduates finding employment in other Dioceses and churches throughout Australia and the world.[13] Most recently, its influence has continued to be felt through movements such as the Fellowship of Confessing Anglicans and the Gospel Coalition, both of which have enormous influence within Sydney, both of which have been influenced by and contributed to by the Sydney Anglican Church.[14]

2. Authoritarian

In waging war, military leaders need to be clear and decisive in alerting their troops to the dangers, and in articulating strategies to defeat the enemy. They also need to exercise authority in an authoritative way in order to instil confidence in the troops, and to inspire them to the necessary sacrifices. Leaders cannot afford to be 'wishy washy' or uncertain, or else confidence in their leadership will quickly evaporate.

The success of movements like the Gospel Coalition and Fellowship of Confessing Anglicans depends upon the strength and conviction of its leaders. In seeking to be authoritative, its leaders have a ready ally in the Scriptures. The Bible presents as authoritative, at least throughout most of its pages. Books like Ecclesiastes might be somewhat more speculative and dialogical, as are some of the Psalms, but large tracts of the Bible present as conveying the very words of God, with the Book of Leviticus a prime example. Almost everything in that book, which includes the prohibition of

---

13 For an in-depth analysis of this trend and its possible implications, see Muriel Porter, *A New Exile? The Future of Anglicanism,* Northcote: Morning Star Publications, 2015.

14 Peter Jensen was one of the driving forces behind GAFCON. He was honorary secretary of the GAFCON Primates' Council and is currently the General Secretary of GAFCON. Peter was also a guest speaker at the launch of an Australian branch of The Gospel Coalition on July 23, 2015.

sex between men, is represented as coming from the mouth of God whose authority stands behind each and all of its prohibitions and permissions.

Those who preach from the Bible often see themselves as speaking God's Word into whatever human situation they are addressing. They are not simply speaking their own words, they are conveying God's words to those listening. God thereby addresses people through their words, and, since God is God, he also exerts authority over them.

Add to this the idea of the clarity or perspicuity of the Bible, and what you have is a recipe for an authoritative approach. This was illustrated for me in a conversation I had with the current Principal of Moore Theological College, Rev. Dr Mark Thompson. I had been preparing a talk on the broad issue of women in ministry,[15] and, to aid me in my preparation, I met with Mark, and also with Jane Tooher. Jane is the Director of the Priscilla and Aquila Centre, which is devoted to encouraging the ministry of women, though not the leadership of women over men, within the Diocese of Sydney. At one point, when discussing both Mark and Jane's understanding of 1 Timothy 2, I asked Mark how probable he thought his interpretation of these verses was. His surprising reply: 'I don't think in terms of probability.' Mark went on to suggest that his understanding of these verses was what these verses mean. I was somewhat startled at the time, but later reflected that Mark has often spoken and written about God being an effective communicator. If the Bible is, in fact, God's word, written to communicate God's will, then we can reasonably expect that God will succeed in making his will clear.

This point was further illustrated to me by an earlier suggestion by one of Sydney Anglican's foremost scholars, Rev. Dr John Dickson. John had suggested, in a booklet he produced, that the word 'to teach' used in 1 Timothy 2:12 may have had a specialised meaning, with unique application to the early church.[16] What I found interesting was not this suggestion, which is a modest one, but the extraordinarily vehement reaction to

---

15   Entitled 'Breaking the Stained Glass Ceiling: a risky but rewarding renovation.' The talk was delivered at Hunters Hill Anglican Church on 21 February 2015, at the request of the Sydney Chapter of the Movement for the Ordination of Women, and Soundings, a discussion group that meets at Hunters Hill.

16   John Dickson, *Hearing Her Voice - A Case of Women Giving Sermons*, Fresh Perspectives on Women in Ministry Series, Zondervan, 2013.

the booklet by a number of other Sydney Anglicans who clearly were uncomfortable with any suggestion that would cast doubt on what they considered to be the clear and certain teaching of these verses. Another booklet was therefore rapidly composed and produced.[17] In it, Dickson is accused of relying on uncertain background information and of 'digging below the text', rather than 'submitting to the text' in its obvious (at least to those authors) meaning. The suggested problem with digging below the text, or with anything that might create uncertainty in the minds of readers, is that God's ability to command obedience is undermined. As one of the contributors, Rev. Dr Peter Bolt put it:

> We are left in the hands of the scholars, hoping that the tentative but informed reconstruction we are following is the correct one (even though the scholar in the cubicle next door disagrees) so we might obey the voice of the living God, and not come under his judgement.[18]

An authoritative approach requires an authoritative Bible which can readily be understood and submitted to. With such a Bible, and with such an understanding, members of GAFCON can confidently declare that same-sex marriage violates the will of God, and that anyone, including gay Bishops, who go ahead and get married, are acting immorally, as is anyone who argues for or condones such behaviour. With such a Bible, and with such an understanding, those who sign up to the Gospel Coalition can confidently proclaim that women must never exercise authority over men in Christian congregations or within the home. Such behaviour is always wrong, and those who encourage it can be called upon to repent for ignoring or seeking to explain away the clear teaching of the Bible.

One can certainly understand this approach, and I have encountered it often. However, there are any number of problems with it. For a start, it is one thing to suggest that the Bible is authoritative, another thing to successfully articulate a sensible and sustainable understanding of Biblical authority, given the issues discussed in Chapters 1 to 3 of this book. Secondly, even if one is successful in forging a sensible and defensible doctrine of Biblical authority, one must ever remain vigilant against the possibility that we have misunderstood what the Bible is saying. Not only is it more difficult

---

17   Peter Bolt, Tony Payne (eds.), *Women, Sermons and the Bible: Essays interacting with John Dickson's Hearing Her Voice*, Sydney: Matthias Media, 2014.

18   *Women, Sermons and the Bible*, 193.

than some might think to successfully exegete Biblical passages, it is often just as difficult to determine what Biblical passages mean for us today. The demands of exegesis and hermeneutics are large, to say the least.

Another ever-present danger of an authoritative approach is that it can, so easily, become authoritarian, which will happen if people are expected to give unquestioning allegiance to the dictates of authoritative leaders or movements. Whenever people are discouraged from independent enquiry, when pressure is placed upon them to accept without reasonable question what the leader or movement claims is the only right interpretation of Biblical texts, then the movement or leader has strayed into authoritarianism. One of the marks of a healthy movement or church is that it encourages questions and questionings. Not only are human beings chronically prone to error in their thinking, and therefore need to be questioned and corrected, they are also prone to be protective of their favoured opinions or theories. A healthy church will also, therefore, be comfortable with the inevitability of different answers to those questions. It won't be threatened by them.

I was quite disturbed, not long ago, by a conversation I had with a recent graduate of Moore Theological College. He told me that while he was at College it was always okay to ask clarifying questions, but not okay, at least with many of his lecturers, to ask more probing questions, especially any that might be seen as an assault (however veiled) on the College's current herd of sacred cows, including the ban on women leading or teaching men. Those who take an authoritarian approach to their religion find it hard to have questions asked of them.

3. Simplifying

Another common and disturbing characteristic of militant, authoritative and/or authoritarian movements is the tendency to simplify complex realities. Movements thrive when black and white, right and wrong, good and bad are clearly and starkly defined. Leaders of movements and preachers of congregations can quickly attract a following if they are uncompromising in their black and white certitude. What makes this situation so troubling is that congregations and movement members often encourage their leaders and pastors to be like this. And because black and white thinking works, it provides a terrible temptation to sacrifice integrity in the pursuit of applause and recognition.

Male/female relationships

I was recently conversing with someone about the meaning of the following words from 1 Timothy 2:

> Let a woman learn in silence with full submission. I permit no woman to teach or to have authority over a man; she is to keep silent. For Adam was formed first, then Eve; and Adam was not deceived, but the woman was deceived and became a transgressor. Yet she will be saved through childbearing, provided they continue in faith and love and holiness, with modesty. I Timothy 2:11-15

My conversation partner, a young and enthusiastic theological student, said to me after we had discussed some of the complexities involved in interpreting these contentious words, 'Don't you think you are over-complicating things, Keith?' He was, I think, of the same opinion as Mark Thompson that the meaning and application of these words is plain to see; not at all complicated, or, at the very least, not too complicated to obediently act upon.

Unfortunately, as almost always, reality is more complex than the simple solutions employed to explain it. Take, for example, the words about Eve being deceived and not Adam. When I was at theological college, my Doctrine One lecturer, then Principal of Moore College, Broughton Knox, toyed with the idea that women were more susceptible to deception than men, which these verses can be read to suggest. In fact, that is how this phrase has been interpreted for most of the last 2,000 years. The earlier phrase, 'Adam was formed first, then Eve', was almost universally interpreted to imply female inferiority. Following are some of the more graphic statements of earlier theologians:[19]

> Chrysostom: '[A man is to have] pre- eminence in every way.[20] [Women are] captivated by appetite. [They are] weak and fickle ... collectively.'[21]

> Tertullian: 'And do you not know that each of you [each woman] is Eve? ...

---

19   I am indebted in what follows to the research of Rev. Dr Kevin Giles for pulling together the following quotes in a lecture entitled, 'Women in history, theology and the churches today', the transcript of which he kindly passed on to me.

20   *The Homilies* '[Women are] captivated by appetite ... [are] weak and fickle ... collectively.' *John Chrysostom: Timothy. Titus and Philemon, Library of the Fathers,* trans. James Tweed, Oxford: Parker, 1853, 63-64.

21   *Homily on 1 Timothy,* 71.

You are the devil's gateway: you are the first deserter of the divine law.'[22]

Augustine of Hippo: 'Whether it is in a wife or a mother, it is still Eve the temptress that we must beware of in any woman… I fail to see what use woman can be to man, if one excludes the function of bearing children.'

Thomas Aquinas: 'Woman is defective and misbegotten, for the active power in the male seed tends to the production of a perfect likeness in the masculine sex, while the production of a woman comes from defect in the active force.'[23]

Luther: 'Adam is approved [by God] as superior to Eve.'[24] 'As the sun is much more glorious than the moon (though the moon is glorious), so the woman was [created] inferior to the man.'[25]

Calvin: '[Women] are born to obey, for all wise men have always rejected the government of women, as an unnatural monstrosity.'[26]

John Knox: 'And such be all women, compared to men in bearing of authority. For their sight in civic rule is blindness, their strength weakness, their counsel foolishness.'[27]

Matthew Henry: 'The natural distinctions God has made we should observe. Those whom he has placed in subjection to others, should not set themselves on a level, or affect or assume superiority. The woman was made subject to the man, and she should keep her station, and be content with it.'[28]

Charles Hodge: '[Man's] superiority … enables and entitles him to command … The superiority of the man is taught in scripture, founded in nature and proved by experience.'[29]

It is noteworthy that almost no Christian theologian today reads or interprets 1 Timothy 2 as implying female inferiority or the propensity

---

22   *The Apparel of Women*, in *Ante-Nicene Fathers*, ed. A. Roberts and J. Donaldson, Grand Rapids, Mich.: Eerdmans, 1972, 3:22.

23   *Summa Theologiae*, trans. E. Hill, New York, NY: McGaw-Hill, 1964, 37.

24   *Commentaries on 1 Corinthians 7, 1 Corinthians 15, Lectures on Timothy*, vol. 28, of *Luther's Works*, ed. H. C. Oswald, trans, E. Sittler and M. Bertram, St Louis: Concordia, 1958, 278-79.

25   *Luther's Commentary on Genesis*, Grand Rapids, Mich.: Zondervan, 1958, 1:34.

26   *The Second Epistle of Paul to the Corinthians and the Epistles of Timothy, Titus and Philemon*, trans. T. Smail, Grand Rapids, Mich.: Eerdmans, 1964, 217.

27   The First Blast of the Trumpet against the Monstrous Regiment of Women.

28   A Commentary on the Holy Bible, Vol. 6, London, Ward, Lock and Co, 1948.

29   *A Commentary on the Epistle to the Ephesians*, London: Banner of Truth, 1967, 312.

to lead others astray. Even though one could reasonably argue that these long-standing interpretations make good sense of the text, and are good candidates for a plain reading of the text, contemporary proponents of female subordination have quietly ditched these earlier interpretations in favour of newer and more 'politically correct' understandings.

In the 1970s a new interpretation of these verses emerged. George Knight III, who Kevin Giles describes as 'possibly the most creative and innovative Reformed theologian of the twentieth century,'[30] suggested that God created men and women as 'equals', but also assigned to them different roles on the basis of their gender.[31] He argued that this role differentiation is grounded in an 'order of creation,'[32] a phrase which is now commonly heard among Christians who describe themselves as 'complementarians.'[33]

Most of Knight's key suggestions were new, suggestive of the need for sophistication in what is a complex process of Biblical interpretation. Moreover the appeal to God's communicative skills to validate contemporary interpretations of 1 Timothy 2 flounders on the fact that nearly all of Christianity's greatest theologians have understood this text differently. Moreover, Knight's attempt to refine and replace earlier understandings has its own nest of problems, some of which will be spelled out in the chapters to come.

The point is that efforts to represent this issue as straightforward and simple are misguided. There are, in fact, all sorts of uncertainties and reasonable alternatives when it comes to an understanding of 1 Timothy 2 and related passages. In answer to the complaint of the young theologian that I and others are overcomplicating things, the simple answer is: things are complicated.

---

30   In his lecture, 'Women in history, theology and the churches today,' 8.

31   Knight's ideas are articulated in this seminal work, *New Testament Teaching on the Role Relationship of Men and Women*, Grand Rapids, Mich.: Baker, 1977.

32   Knight further argued that a God-given permanent subordination of women in role and authority in the church and the home is mirrored in the eternal subordination of the Son to the Father. He spoke of a 'chain of subordination' between men and women and between the Father and the Son, *New Testament Teaching*, 33.

33   The term 'complementarian' was coined by John Piper and Wayne Grudem while editing the symposium, *Recovering Biblical Manhood and Womanhood: A Response to Evangelical Feminism*, Crossway, 1991.

Homosexuality

Christians are increasingly willing to accept that the issue of male/female relationships is a complex one; and that this is an issue over which Christians quite reasonably differ. But many, probably most, Christians are not so willing to remove the issue of homosexuality from the category of a black and white issue. The Bible's teaching seems so straightforwardly plain. There is no simple way, surely, to get around a verse like the following:

> You shall not lie with a male as with a woman; it is an abomination, Leviticus 18:22.

That is as clear a prohibition as one will find in the Bible. Moreover, this prohibition appears to be in the background of the other few Biblical passages that appear to touch on the issue of same-sex sexual relationships. I don't think it is possible to successfully argue that the Biblical authors had anything other than a negative evaluation of same-sex sex, but that is not to say that there are not greys, greys that have everything to do with efforts to understand *why* the Biblical writers were so negative in their evaluation. That is where it starts to get complicated.

And there are puzzles. There are other apparently black and white prohibitions and permissions found in the book of Leviticus that we no longer take notice of, for very good reason. Some of these are picked up quite humorously in a now famous episode of the West Wing, where the President of the United States has an audience with a Christian talk show host.

> *President Josiah Bartlet:* Good. I like your show. I like how you call homosexuality an abomination.
>
> *Dr Jenna Jacobs:* I don't say homosexuality is an abomination, Mr. President. The Bible does.
>
> *President Josiah Bartlet:* Yes, it does. Leviticus.
>
> *Dr Jenna Jacobs:* 18:22.
>
> *President Josiah Bartlet:* Chapter and verse. I wanted to ask you a couple of questions while I had you here. I'm interested in selling my youngest daughter into slavery as sanctioned in Exodus 21:7. She's a Georgetown sophomore, speaks fluent Italian, always cleared the table when it was her turn. What would a good price for her be? While thinking about that, can I ask another?

My Chief of Staff Leo McGarry insists on working on the Sabbath. Exodus 35:2 clearly says he should be put to death. Am I morally obligated to kill him myself, or is it okay to call the police? Here's one that's really important 'cause we've got a lot of sports fans in this town: Touching the skin of a dead pig makes one unclean. Leviticus 11:7. If they promise to wear gloves, can the Washington Redskins still play football? Can Notre Dame? Can West Point? Does the whole town really have to be together to stone my brother John for planting different crops side by side? Can I burn my mother in a small family gathering for wearing garments made from two different threads? Think about those questions, would you? One last thing: While you may be mistaking this for your monthly meeting of the Ignorant Tight-Ass Club, in this building, when the President stands, nobody sits.

One thing you quickly learn as you read through the Bible is that many things that are said and commanded in earlier stages of the Bible's composition are modified, and in some cases overturned, in later Biblical texts. There is a dynamism to the Bible that is masked by its current packaging in a single volume. New understandings and new experiences frequently occasion new appropriations of the earlier material. The big question facing contemporary Christians is whether new understandings of homosexuality, itself a recent concept, will combine with a deeper understanding of the Bible to create a new and hopefully transformative approach to this hugely important issue.

4. Paternalistic

Another common and perhaps understandable characteristic of defensive movements is paternalism. People under threat need protection, even from themselves, and when those doing the protecting have a clear sense of what the dangers are, and of their own essential rightness, they will quite naturally want to protect those they feel responsible for. And because they have already determined what is right and wrong, they will be reluctant to give air to alternative understandings, because of the fear that these will lead people astray. Hence the likelihood of a paternalistic approach, exemplified in the following ways:

Restricting the flow of information

One very effective way to 'protect' the thinking of people is to restrict the flow of information. This has long been recognised as essential for the maintenance of totalitarian political and religious regimes. Knowledge is power, and if you can control the dissemination of desirable 'knowledge,' while inhibiting access to alternative 'knowledge,' then you can go a long way to determining the opinions of those you are seeking to control or protect.

This, of course, is more easily attempted than achieved, even in the most strictly censored of regimes. The internet has all but stymied efforts to keep people ignorant of alternative ways of understanding and dealing with reality. However, at least some control over people's thinking can occur if one succeeds in restricting the flow of information. In my own Anglican church setting here in Sydney, churches receive a monthly magazine called *The Southern Cross*. It is (or has been) a highly censored magazine. I can't remember the last time it included articles expressing a different point of view from that espoused by the conservative and totally dominant evangelicalism of the Diocese. Some room for slight difference on some issues is allowed, but otherwise strict censorship is maintained.

By contrast, the equivalent Anglican magazine in Melbourne, *The Melbourne Anglican*, allows the expression of a range of alternative Christian views, reflecting the diversity of that Diocese. Now one could argue that a church's newsletter should reflect the dominant ethos and beliefs within that church. That makes sense, but it fails to take account of the fact that even within the Sydney Anglican church there is a wide range of opinion on a host of relevant issues, with potential contributors to its magazine constantly being knocked back because the views they are hoping to express are considered unacceptable.

And these efforts to restrict the flow of information are likely to be at least partially successful. Not only do parishioners not have the benefit of a range of views to sift through and assess, they are also given the strong and intended message that only some points of view are acceptable.

Discouraging independent investigation

Similar to the previous point of restricting the flow of information is pressure applied to discourage people from thinking for themselves. There are all sorts of ways of doing this. People can be warned off listening to different points of view or told not to attend events where alternative understandings are articulated and where they might be influenced to think a different way. Another way to discourage independent thought is to demonise doubters, those who dare to question the dominant point of view; those who give a sympathetic hearing to those who think differently. There are any number of ways to discourage independent or critical investigation.

I must say I find it almost impossible to empathise with such behaviour. I can understand why people act in such way - just - but empathize, no. Ever since I was a teenager, I adopted what became a life-long habit of not believing something simply because I'd been brought up to believe it, or because significant others believed that way. I endeavoured to carefully and respectfully consider alternative points of view. I figured that if something was true, it was likely to commend itself to me as true, and if truth mattered to me, which it did, I must not put my head in the sand and refuse to consider the possibility that I might be wrong on this or that matter of belief.

In fact, efforts to prevent independent thought are good evidence that the position being so 'defended' is shaky. Efforts to control the thinking of others is tell-tale evidence of deep and often unacknowledged insecurities of belief. The need for critical questioning is even more urgent in situations where independent or critical investigation is discouraged.

The temptation to paternalism is powerful, however, and hard to resist. This was illustrated for me in a recently published report of the Sydney Diocesan Doctrine Commission. It is entitled, *Human Sexuality and the 'Same Sex Marriage' Debate*. The report begins promisingly with the following statements made in the report's Preface:

> It was particularly important for each of us [the Report's contributors] to read with generosity and sympathy the contributions of those, both inside and out-side the circle of Christian faith and fellowship, who most seriously and strong-ly disagree with us. Nothing is to be gained in this debate by creating straw men or women – on either side – or simply repeating tribal shibboleths.' [34]

Despite this promising beginning, the report evidenced almost no engagement with well-considered alternative points of view. A small number of arguments to alternative conclusions are briefly mentioned, and just as briefly dismissed,[35] conveying the strong and possibly intended

---

[34]   Mark D Thompson (ed.), *Human Sexuality and the 'Same Sex Marriage' Debate*, Sydney: Anglican Youthworks, 2015, 6.

[35]   The anonymous author of the chapter 'Applying the Bible to Same-Sex Relationships' borders on rudeness in his dismissal of the argument that the New Testament might not be

impression that such arguments are not worthy of consideration.[36] There are only two footnotes in the entire work referring to just three books presenting an alternative point of view. There are no other such references. The 'For Further Reading' list at the conclusion of the book contains six books, all of them conservative. Clearly, the authors of the report did not trust their readership to carefully consider the alternatives themselves. Nor have they supplied a model of respectful engagement.

5. Conformist

Those with a vested interest in restricting the flow of information and who discourage independent and critical thinking, and who are inclined to authoritarian and black and white approaches, will also need to rely on the indispensable support of group pressure. No leader can lead without followers willing to fall into line with his own and the group's expectations. No movement can succeed without the creation and safeguarding of solidarity, without a clear sense of 'us' and 'them'. Movements flourish when the boundary lines between 'us' and 'them' are clearly defined.

Human beings are known to congregate in like-minded groups. We are tribal animals. We feel most comfortable with people who are like us. One of the strongest of all forces operating within our families, clans and cultures is the principle of 'homophilia', which is love for, and attraction to, what is similar to oneself. Just as potent a force is its opposite, 'heterophobia', fear of the other.

Homophilia and heterophobia are powerful tools in the hands of those seeking to protect and entrench their particular in-group. But there is another factor involved here. We humans appear to need those who are not like us to help us discover who we are. We need the 'other' to enable us to

---

directly addressing homosexuality as we now understand it. He writes, "Thus, the *supposedly* [my emphasis] very different form of homosexual practice being discussed today ...' 43. He stoops to sarcasm in a footnote on the same page, where he describes as 'ingenious' an argument he clearly does not consider ingenious, except sarcastically.

36   After quickly disposing of alternative points of view, the author goes on to imply that any such attempts are doomed in the face of the clear teaching of the Bible: 'What are we to make of these objections? And given the doubts they raise, how are we to have any confidence as Christians that the apparently clear teaching of the Bible about homosexuality is in fact clear ...?' 44.

forge our own identities as individuals and groups. But within this perhaps necessary process are the seeds of prejudice, exclusion and violence.

Because the 'other' is 'other,' they can so easily become a stereotype, which we then demonise and stigmatise. We turn the 'other' into an enemy, someone to be afraid of; someone to be excluded from our group or movement. It is, no doubt, a risky thing to allow one's enemy to remain within one's in-group, because of the chance they might initiate a resistance movement, a possibility too dangerous to allow. And so a process of exclusion is necessary to keep the movement pure.

A former student of Moore College once described his experience of witnessing this process in action within his year at College:

> I found a general level of competitiveness and 'you're out till you're in' that made college a hard and bruising place. A couple of conversations I had fairly early on knocked the wind out of me. Friends and people I had looked up to were, I was told, 'on the outer' and 'not to be trusted.' When I asked why, it was on the basis of others saying this should be their approach. I was shocked that the network had such a powerful effect. This wasn't people merely being 'not liked.' They were considered dangerous, heretical, with no basis I could see. They continue in fruitful ministry in the Diocese now.[37]

The weapon of exclusion is a powerful one, wielded by many. It is, in many ways, the ultimate weapon, and the reason for that is that it plays upon one of humankind's deepest and most potent fears; the fear of being expelled from one's group. In my role as a parole officer, I often come across people who have been disowned by their parents to spectacularly destructive effect. Sociologists suggest that connectedness within our families and other groupings is as fundamental to our well-being as is our need for shelter and sustenance.[38] Without it, we die. Separation is a form of death. The pain or

---

37 This was just one of hundreds of responses to an Open Letter, written by me, calling for reform in the Diocese sent out in November 2006. For more details, see *A Restless Faith: Leaving Fundamentalism in a Quest for God*, 2012.

38 See, for example, R. F. Baumeister, M. R. Leary, 'The need to belong: Desire for interpersonal attachments as a fundamental human motivation,' *Psychological Bulletin*, 117, (1995), 497-529, M. J. Bernstein, D. F. Sacco, S. G. Young, K. Hugenberg, E. Cook, 'Being "in" with the in-crowd: The effects of social exclusion and inclusion are enhanced by the perceived essentialism of in-groups and out-groups,' *Personality and Social Psychology Bulletin*, 36, (2010), 999–1009.

grief of separation is more intense than almost any pain, and so we try to avoid it at all costs.

It is no wonder that exclusion is so powerful a weapon of control. To exclude someone from a group that once nurtured them is the strongest of punishments. The threat of exclusion is normally enough to bring people into line, at least during the more successful phases of any movement, before counter-movements have begun to erode confidence in the reigning paradigms, thus providing alternative in-groups to which people can belong.

6. Fearful

A final likely characteristic of movements of defence, such as the Gospel Coalition and the Fellowship of Confessing Anglicans, is fearfulness. These movements have been brought to birth by fear. Their defining characteristics have been formed by fear. They are driven and sustained by fear, one of the most powerful human motivators.

Generating much of this fear is anxiety about what might be lost if attacks against traditional forms of the faith are successful. I was speaking recently with a friend about the flight of Israel from Egypt described in the book of Exodus, and drew attention to something of which she was well aware, which was that independent evidence for this event is all but non-existent – so much so that even the more conservative and cautious of archaeologists working in this field have serious doubts about its historicity. As with the story of Noah, a term increasingly being used to describe this and other Biblical stories is 'fictionalised history' or 'historicised fiction.' This friend said to me, 'If the Exodus did not occur, however exactly we construe its details, I can no longer be sure who God is.' In other words, any confidence she might have had that she knew God would be lost. And so this person continues to believe as she always has, with a key motivator being the fear of what she might lose.

That there is a risk of losing 'y' if one believes 'x' is not a reason for 'y.' It does not provide independent support for 'y.' It is, in fact, an instance of the 'slippery slope' argument, which has something like the following form:

> I won't believe x, because if I do believe x, then I might also have to believe y, and that is scary!

As an instrument of social control it would take this form:

> Don't believe x, because if you do believe x, then you will also have to believe y, and, if you do, you will no longer be one of us.

Peter Enns points out the danger of such an approach:

> The familiar slippery slope argument should be rejected by thoughtful evangelicals. Arguing for a position on the basis of what might be lost if that position is not retained is not an argument, but an expression of fear, which, when allowed to reign, leads to anger, either directly, or indirectly by means of manipulation, passive-aggressiveness and … emotional blackmail.'[39]

Anger and fear often go hand in hand. When we think we can't have something, or might lose it, we get angry, and anger is hard to hide. Diarmaid MacCulloch, in his monumental work *A History of Christianity: The First Three Thousand Years*, notes the obvious and pervasive presence of anger amongst contemporary religionists:

> Throughout the world at the present day, the most easily heard tone of religion (not just Christianity) is of a generally angry conservatism.

MacCulloch tentatively suggests a reason for the anger:

> I would hazard that the anger centres on a profound shift in gender roles which have traditionally been given religious significance and validated by religious traditions. It embodies the hurt of heterosexual men at cultural shifts which have generally threatened to marginalize them and deprive them of dignity, hegemony or even much usefulness – not merely heterosexual men already in positions of leadership, but those who in traditional cultural systems would expect to inherit leadership.'[40]

MacCulloch may be right. The vehemence with which issues of female leadership and homosexuality are being pursued by social and religious conservatives suggests the presence of deeper motives as patriarchy continues to come under pressure from liberal and emancipatory elements within society and church.

---

39   Peter Enns, 'Inerrancy, however defined, does not describe what the Bible does,' *Five Views on Biblical Inerrancy*, 89.

40   D. A. MacCulloch, *A History of Christianity: The First Three Thousand Years*, London: Allen Lane, 2009, 990.

Whether this is so or not, fearfulness is clearly a key motivator for movements of defence. It is also used to safeguard and sustain such movements, who all too often trade in the currency of fear: fear of the menacing outside world and of its multiple inroads, fear of liberals bringing the Trojan horse of atheism and unbelief into the church, fear of anyone, even those closest in Christian belief, who might lead one astray from the truth as it has been tightly defined by one's in-group.

The use of fear is a very effective method of social control; of keeping the troops committed and in line. This was disturbingly illustrated for me when I first read the Sydney Diocesan Doctrine Commission report: *Human Sexuality and the 'Same Sex Marriage' Debate*. The authors of the report, in seeking to account for the speed with which western societies have come to accept the legitimacy and normalcy of homosexual relationships, suggest that the reason this has happened so quickly is because of a highly successful campaign of 'social engineering' by lesbian, gay, bi-sexual, transgender and inter-sex (LGBTI) activists.[41]

There is no doubt that highly effective campaigns have been waged by and on behalf of LGBTI people, and that these have contributed to what has been, without a doubt, extraordinarily rapid social change. Moreover, the report is rightly critical of efforts to censor debate on this issue, and to vilify those who in good conscience think differently, thereby making it less likely that thoughtful dissidents will be heard. However, what struck me about the report, and what disturbed me, was that its authors appeared to be as guilty of attempted social engineering as those they criticised.

The report was written, at least in large part, for the benefit of Sydney Anglicans, and so there was pressure from the start for it to be uncompromising in its rhetoric and stance. It certainly was that. But if any of its readership were of a mind to consider alternatives to the Sydney position, they would have been disappointed. As noted above, alternative points of view were quickly and almost contemptuously dismissed, deemed unworthy of consideration. Just one of many possible explanations for Biblical prohibitions against men having sex with men is offered; a version of complementarianism. The authors convey the impression that almost nothing good has come of efforts by LGBTI people to be heard and to have

41   *Human Sexuality and the 'Same-Sex-Marriage' Debate*, 101. The argument to this conclusion is presented in Chapter one of the report.

their situation and struggles understood. Moreover, the authors appear to lament the success of efforts to decriminalise sex between people of the same gender,[42] while appearing to imply that earlier understandings of homosexuality as a mental illness were illegitimately overturned.[43]

I got the impression, whether rightly or wrongly, that chapter one of the report was patterned on chapter one of Romans with its description of gross human sinfulness. LGBTI people are consistently portrayed as militant, deceptive, corrupt and seeking to corrupt others.[44]

What is almost entirely lacking in the report, certainly in its early chapters, is empathy or understanding of the huge and often suicidal struggles of LGBTI people,[45] including Christians whose stories are not told and are hardly acknowledged. Nor is there a hint of an apology for Christian contributions, whether by attitudes or misguided teachings, to the pain and suffering of our LGBTI sons and daughters. The document thus contributes to this millennia-long abuse.

Chapter one of the report concludes by noting how huge is the challenge facing 21st century Christians in their efforts to swim against the cultural tide, and by asking:

> How do we even begin to engage in dialogue on these issues, let alone expose the ruse that has been perpetrated by gay activists, when freedom to question the cultural consensus or engage in genuine debate seems to be at an all-time low?[46]

It is a fair enough question, although it again vilifies gay activists as those chiefly responsible for deceptively misleading the western world.[47] However,

---

42 *Human Sexuality and the 'Same Sex Marriage' Debate,* 19, 20.

43 *Human Sexuality and the 'Same Sex Marriage' Debate,* 20.

44 *Human Sexuality and the 'Same Sex Marriage' Debate,* 18, 19, 25, 26, 27.

45 There was just one slightly empathetic sentence in the whole of chapter one, that I could find, this one: 'At its inception, the gay rights movement was, in many ways, both a legitimate and necessary response to a range of social problems and genuine injustices (including acts of violence) experienced by homosexual people.' *Human Sexuality and the 'Same Sex Marriage' Debate,* 22.

46 *Human Sexuality and the 'Same Sex Marriage' Debate,* 35.

47 This is a scandalous example of scapegoating, and it fails to acknowledge that our growing acceptance of, and care for homosexual people, which the report itself tries to contribute to, is the result of contributions by many people and groups, including Christians.

and just as disturbingly, the author of these words appears oblivious to, or culpably ignorant of, the almost entire lack of open and honest dialogue happening within his own Sydney Anglican Church, the report's sponsor. There has been no permission given, no encouragement for Sydney Anglicans to question or to engage in critical dialogue with the Diocese's own cultural consensus, certainly not from the leadership of the Diocese, and this report simply reinforces the impression that it would be highly dangerous to do so. The report is thus hypocritical in its call for genuine and open dialogue.

Over the last year or two, I have spoken to many Sydney Anglicans, including people of power and influence, including its thought leaders. More than once, reservations have been expressed about the Sydney Anglican stance on homosexuality, but just as often those confiding in me have said they would not dare express those reservations publically or within the hearing of fellow Sydney Anglicans. They are too scared. They have too much to lose, careers to protect.

It is almost the same with the issue of women's leadership within the church. Many more times than once I have come across clergymen, at all levels of the ecclesiological hierarchy, who have admitted, often in hushed tones, that the case against the ordination of women to the priesthood and episcopacy is nowhere near as strong as is claimed by its more ardent advocates. The reason the anti-ordination case has been so widely accepted by Sydney Anglicans is not because of the inherent strength of the complementarian case,[48] but because a sustained and highly successful political campaign has been waged over the last ten to twenty years.[49]

The predictable outcome of campaigns of all sorts, especially those which deliberately set out to mute dissent, is fear. Fear will always be the guiding motivation of those who are embedded in groups where certain topics of

---

[48]   As I will seek to show in the chapters which follow.

[49]   A host of inter-related tactics have been employed, including stacking the boards and committees of the Diocese with acceptable, that is, anti-ordination candidates, impeding the career progression of those who think differently, organising multiple conferences to promote a complementarian understanding of the relevant Biblical passages. So successful has this campaign been that Moore Theological College has adopted complementarianism as its official position, making it increasingly unlikely that those attending Moore College (which they must do to be deaconed or priested in the Diocese) will adopt any other position.

discussion, or conclusions about those topics, are taboo. Fear will almost always be the guiding motivation of movements of defence. It will inform and shape the characteristics of such movements, including militancy, simplification, paternalism and conformism. Fear is also likely to produce its fair share of casualties, which will be the topic of the next chapter.

CHAPTER FIVE

Casualties

It is understandable that Christians are fearful at the moment. There are reasons to be afraid, and that fear has gripped me at times. It is not good to have the faith of one's youth beset by so many significant challenges all at once. It is understandable that movements of defence have sprung up to meet those challenges and to protect the embattled faithful. It is understandable that cultures born of fear and sustained by fear should have the sorts of characteristics discussed in the previous chapter. However, such cultures create casualties, including the following:

Christian leaders are prime candidates for becoming casualties of their own frantic efforts to man the barricades of Christian defence. Popes and Archbishops, Bishops and elected leaders of denominations clearly have the most to lose if those barricades are breached. They have built their lives and careers on particular understandings of the Christian faith. The houses they live in, the stipends they receive, the reputations they've built, the struggles they've survived, and the tears shed, are an enormous personal and spiritual investment they are not likely to surrender without a fight.

Once again, fear of loss is a powerful motivator. How hard it must be, especially later in one's life, to admit to oneself and to others that you have been wrong. I had lunch once with a highly successful minister whose ministry has touched the lives of thousands, and who, because of that, had been entrusted with greater powers to influence even more people. He said to me:

> If you are right and I am wrong, then the integrity of my whole ministry will be undermined. The things I thought I had achieved will be meaningless.

Worse than that, they will have damaged those I thought I was helping.

Leaders of institutions quickly and easily become identified with those institutions to the point where their personal investment in those institutions threatens to compromise them. And it is not just allegiance to an institution or a movement that is a factor, it is also the built-up network of friends, allies and co-combatants. The pressure to stay in the movement or institution, and to not weaken, or express doubts, is enormous, especially for leaders. To become soft or to waver is to quickly be discarded, and that possibility is much too frightening to even countenance for many. And what that means is that problems or difficulties with the movement or institution will be minimised or swept under the carpet, as has happened to scandalous proportions with sexual abuse cases still wracking the institutional church.

The watching world looks on with increasing distaste as story after story emerges, not just of unending instances of abuse by trusted clergy and church workers, but of systemic and prolonged efforts to protect the perpetrators, to silence victims, while resisting calls for justice, all in the misguided and ultimately counter-productive cause of protecting the 'good name' of the church. Hans Küng, in his provocatively entitled book *Can we save the Catholic Church?* (2013),[1] draws attention to a formal letter sent out in May 2001 to all Catholic Bishops by the then Pope, Benedict XVI. According to this letter, cases of abuse were to be classed as *secretum pontificum* – a pontifical secret. Those who made them public, apart from the abused themselves, were threatened with dire church sanctions. The reason that cases of sexual abuse in the church have taken so long to come to the light of day is that powerful, self-protective, and mostly male networks have actively hidden the truth, or, just as culpably, turned a blind eye to the evil around them, too afraid to rock the ecclesiastical boat which they know is capable of treating them with the same callous cruelty.

Leadership can be a poisoned chalice of insidious temptations. A joke going around when I was in training for the ministry – which I am sure has existed for as long as the church has been around – was that to become a bishop you needed to first have an operation to remove your spine. The higher up the ecclesiastical ladder you climb the greater the likelihood that you will have had to compromise your core convictions. And there is a

---

1   Hans Küng, *Can we save the Catholic Church? We can save the Catholic Church!* London: William Collins, 2013.

good chance you will also have stopped thinking independent thoughts, especially thoughts which might be subversive to the institution you have come to depend on. It is quite sad, actually.

Roger Olson, in his book *How to be an Evangelical without being Conservative*, argues that we need to keep re-examining Christian doctrines, which he rightly observes are man-made. He notes that for many people this process stops once they become embedded in organisations which discourage such re-examination. People who were questioners in their youth get to a point where they no longer ask probing or dangerous questions. In his words:

> [Once] they are ensconced in a seat of authority, they tend to suffer from 'hardening of the categories,' by which I mean a rigidity and narrowness that disallows what they once practiced – open [and] honest ... questioning of traditional beliefs and practice.[2]

Christian leaders all too commonly become locked within the lofty towers of their own success, unable to think creatively, except within the narrow confines of what is safe.

Theological lecturers and other Christian academics face similar temptations to mute their more inquisitive theological instincts. They face the scary prospect of losing their jobs, or of not even being offered a job if they or their ideas are considered dangerous.

Sometimes theological institutions require those who teach at them to sign up to certain beliefs considered non-negotiable to the theological tribe doing the hiring and firing. I am somewhat ambivalent about the need for this. When I was being interviewed for a teaching position at Moore College, way back in 1991, I was asked a number of questions, for example, whether I believed in hell or the devil, and whether I understood the Bible to be the Word of God, but I was not required to sign up to anything. I was glad of that because at no time during my fifteen years of teaching at Moore College did I feel under any great pressure to stop thinking. There was, I thought, a reasonable degree of freedom given to explore and re-think issues, as one would hope would be the case within an academic institution. If I had applied to teach at Wheaton College, an evangelical liberal arts college in the US, I would have been required to sign up to a Statement of Faith that included the following beliefs about Adam and Eve:

---

2   R. Olson, *How to be an Evangelical without being Conservative*, Zondervan, 2009, 37.

WE BELIEVE that God directly created Adam and Eve, the historical parents of the entire human race; and that they were created in His own image, distinct from all other living creatures, and in a state of original righteousness.

WE BELIEVE that our first parents sinned by rebelling against God's revealed will and thereby incurred both physical and spiritual death, and that as a result all human beings are born with a sinful nature that leads them to sin in thought, word, and deed.

Even as an undergraduate at Moore College I wouldn't have been able to sign to say that I believed this. Even at that early point in my life, I had doubts about whether the Adam and Eve story should be taken literally.

Having said that, I do think that institutions, even academic institutions, have the right to require certain beliefs or convictions of those they employ. Holocaust deniers are unlikely to be hired by any self-respecting educational institution. Creation scientists are unlikely to be hired to teach biology or geology, or in any of the scientific departments of most universities, and not just because their conclusions run so completely counter to those of mainstream science, but because their methods would be considered unscientific.

Theological colleges or seminaries often describe themselves as 'confessional', which is to say they adhere to certain beliefs and practices which are essential to them as a religious grouping. They see themselves as having come into being by what is essentially a divine process of being called and chosen, and therefore what they 'confess' is allegiance to that calling and all it implies. Sometimes this is expressed in gospel terms. It is by means of the gospel that God calls faith communities into being. Statements of faith, including the various creeds, define the self-understanding of those who have received that gospel call.

So it makes sense to have statements of faith, and even to expect those involved in training ministers of the gospel to sign up to statements of faith. It does make sense. But problems come when those statements become so set in concrete that they cannot reasonably be questioned or modified. Statements of faith are always going to be contingent and limited by sometimes faulty understandings, which, although they may have made good sense at an earlier time, need to be rethought and reformulated in the light of new discoveries.

This can be illustrated by the experience of Peter Enns, currently Professor of Biblical Studies at Eastern University in St Davids, Pennsylvania. Enns had earlier studied and taught at Westminster Theological Seminary in Philadelphia, Pennsylvania. When he began teaching at Westminster, in 1994, he was required to take an oath affirming his *ex animo* (from the heart) allegiance to the Westminster Confession of Faith, a document drawn up between 1646 and 1648, during the Protestant Reformation. This oath of allegiance was required of all faculty members.

During his time at Westminster, Enns explored ideas which had the potential to raise questions about the adequacy of the Westminster Confession, though he did not, as far as I know, ever address those questions directly to the Confession. Instead, he drew on what is now a wealth of information about the life and times of the Bible which has emerged since the Confession was written. These ideas were explored openly and honestly in class, with the knowledge and approval of his fellow faculty, or, at least, most of them. However, it was the publishing of these ideas in a book, *Inspiration and Incarnation: Evangelicals and the Problem of the Old Testament* (2005),[3] which became the catalyst for an already brewing conservative or fundamentalist pushback.

In his book, Enns noted, as we have done earlier in this book, that the ancient authors of the Bible presupposed an ancient cosmology. He drew attention to striking similarities between the early stories of Genesis and earlier-still Ancient Near Eastern myths, raising reasonable questions about the historicity and genre of the Biblical stories.[4] He cited linguistic evidence suggesting that Moses was not the author of the Pentateuch,[5] and drew attention to differences of theological outlook amongst the various Old Testament authors.[6] Enns concluded his book by exploring what may appear to us to be strange ways in which New Testament writers used their Scriptures, pointing out instances of apparent *eisegesis*; reading into

---

3   Peter Enns, *Inspiration and Incarnation: Evangelicals and the Problem of the Old Testament*, Grand Rapids: Baker Academic, 2005.

4   Enns devotes chapter two of his book to exploring relationships between the Old Testament and Ancient Near Eastern Literature.

5   *Inspiration and Incarnation,* 51-52.

6   Enns devotes chapter three of his book to exploring instances of theological diversity in the Old Testament.

texts meanings not likely to have been intended by the original authors, a practice which he pointed out is consistent with hermeneutical approaches prevalent in Second Temple Judaism.

Enns's stated purpose for writing his book was 'to bring an evangelical doctrine of Scripture into conversation with the implications generated by some important themes in modern biblical scholarship ... over the past 150 years.'[7] I think he does that admirably, and responsibly.[8] Even his critics acknowledge that the material he discusses is mostly uncontroversial. Enns is well versed in the results of modern biblical scholarship. And many, myself included, have been hugely helped and stimulated by *Inspiration and Incarnation*. The book was designed to be a conversation starter. It certainly succeeded at that level, but it also got Enns into a deal of trouble.

The, at that stage, recently appointed President of Westminster Theological Seminary, Peter Lillback, summed up the reaction to the book in these terms:

> [*Inspiration and Incarnation*] has caught the attention of the world so that we have scholars who love this book, and scholars who have criticized it very deeply ... We have students who have read it say it has liberated them. We have other students that say it's crushing their faith and removing them from their hope. We have churches that are considering it, and two Presbyteries have said they will not send students to study under Professor Enns here.

Lillback's words have something of an ominous feel, especially in the light of what was about to happen to Enns. Strong undercurrents of concern were clearly running. Two years earlier, the previous President of Westminster, Samuel T. Logan, had had his tenure as President terminated by the Board of Trustees, because of concerns that he was too accommodating of contrary Christian views. A number of new faculty who subsequently joined Westminster were sympathetic to the view of the Board, which considered Enns's book to be inconsistent with the high view of Scripture articulated in chapter one of the Westminster Confession of Faith. High

---

7   *Inspiration and Incarnation*, 13.

8   Enns was, in fact, simply playing his part in a long-standing practice at Westminster of attempting to synthesize biblical scholarship and the school's confessional tradition, a practice going back at least to the 1950s and being then practiced by the Biblical department as a whole, including such scholars as Ray Dillard, Tremper Longman and Moises Silva.

profile evangelical scholars, including Bruce Waltke,[9] D. A. Carson, Paul Helm, G. K. Beale and John Frame were critical of the book, claiming that it abandons the traditional evangelical doctrine of biblical inerrancy.

Something of a storm erupted, and, over a period of two years, two reports were commissioned. One of those reports argued that Enns's teaching and book did not violate his oath of allegiance to the Westminster Confession, a conclusion supported by a majority of the faculty.[10] Another of the reports argued that the oath was violated.[11] The Board of Trustees was then convened, and, on 26 March 2008, voted 18-9 to suspend Enns from his professorship on the basis that a majority of the Board were convinced the book was incompatible with the Confession.

Was the Board right to do this? It certainly had the right. The board of any educational or religious institution has the right to govern in accordance with its governing documents, as already acknowledged. Nevertheless, Enns still qualifies as a casualty. He was a tenured professor and lost his job, despite having majority support from his fellow faculty. He was being academically responsible. That wasn't questioned. The information he shared was not contested, by and large. He had been teaching the content of *Inspiration and Incarnation* for fourteen years, without controversy. His sacking thus had nothing to do with responsible scholarship or the honest pursuit of theological understanding, in which he and most of his fellow faculty had long been involved. It wasn't about theology, ultimately. It was about politics and the transgression of tribal boundaries.[12]

---

9   Waltke had strongly endorsed the book initially, on the back cover of *Inspiration and Incarnation*, but in 2006 denounced it.

10   Almost two-thirds of the faculty voted in favour of Enns on this. The vote was 11-7, and the moderator, who wasn't able to vote, also favoured Enns.

11   After both reports were tabled, a motion was proposed declaring that Enns's writing and teaching lay within the bounds of his faculty oath. This motion was approved by the faculty, 12-8, in December 2007.

12   Westminster was founded in 1929 as a break-away school from Princeton Seminary. Essential to its founding ethos was a spirit of defensiveness in the face of perceived liberalising threats, along with a strong sense of its own rightness and superiority over other expressions of the faith. That spirit has persisted. By way of illustration, just a few years prior to the Enns controversy, Richard B Gaffin, a former professor of the school, wrote an article in the *Westminster Theological Review* (65, 2003) in which he asserted, 'All sound religion is Reformed in its essence and implications. Reformed distinctives are truth held in trust for the other traditions, and Reformed theology, while it is certainly capable of growth and of

Tribal boundaries become a problem when the boundaries are so inflexible they cannot be questioned or modified in the light of new and better understandings, and as a result academic integrity is lost. Moreover, Enns's suspension would have sent a powerful message that questioning might be okay, but only ever up to a point. Challenging tribal boundaries is taboo. As a result, people either stop thinking or they become dishonest, both of which are inconsistent with scholarship and the pursuit of truth.

Theological students at Westminster Theological Seminary would undoubtedly have been affected by the dismissal of their high profile Professor of Old Testament and Biblical Hermeneutics; as they would be by the resignation of nine Trustees following the decision of the Board; as they most certainly would have been by the departure from Westminster of eleven of the twelve faculty members who had supported Enns, eight of them within nine months of his departure, followed soon after by another. Since then, two more have either resigned or been forced out. Students were doubtless aware that a purge had occurred, that battle lines had been drawn, and that they needed either to submit their thinking to a literalistic understanding of a 17th century articulation of the faith, or be willing to take the riskier course of being open to new and obviously subversive understandings of the faith. They would, without doubt, have felt pressure to mute their questionings, at least in class, or within ear-shot of prospective employers who might, or might not, hire them, depending on whose side they were on of the recent battle for Westminster.

Enns's experience is not isolated, sadly. Robert Crotty, mentioned in chapter four, was another casualty of political or religious correctness. Within a few years of Vatican 2, he was accused by a fellow Catholic priest of having a suspect doctrine of revelation, apparently because of his far too positive attitude to critical Biblical scholarship. Crotty had tried in his teaching to be sensitive to the convictions and beliefs of those he taught, but he also felt duty bound to pass on relevant information, even if it meant challenging older ways of thinking. In his words:

> [My] teaching, whether to Australian seminarians or to lay audiences, had al-

---

learning from other traditions, is not so much working together with those traditions out of a common theological orientation, as is seeking to correct them,' 328. An essential part of that tradition, according to its defenders, was inerrancy. The fear of a slide into theological liberalism appears to have been the driving force behind efforts to remove Enns.

ways been restrained and judicious. I was always mindful [that I did not need to disclose] all that I was thinking. I did not set out to destroy commitments or to belabour beloved and entrenched beliefs with which I might have disagreed. However, I considered it my duty as an educator to challenge people, to provide them with a new way of thinking and to lead them towards what I was thinking, if that is what they wanted. But I think I did it gently and with consideration.[13]

Whether gently or not, Crotty was brought before a hearing organized by his diocesan archbishop, which had deliberated for six weeks prior to Crotty being brought before it. Unexpectedly, he was acquitted, purportedly because of a lack of evidence, but Crotty later admitted he was 'guilty' as charged, and decided to leave the priesthood. As he put it:

Exhausted by the intrigues, the subterfuges, the constant need for vigilance and the fact I saw no sense in changing people who did not want to be changed, in early 1972 I voluntarily resigned from the Catholic priesthood and moved back to secular life at the age of 35.[14]

Once again, as with Enns, it was Crotty's students who were thus deprived of his scholarship and gentle integrity. They would also have learnt the important life lesson of keeping their heads down if they began thinking dangerous thoughts.

One final and more current example. On 29 June 2015, just days after the US Supreme Court brought down its ruling on same-sex marriage, Daniel Kirk, a New Testament lecturer at Fuller Theological Seminary, in Pasadena, California, posted a blog, some of which I've reproduced below. In 2011, he had published a book which included a chapter on homosexuality. At the time, it received positive feedback from fellow faculty.[15] One faculty member, who would later become president of the seminary, specifically mentioned the chapter in his endorsement of the book. When he became president, he invited Kirk to participate in a panel formed to discuss a 2013

---

13   Robert Crotty, *Three Revolutions: Three Drastic Changes in Interpreting the Bible,* Adelaide: ATF Press, 2012, 142.

14   *Three Revolutions*, 143.

15   J. R. Daniel Kirk, *Jesus have I loved, but Paul? A Narrative Approach to the Problem of Pauline Christianity,* Grand Rapids: Baker Academic Press, 2011. The chapter on homosexuality is extraordinarily gentle and, I would have thought, uncontroversial.

Supreme Court decision[16] which had implications for the wider acceptance of same-sex marriage. On leaving the seminar, Kirk was told by some of his senior colleagues that his writing on homosexuality, specifically this chapter, was going to be a profound hindrance to their ability to support him should he apply for tenure, which warning was realized in 2015, prompting his blog entitled *Fuller and Me*:

> When I came to Fuller seven years ago, not one (ok, maybe one) of my Biblical Division colleagues believed in inerrancy. Fuller had given up that shibboleth years ago. [After completing my 'theology exam,'] I had started researching Theological Interpretation of Scripture. I was frustrated by the literature, because it seemed to be largely coming up with fancy ways to ignore historical and critical scholarship in order to give primacy of place to the church's theological traditions as guides to reading the Bible.
>
> I read scripture theologically. But as a New Testament scholar, I see my job as always listening first and foremost to the text in its historical context, and allowing its theology to be the first voice to which we respond. In the end, I will affirm creeds or confessions, if I do, because I believe they contain the right things to say at a given moment in time in which they were written, in light of what scriptures says. In this, I thought I was just being a normal biblical scholar. And Protestant. And Evangelical.
>
> However, a couple of my senior Bible colleagues found this disturbing. It was not enough to affirm that some confessions were correct. One had to start with the confessions and use them as hermeneutical guides in the strong sense. One had to like the idea that we define Christianity by what we believe. (All this despite the fact that we have Baptists and Anabaptists on faculty.)
>
> Integrity is crucial for both of us. I define integrity as being true to historical critical scholarship and bringing that into theological dialogue with the church. They define integrity as being true to the 'Grand Tradition of the Church' and allowing that to guide what we see in and say about history. My senior colleagues and I give different answers to the question of how we relate the Bible to the theology of the church? And this is one major reason why next year will be my last at Fuller.

---

16   Which struck down the Defense of Marriage (DOM) Act and Proposition 8. The DOM Act had defined marriage as a union between a man and a woman, thus denying federal benefits for gay couples whose marriages were recognized at the state level. Proposition 8 was a California ballot initiative prohibiting same-sex marriage by amending the state's constitution.

When I wrote, *Jesus Have I Loved, but Paul?* I knew that it was something of a risk to write on homosexuality. It's basically the only chapter anyone ever reads. But it was well received among my colleagues. It has been used in Fuller classrooms. One colleague overstepped reality by calling it 'brilliant.' But I appreciated the encouragement.

The more I study the question of homosexuality in scripture and the ancient world, the more complex I realize the issue is. I have worked some of those questions out here, publicly, expressly to help uncover that things are a lot more complicated than simply delineating what sexual practices are ok and which are not. Historical critical scholarship has made me question, and realize the need to question, what we say theologically and ethically.

For a number of my colleagues, it is not ok to ask these questions unless the answer we already have decided upon follows close on their heels. Anyone at Fuller can tell you that over the past year to eighteen months clear signals have been sent that sexuality is not something that is open for any sort of conversation, much less debate.

For everyone, living with integrity is important. For a small window of time, I caught sight of a Fuller in which integrity on the sexuality issue meant having conversations whose faithfulness was measured by standards of academic investigation and conversation. For now, Fuller has chosen a different route. Integrity means ensuring that the stated position of the school is upheld and affirmed and not called into question.

These are different ways of measuring integrity. Neither is right or wrong. But I am disappointed that Fuller has chosen its way, as indeed a number of colleagues are disappointed with the route I chose. Most of all, I am disappointed that we cannot hold these differences in creative tension. This difference is a major reason why I will not be at Fuller after next year.[17]

It is too early to tell what impact Kirk's decision will have on his fellow lecturers and students, not to mention the seminary's wider Christian constituency. But clearly, a decision as public as this is likely to have significant repercussions and ripple effects. Those wanting to follow in Kirk's footsteps will have some additional pressure to not do so; pressure to conform or leave.

Theological students, within any theological institution, conservative or liberal, will face pressure to conform to the reigning paradigms. Some of

---

17 http://www.jrdkirk.com/2015/06/29/fuller-and-me/

that pressure will come from above, from administrators and lecturers and the various hiring bodies. Some of it will come from fellow students, who often will have come to the seminary or college from churches with very clear ideas of what is acceptable and what is not; of what they can believe and what they must not believe. That puts pressure on any student who is, or might become, a dissenter from the dominant way of understanding the faith.

Pastors of congregations can become casualties of efforts to reign in theological or ethical differences, as they can by controlling and fear-driven Christian cultures. It can happen in a host of ways. It can happen if they stop asking questions. It can happen if they keep asking questions. Either way, they and their congregations stand a good chance of becoming casualties.

Within my own Anglican Diocese of Sydney, asking questions can most certainly get you into trouble, not only whilst at college, but out in ministry as well. The pressure to conform and to mute one's questioning is continuingly strong for those involved in pastoral leadership in the Diocese. People are afraid to question the status quo or rock the boat. Exacerbating that fear has been the emergence of a new and troubling narrative about the inevitability of falling away from orthodox faith if one strays even a step from it. Rev. Andrew Katay, a prominent Sydney Anglican clergyperson, who is not convinced by this narrative, articulated it in the following terms prior to the election of Sydney' current Archbishop, Glenn Davies:

> Human sinfulness means that all people, and therefore all organisations and institutions, tend to depart and drift from godliness. The way this drift happens is observable and inevitable. Even when an organisation has good, gospel-minded, theologically sound and godly leadership, a change can take place. It is a subtle but decisive change. The change is the move from what could be called 'closed,' or 'hard' conservatism, to 'open' or 'soft' conservatism.
>
> The difference between the two might not necessarily be in terms of the content of their convictions, but in the manner in which they are held. Open or soft conservatives are, well, more open to new ideas, and softer towards difference; this is their way by temperament. They tend to be centre defined, not boundary defined.
>
> But that very openness, softness, tolerance, means that there is an inevitable move from soft conservatism to liberalism. It can't be helped, and it can't be stopped. It will, as a matter of necessity, happen. This is the story told in the

book *The Dying of the Light*,[18] about seventeen US colleges and universities which started out as theologically reformed, orthodox and conservative, but have since entirely lost their way.

And because this move is unavoidable, it means that the only way to stop the drift to liberalism is to oppose soft conservatism as though it were in fact liberalism– with the same vigour and passion.

In the *Dying of the Light*, its author, Fr James T. Burtchaell, a Roman Catholic priest and an outspoken opponent of any liberalising in attitude towards homosexuality, described what he believed was the gradual, but irreversible secularisation of formerly Christian colleges and universities, a significant factor in which was the acceptance of 'soft' members who were open to extra-biblical influences, effectively compromising gospel-directed scholarship. Irrespective of the historical accuracy, or otherwise, of Burtchaell's thesis, a narrative such as this is likely to be a potent source of fear and mutual suspicion. According to the narrative, it is those who are closest to you, the 'soft' conservatives, who are the most dangerous, in large part because they are the ones who are most likely to entice you away from the straight and narrow, and into an inevitable and irreversible slide into liberalism and apostasy. They are the ones you need to be most suspicious of, not warmly embraced as sisters and brothers, but kept at arm's length until you can be sure that they are safe and sound.

The impact of this narrative has been massive within the Sydney Anglican Church. It has been articulated often by some of its leaders, notably the Jensen brothers. If the great fear is that taking even a small step away from orthodoxy will inevitably lead to destruction, then, for those who accept this narrative, questions and doubts simply must be quashed; in oneself and others. And that is what is happening right across the Diocese, sadly. As an instrument of social control, it is brilliant, but it is also hurting people, creating scores of casualties.

I attended a meeting in early July 2015 of people who were deeply concerned about the culture of the Diocese, some to the point of despair. One talented young mother, well into doctoral studies in theology, shared her experience of often going home from church in tears because of the stifling dominance of the complementarian view on gender relations within the church she

---

18   Fr James T. Burtchaell, *The Dying of the Light*, Grand Rapids: Eerdmanns, 1998.

was attending. She felt devalued and demeaned, which was the experience of all the women who attended this meeting. She said that her senior pastor was open to discussing the issue of who could preach and lead and who couldn't, but felt constrained (to the point of inaction) by his peers in ministry and by his congregation, many of whom now shared the Diocesan view. And it wasn't so much the difference of views which was the issue. After all, complementarians might be right. It was the widespread belief that any 'softening' on this issue was dangerous. Another person shared her experience of coming under suspicion, and of even having her Christian faith questioned because of her belief that women can be priests and bishops. She had become an outsider, someone not to be trusted, despite the fact she had trained at Moore College. She is also a talented preacher and theologian.

It is a grim situation, and not easily countered. What gives credence to this pervasive narrative is that it contains more than a grain of truth. It *is* likely that those who start questioning and who are open to differences and to new knowledge will come to see the problems with literalism and inerrancy. They will begin to wonder about the implications of evolutionary theory. They are more likely to give a more sympathetic hearing to egalitarian arguments, and to listen with greater attentiveness to LGBTI people, whilst also being more open to reconsidering traditional understandings. It is true that there is a certain inevitability that people will stray from their fundamentalist moorings if they begin to question those moorings.

This loosening of belief in the face of questions has always been true of conservative movements when older paradigms are replaced by newer ones. It is a fragile faith that isn't willing to go through this questioning process, wherever it might lead, no matter how scary the possible outcomes.

I was one day speaking to a work-mate, who, like me, had been involved years previously in full-time Christian ministry, in his case, in the Methodist Church. This friend had gone to theological college two years after becoming a Christian and joining a Christian commune. He entered college to train for the Christian ministry to which he felt called. Attending lectures was initially unsettling, but later exhilarating, as a host of new questions and ways of seeing the faith were introduced to him. But a strange thing happened not long after he had begun training. He returned to the commune and was told in hushed tones that the leader of the commune had been warning people off him because he was attending a 'liberal' college. This leader had been through the same college, but vowed from the beginning that it would not dislodge him from his literalistic and fundamentalist faith. He kept his vow.

My friend, who was a question asker, went out into ministry in country New South Wales to become the pastor of a small-town Methodist Church. He quickly became aware of the gap between his own studies of the Bible and his parishioner's understandings. He one day led a Bible study on the book of Revelation and believed he was doing a reasonable job introducing people to the likely historical background, and to the heavy use of symbolism which cannot sensibly be taken literally. However, he was then taken aback by a question from one of those attending the group, a bank manager. Appearing not to hear anything my friend was saying, he asked, 'What I want to know is, will Jesus be coming back on a horse or a cloud?'

A much more serious challenge to my friend's non-literalistic faith occurred when he moved to a slightly larger country parish where a small group of his parishioners charged him with heresy. He had preached a sermon on the temptations of Jesus, and had not mentioned the devil. He had earlier been persuaded that the devil is best taken as a symbol for the evil that can so readily afflict individuals and societies, but who must, nevertheless, take full responsibility for that evil. Blaming the serpent just isn't an option within the non-dualistic world view articulated in Genesis, for example. And so my friend pursued the line of asking whether we would recognise evil if it materialised in front of us. He used a photo of a German Bishop saluting Hitler to make his point. I would have liked to have heard the sermon, but a small group of his congregation approached him after the service to demand an answer to their question, 'Do you believe in the devil?' They tried, unsuccessfully, to have him charged with heresy at the next Parish Council meeting. This completely floored my friend. It was, for him, the beginning of the end of his time in Christian ministry. He had become a casualty of his willingness to countenance new possibilities, to understand his faith in different terms.

There are other casualties. They are the pastors who are too afraid to do what my friend did and be honest about their evolving (or not evolving, because that is too scary) understandings of the faith. Someone once told me of a minister who confided in him that if he disclosed to his congregation the things he had learnt about the Bible at theological college, half of his congregation would leave. He felt he was forced to be dishonest. Both he and his congregation thereby became casualties of his lack of integrity and courage.

Churchgoers are too often the last ones to be told about developments in Biblical studies, though it should also be said that ordinary, churchgoing Christians are sometimes better informed, more widely read and better educated than are their pastors, and therefore bemoan the often patronizing manner in which graduates, and especially recent graduates, speak down to them as if they aren't theologically competent. I know of at least one highly competent scientist who is repeatedly disappointed when the early chapters of the Bible are preached about, because issues of the relationship between the Bible (very often taken literally) and contemporary science are simply ignored; and when they are engaged, they are engaged inexpertly, leaving those who are more scientifically informed scratching their heads in frustrated bemusement.

What is equally frustrating for many is that when they do have sensible questions about the Bible, about its composition, about the historicity of its stories, they are fobbed off or told to just believe. Worse still, they are treated with suspicion, with questions raised about whether they truly belong to the group, or are even Christian. That, for me, is one of the most troubling examples of unwarranted tribalism; people being ostracized or looked down upon by fellow church goers because they have the temerity to ask probing questions or express doubt. Doubts and questions are treated like a sickness or a virus, and, because of this, those who ask or express them are quarantined or excluded from the community, to prevent the virus from spreading.

In cases like these, both parties become casualties of the accompanying fear and defensiveness. The questioner feels excluded and not understood. Those doing the excluding are also good candidates for our sympathy, because the beliefs they so confidently assert, and then use as weapons of exclusion, are often built upon shaky ground. The whole community suffers because it passes up on the opportunity to learn and grow.

Church-leavers are also casualties of the fear and defensiveness currently gripping many churches. People leave church, often never to return, for a variety of reasons. Some suffer directly and personally from the suspicion, exclusion, and lack of love, or love-with-strings-attached they have encountered in church. Some become disillusioned or burnt out by expectations they no longer feel they can meet. Others leave because they are no longer satisfied with the answers being given to contemporary challenges. Or they are expected, as a condition of being a member of their church, to sign up to beliefs they no longer find credible. There are a host of reasons why people are leaving church as they currently are in their droves - certainly in first world countries. In the US, for example, young Americans are increasingly choosing not to go to church, including young evangelicals, about half of whom lose their faith after they leave high school and begin tertiary education.[19] And it is not just the young who are losing faith. An estimated 80% of churches in the US are flat or declining, 5,600 closing every year.[20] In the UK, Christian congregations are shrinking and closing at such a rate that, if the present rate continues, Christians will become statistically invisible by 2067.[21] In Australia, churchgoing has been in steady and serious decline for decades, with no sign of that trend stopping or reversing any time soon. Church is fast becoming an archaic institution in Australia, as it is already in many European countries.

A powerful illustration of this trend can be found in the experience of the son of the couple who told their story in the *Introduction* to this book. We will refer to him as Matthew, but that is not his real name. The details of his story are real, and all too common.

Matthew was born into a loving and deeply impressive Christian family, of parents he loves and remains close to. In all sorts of ways, he had a near perfect introduction to life, but at the young age of five he became aware of an attraction towards people of his own gender which came to full flowering in adolescence. He was gay, he believes from birth, but he was also born into a smallish country town where attitudes towards those who were brave enough to identify as homosexual were disapproving, to

---

19   Denis O. Lamoureux, 'No Historical Adam: Evolutionary Creation View,' in Matthew Barrett, Ardel B. Caneday (eds.) *Four Views On The Historical Adam*, Grand Rapids: Zondervan, 2013, 18.

20   According to 'America's Changing Religious Landscape,' a Pew Research Center survey published in May 2015.

21   '2067: the end of British Christianity,' *The Spectator*, June 13, 2015.

say the least. Matthew felt he could not talk to anyone about his feelings and emerging desires, including his parents who attended a conservative Christian church. He felt he had to hide who he was. His identity became an increasingly guilty secret because he knew his church and community disapproved of gays, in the case of the church, believed them to be hell-bound. Early adolescence was tough for Matthew. He became suicidal, started taking drugs, and was constantly miserable and alone in his struggles and torment. He was referred to counsellors, and would see them frequently, but none raised the possibility that his misery was connected to his struggles as a gay teenager.

At the age of 17, he had the opportunity to leave the country town he had come to hate, and to enter an evangelical organisation dedicated to taking the gospel mainly to youth. Matthew grabbed this opportunity with both hands, and entered into ministry and evangelism with gusto. The faith of his youth was rejuvenated, and for the next seven years he managed to remain celibate, resisting the continuing urge to find sexual fulfilment with men. He was happier than he had been for years and was enjoying working with Christians he admired and respected. He was even able to use his own experience in evangelistic encounters. Early on, his testimony was, 'I used to be gay, but God made me straight.' He knew, even then, this wasn't right, so he changed his message to, 'God restored me to being straight, but I still struggle with temptations to have sex with men.' This also didn't seem right, and, towards the end of his seven years with this evangelistic organisation, he again changed his message to, 'I am gay, and God is okay with that.'

Matthew's painful journey was a gradual journey towards self-acceptance, though for most of his early years, he longed to be different, longed to be straight. He constantly and for years prayed that God would heal him of his homosexuality, but with no answer coming, only silence - with unrelenting accusations from his Christian friends and his own conscience. This precipitated any number of crises of faith.[22] One such crisis he recorded in a diary entry on the occasion of his twenty-fourth birthday. This is what he wrote:

---

22   For an equally powerful and poignant story of a young and enthusiastic evangelical Christian whose life-long wrestling with this issue was very similar to Matthew's, I'd heartily recommend, Justine Lee's *Torn: Rescuing the gospel from the gays-vs-Christian Debate*, New York: Jericho Books, 2013.

I don't believe in the God on my lips. I don't believe He <u>really</u> loves me personally. I don't believe he <u>really</u> cares about my problems. I don't know if I ever knew that God. I don't know if I ever will. Supposedly, the Christian God can handle this sort of thing. I'd rather he kick my ass. At least then I'd know he cared. I'm 24 today. I still lust after guys.

I guess I thought it would get easier, that maybe, just maybe the blood of Jesus would work for me too. That's why I question my allegiance to a supposedly loving and caring personal god. I'm really bitter at you God, and I'm not sorry. You're meant to be loving. So love me. You are meant to be caring. So speak to me.

If I worked as a volunteer for an earthly king, if he didn't ever talk to me, but just gave me a book of guidelines to read, if he didn't answer my requests for help, if he was distant, hard to talk to, you know what I would do? I'd quit my job for him and work for someone real. Why don't you answer me? Why don't you change me?

Matthew's journey continues, but he almost never attends church; and the questions he posed to God on his twenty fourth birthday remain a significant obstacle to him.

Those who aren't Christian are less and less likely to go in the opposite direction and turn up at church. Some do buck the trend out of inquisitiveness or need or because they are invited by a friend, but, for increasing numbers of people, even the thought of going to church is alien and unattractive. And there are a host of reasons for this.

For some, it is the controlling and fear-driven nature of churches that has alienated them, with attempted cover-ups of sexual abuse a powerful symbol of the unacceptable misuse of fear and control. A Christian media group,[23] led by a Baptist pastor in Sydney, carried out a survey in October 2011. One thousand Australians were interviewed, and the purpose of the survey was to identify what were the major 'blocker issues' standing in the way of people considering Christian faith. The biggest blocker of all, not surprisingly, was church abuse. 76% of interviewees identified abuse by the church and its officials as a 'massive' or 'significant' negative influence on their attitude towards Christianity and the church.

---

23   Olive Tree Media.

One of the reasons the abuse issue is so significant is that it goes to the heart of the church's credibility. It raises reasonable questions about honesty and transparency; and gives credence to the idea that the church might be similarly dishonest about other of its practices and beliefs. The church is no longer a trusted institution.

Just under church abuse as a blocker issue were doctrines and practices about homosexuality, with 69% of respondents identifying this issue as a significant reason for not embracing Christian faith. The way Christians speak about or act towards those who are homosexual is sensibly perceived as an instance of abuse, because it leads to countless examples of the sort of agonizing struggles Matthew experienced. The general perception, among Australians in general, including Christians, is that Christianity is anti-gay. Among younger people, that perception is almost unanimous.[24]

Under church abuse and homosexuality, other issues inhibiting Christian belief were doctrines about hell and condemnation (66%), the role of women (60%), suffering (60%), science and evolution (57%), as well as hypocrisy, judging others, religious wars and exclusivity.

Of the thousand people interviewed, only 50% identified with a religion; only 40% declared themselves to be Christian. Thirty-one percent did not identify with any religion or spiritual belief, while 19% said they were spiritual, but not religious. These figures represent a somewhat bleaker picture of how Christianity is faring than the results of the 2011 Australian census, where 61.1% of those surveyed declared themselves Christian,[25] with another 7.2% identifying with other religions, and 22.3% describing themselves as having 'no religion', with this figure up from 18.7% in 2006, which, in turn, was an increase from 15% in 2001.

Christianity is rapidly declining in Australia, both in numbers and influence. Admittedly, Australia is one of the world's most secular nations. According

---

24   In 2007, David Kinnaman, president of the Barna Group, published a book entitled, *UnChristian: What a new generation really thinks about Christianity*. Kinnaman noted that attitudes to gays among churchgoers has created a negative image of the Christian faith among people ages 16-29. The vast majority of non-Christians within this age group (91%) said Christianity had an anti-gay image. Even 80% of active churchgoers agreed with the anti-gay label.

25   The percentage of Australians reporting affiliation with the Christian religion dropped from 68% in 2001.

to a worldwide poll conducted in 2012 by Win-Gallop International, Australia was placed in the bottom fourteen nations in the world for religiosity, judged in terms of attitudes and practice. We were placed in the top eleven for atheism, with 10% of Australians describing themselves as 'convinced atheists.'

There are, no doubt, particular reasons for Christianity doing so poorly in Australia, which are not reflected elsewhere, where Christianity continues to thrive. However, the fact that Christianity is doing so poorly in Western or traditionally Christian nations such as Australia is cause for serious concern. It appears that Enlightenment and post-Enlightenment ways of thinking, and discoveries that have been made using the sharpened tools of the Enlightenment, are putting Christianity under such pressure that its future as an intellectually viable option is rightly being called into question. Christianity will live on, no doubt, but in what shape? Does it have the capacity to reconfigure in such a way as to once again commend itself as a way of thinking and living which will rightly attract new adherents, and in such a way as to reverse the current hemorrhaging afflicting its intellectual heart?

CHAPTER SIX

The Courage to be Honest

One of the reasons for writing this book is that after writing my previous book, *A Restless Faith* (2012), by far the most common responses were questions to the effect, 'If what you have written is correct, then what form of Christian faith is possible? What changes to my own faith will be necessary? Can I even have faith?' Those are good questions, and they certainly were not answered in *A Restless Faith*.

I won't pretend that I will ever fully know the answers to those questions. This is a project far larger than any one person could successfully complete. The best I can offer, from the vantage point of my own very limited talents and perspective, are some suggestions for a way forward. Many others will need to make their contributions to what is a complex, and, I think, never ending project of developing forms of Christian faith that will rightfully win a following in each successive age. The question is not whether Christianity will survive. The question is whether people will be able to sign up to Christian faith with intellectual and moral integrity. Will they be able to be honest with themselves and others? That is the first and most important question, and it is the subject of this chapter. In the following chapters, I will suggest some further characteristics for which Christianity will need to become known if it wants to commend itself for acceptance in a contemporary context.

Honesty is a beautiful thing. In recent years, I have attended a number of reunions; school reunions, college reunions, friendship reunions. A year or two back, my wife and I attended a reunion of friends we had met and attended church with in Hay, a small, but special town in south western New South Wales. Many of us had begun our families there; and now those families had grown up, and we ourselves were noticeably the worse for wear! The only hairs not yet grey have been dyed that way. But the very best thing about that reunion, and the others as well, was the honesty with which people shared their many and sometimes heart-breaking struggles; struggles of faith, struggles of life, struggles of death.

Honesty like this is an expression of vulnerability. It invites care and empathy. It encourages honesty in others. But it also requires courage, the courage to admit we were wrong, or that we did wrong, and have needed to ask for forgiveness. We weren't the bullet-proof people everyone thought we were. Nor were our beliefs, which we so passionately, and perhaps arrogantly, once spouted. We will probably have to admit that there are greys of belief to match our greying hair.

Being honest about literalism

Those who, through all of their lives, have adopted a literalistic approach to the Bible need to have the courage to admit that this approach does not work. Literalism may have worked – just - at the time of Luther when he encouraged his followers to accept the literal truth of even the most fable-like of Biblical statements. We can no longer follow his advice. We don't believe, as he did, and as the ancients did, that the dome of the sky is solid, and that above it are storehouses of water. We don't believe, as he did, that the sun and stars rotate around the earth. We no longer read our Bibles to help us plot the origins and distribution of human beings spreading out from the Garden of Eden. We have come to accept, or, at least many of us have, that the earth came into existence not thousands, but billions of years ago. And the reason for this gradual, but real and irreversible jettisoning of literalism is the steady accumulation of overwhelmingly strong evidence from multiple and complementary fields of enquiry.

Christians need to face up to this. Many do not. Literalism continues to thrive, and is stronger than ever in some quarters. And one of the reasons it survives is that people forget, or don't realise, that they themselves have steadily surrendered earlier-held literalistic beliefs. They certainly have not been consistent in their literalism. Sydney Anglicans, for example, don't tend to believe in a young earth, and are mostly accepting of some form of evolution. They don't look for guidance to the genealogies of the Bible to work out the age of humankind. They are, for that reason, inconsistent literalists. In order to appear more consistent than they are, they will often appeal to genre as a way of avoiding the charge of inconsistency. That can work to a degree, and genre is important in determining what actually is being asserted in any given passage, but there are problems even with this approach because Jesus and the apostles appear to have believed in a young and flat earth, in stars that can fall to the ground when dislodged from the firmament above, in a world-wide flood, in Adam and Eve, in the literal truth of the Bible's cosmological and historical statements. There is no hint of an appeal to genre by the authors of the Bible itself, certainly when it comes to the Bible's major storyline.

We need to be honest about this. We need also to have the courage to admit that many of the Biblical stories that we may once have thought were straightforward descriptions of what happened in the past are unlikely to be factual in that straightforward sense, or, at the very least, we need to be upfront in admitting that independent evidence for the occurrence of these events is often weak or lacking. That takes courage. The temptation will always be to talk up the evidence for what we believe; to refer to this or that expert, while conveniently glossing over the difficulties or contrary evidence. When we do this we are culpably dishonest.

Being honest about inerrancy

Christians need to acknowledge that the Bible does contain errors. It cannot reasonably be said that the Bible is 'free from all falsehood and mistake … in all of its assertions … [including] all matters historical and scientific.'[1] This is simply not true, and in defence of this idea, all sorts of embarrassing endeavours have been spawned. For example, Article 12 of the Chicago Statement on Inerrancy makes the following assertion:

> We further deny that scientific hypotheses about earth history may properly be used to overturn the teaching of Scripture on creation and the flood.

Statements such as these have backed many a person into unwinnable corners. People have felt they simply have to believe in Noah. Jesus did. Their doctrine demands it. Davis A. Young, Professor of Geology Emeritus at Calvin College in Grand Rapids, Michigan noted back in 1995 that 'recent conservative scholars have almost universally characterized the flood narrative as the record of a literal, historical event, with most insisting

---

1   Peter Jensen, *The Revelation of God*, Nottingham: Inter-Varsity Press, 2002,199.

on both geographical and anthropological universality.'[2] They argue, Young points out, that the possibility of a local flood is ruled out by God's promise to never again flood the earth, which he most certainly has done many times at local or regional levels. The reasoning is sound and their consistency in adhering to inerrancy is admirable. The trouble is that no such universal and universally devastating flood has ever happened in the history or pre-history of humankind, as noted previously.

Young notes that in the face of mounting evidence against a literal or historical reading of the Noah story, conservatives have adopted a number of strategies. Some have appealed to miraculous intervention, for example, to transport the animals back to their native habitats. Others have launched an appeal to ignorance and to the uncertainty of scientific knowledge. Many have continued to present distorted or outdated scientific findings. Young laments all of these strategies, and sees them as amounting to intellectual and moral compromise.

> Unfortunately, the evangelical community has been too willing to assess the credibility of its experts on the basis of the conclusions they reach rather than on the basis of the means by which they have reached them. Again and again conservative exegetes have turned to the work of catastrophists such as Price, Rehwinkel, and Whitcomb and Morris because their findings are compatible with a literal reading of the Bible, and heedless of the fact that their research methods, such as they are, fall outside the canon of acceptable scientific pro-cedure. In fact, few flood geologists can lay claim to any significant expertise in geology, palaeontology, anthropology, or biogeography. Evangelicals are compromising the integrity of their biblical scholarship to the extent that they base their exegesis on this sort of questionable secondary scholarship.[3]

This is but one instance of many where the doctrine of inerrancy has pushed Christians into corners they cannot back out of except by becoming intellectually dishonest, or, more sensibly, by jettisoning their unsustainable doctrine of inerrancy. My guess is that current debates about whether Adam and Eve were real people, as St Paul appeared to believe, will generate similar struggles of conscience and intellect. It surely has already.

---

2   Davis A. Young, *The Biblical Flood: A Case Study of the Church's Response to Extra-biblical Evidence*, Grand Rapids, Wm. B. Eerdmans Publishing Company, 1995, 180.

3   *The Biblical Flood,* 301.

This was illustrated for me quite starkly in May 2015 when Moore College's Priscilla and Aquila Centre hosted a public lecture on the historicity of Adam and Eve. One of Moore's younger faculty, Rev. Dr Andrew Leslie, was given the challenging task of addressing this current hot topic. He did an admirable job, given the complexity of the issues involved. His hermeneutical starting point was the inerrancy and perspicuity (clarity) of the Scriptures, which he said would guide his theorising, which it did. However, he almost immediately encountered difficulties because he also acknowledged, at least in broad terms, the reality of evolution as articulated by mainstream evolutionary science. He accepted that modern humans have evolved from pre-human forms of life over a period of millions, not thousands of years. He accepted that human and animal death has been a constant and integral presence throughout the long evolutionary process. But he also affirmed the view that Jesus and the apostles and the various authors of the Bible are likely to have believed in Adam and Eve as discrete and historic individuals through whom death and condemnation descended upon the human race.

It was at this point that the clarity of Scripture began to be muddied. These two pictures appear to be entirely at odds with each other, which was progressively made clear as the lecture continued, and as questions from the floor began to be asked. I admired Andrew for his honesty, humility and for his brave efforts to bring his theological assumptions into alignment with what he reads in the Scriptures, and also with what he has come to believe from extra-Biblical sources, including evolutionary science. His tentative suggestion was that at some point in the evolutionary process, God created two innocent and uncorrupted individuals, Adam and Eve, who were placed in a garden (whether literally or figuratively) and given the unique privilege of representing humankind in what was obviously a failed quest to be obedient, and to earn everlasting life for themselves and the rest of the human race. This is, without doubt, a valiant effort, but it faces formidable difficulties. It does not line up terribly well with what is said about Adam and Eve in the Bible, where Adam is described as the 'one ancestor' from whom all the nations of the world descended (Acts 17:26), and where death appears to follow from, and not precede, their foolish choices, subjecting the creation itself to futility (Romans 5:12-14, 16-17; 8:18-22). Moreover, the suggestion is unfalsifiable. There is no way of knowing that this is what happened, and no way of proving it did not.

Andrew Leslie's lecture illustrated for me two major difficulties with inerrancy. Firstly, those who subscribe to it will almost inevitably be required to engage in mental gymnastics. This is likely to happen in at least two ways. Firstly, the definition of inerrancy will need to be continuously tweaked and fine-tuned so that advances in understanding can be accommodated without error-producing contradiction. Secondly, extraordinary levels of creativity will be required to align ancient and contemporary understandings of world and text. To Andrew's credit, he acknowledged the magnitude of the challenge he faced.

A second and perhaps more serious difficulty, alluded to above, is that inerrantists adopt an interpretive method which prevents them, in principle, from accepting conclusions about the world or the text which imply an error or contradiction. They simply must hold out against threatening advances in understanding. Lack of error becomes an overriding standard for assessing the plausibility of interpretive options. What this inevitably does is to prejudice interpreters against conclusions which would otherwise be very reasonable, and even probable, taking account of all relevant evidence. Stephen L. Young notes that adopting inerrancy, which he helpfully describes as a 'protective strategy', serves to 'block analysis of the Bible through ordinary historical, social, anthropological, and scientific methods should they yield findings about the Bible that transgress how inerrantists understand the Bible's claims – especially that the Bible is inerrant.'[4] They thereby stack the methodological deck in favour of inerrancy, effectively quarantining their positions from critique, and closing off options which would otherwise be persuasive.[5]

This is, I think, a serious problem because Christians who adopt this strategy are not likely to become known as people who love and seek after the truth. As noted above, we are better known for having consistently resisted the truth, most famously in our reactions to Copernicus and Darwin.

---

4   Stephen L. Young, 'Protective Strategies and the Prestige of the "Academic."' A Religious Studies and Practice Theory Redescription of Evangelical Inerrantist Scholarship,' *Biblical Interpretation* 23 (2015), 24.

5   *Protective Strategies and the Prestige of the 'Academic,'* 16.

Being honest about pseudepigraphy

Admitting that some of the Biblical books may not have been written by the claimed author of those books is likely to be difficult for many Christians. Speaking for myself, I grew up believing that Moses wrote all but a few verses of the Pentateuch, the verses describing his death. I thought Isaiah was written by Isaiah, Daniel by Daniel, the Pastoral Epistles by St Paul. It was unsettling to be told that perhaps none of these books and letters was written (or fully written) by the claimed author, and that they are therefore misleading and possibly deceptive.

Courage and honesty is required of those who come to that conclusion. It is also required of those who conclude otherwise. When I was a theological undergraduate, one of our lecturers used to signal his sensible uncertainty on various issues by saying, 'On Monday to Wednesday, I think x. On Thursdays to Sunday I think y.' As students, we appreciated this. It encouraged us to be careful in coming to conclusions, and modest in expressing them.

Being honest about the leadership of women

It takes honesty and courage to admit that efforts to prevent women from assuming leadership positions in the church might be misguided or poorly grounded. That the Church has been misguided on this issue is a conclusion Christians have increasingly come to embrace, certainly within Protestant denominations, but also within Roman Catholic and Orthodox circles, and even amongst evangelicals. But there has also been fierce resistance, certainly within my own Sydney Anglican Church, and in other churches as well around Australia, some of them influenced by the strong line taken by Sydney. In such circles, courage is most certainly required by those who take a contrary line.

What has amazed me, as I have observed the strength of opposition to female leadership, is that this strength is not matched by the strength of the case mounted in its favour. Within Sydney, the case goes something along of the following lines:

> Women should not teach or have authority over men because St Paul said they shouldn't. He said this most clearly in 1 Timothy 2:1-15 where he justifies his prohibition by an appeal to Genesis 2 and 3, thereby implying that these instructions are not cultural, occasional or temporary, but are grounded

in the created nature of men and women. Men are created to lead, women to submissively follow. The verses from Timothy, because of their clarity, are used to understand and interpret other Biblical passages; not the other way round. Other Biblical passages, when read through this lens, add support to this interpretation.

I once argued this case,[6] so am reasonably familiar with it. But I am also now unconvinced by it, largely because it crucially depends upon a series of doubtful assumptions. The case is quite fragile, in fact, for that reason.

Doubtful assumptions

One assumption that appears to be necessary for this case to hold together is that there are no instances of women teaching or having authority over men in the New Testament. If women are observed to teach and to have authority over men in the New Testament without any implied or explicit criticism, or, more decisively still, with approval, then the case for saying that the instructions of 1 Timothy are not simply occasional or restricted in their application is considerably weakened.

The New Testament does appear to countenance the possibility and acceptability of women teaching and having authority over men. In what follows, I rely on an excellent article by Kenneth E. Bailey, an expert in Middle Eastern cultures.[7] Bailey draws attention to instances of women teaching men, including Priscilla, and her husband Aquila, who, in Acts 18:24-26, expound the way of God more fully to Apollos. Apollos was a high profile preacher who is praised in these verses for his knowledge of the Scriptures and for his familiarity with the 'things concerning Jesus.' Here is a case of a woman, mentioned first, teaching a respected male evangelist. Bailey also mentions the case of Phoebe, referred to by St Paul in Romans 16:1-2 as a deacon of the church of Cenchreae. She is a deacon, not a deaconess, suggesting that she held a recognised office of the church. C. E. B. Cranfield, in his commentary on Romans, asserts:

> [We] regard it as virtually certain that Phoebe is being described as *a* or possibly, *the* 'deacon' of the church in question, and that this occurrence of *dia-*

---

6   When I was a young curate at South Tamworth in the Anglican Diocese of Armidale, way back in the mid 1980's, I argued against the ordination of women to the priesthood using this very case.

7   Kenneth E. Bailey, 'Women in the New Testament: A Middle Eastern Cultural View,' Theology Matters, Vol. 6, No. 1, Jan / Feb 2000.

konos is to be classified with its occurrence in Philippians 1:1, and 1 Timothy 3:8 and 12.[8]

Not only is Phoebe described as a deacon, she is referred to as a protectress or patroness to many, including St Paul. The Greek word used, *prostasis*, is used in its masculine form to describe governors, chieftains and leaders in a democracy. The word is used to describe Jesus.[9] Phoebe was clearly a very impressive woman, and is likely to have exercised her considerable authority in the context of the church at Cenchreae.

Bailey notes that women also assumed the role of prophet in New Testament churches. Given the foundational role of 'apostles and prophets,'[10] women clearly occupied an elevated place in the life of the early church. Moreover, they exercised that ministry in a context of mixed public worship, as is clear from 1 Corinthians 11:4-5. Men and women, not all of them prophets, were speaking words from God to men and women in church.

Bailey also mentions the intriguing case of Junia who, in Romans 16:7, is described along with Andronicus, as 'notable among the apostles.' Chrysostom, preaching on this text, noted:

> To be an apostle is something great. But to be outstanding among the apostles, just think what a wonderful song of praise that is! Indeed, how great the wisdom of this woman must have been, that she was even deemed worthy of the title apostle.[11]

To be an apostle was to be a member of a select group, heading the list of church orders in 1 Corinthians 12:29. It is almost inconceivable that, as an apostle, Junia would not have taught or had some degree of authority over men. It is hard to imagine her silently sitting beside Andronicus, quite possibly her husband, whilst he and not she addressed Christian congregations where they attended or visited.

---

8   C.E.B. Cranfield, *Romans: A Shorter Commentary*, Eerdmans, Grand Rapids, 1985, 374.

9   In 1 Clement 36:1 and 61:3.

10   See, for example, Ephesians 3:20.

11   B. Booten, 'Junia: Outstanding among the Apostles' (Romans 16:7) in *Women Priests: A Catholic Commentary on the Vatican Declarations*, eds. L. and A. Swindler, NY: Paulist Press, 1977, 141.

It is of course possible, and no text says otherwise, that Junia (and Phoebe and Priscilla) did sit quietly in church, being careful not to teach or be seen to exercise authority over men. The above-mentioned passages can, though with some effort, be squeezed into the mould of a restrictive interpretation of 1 Timothy. However, to do such squeezing would require one to rely upon a **second** doubtful assumption, which is that 1 Timothy is clear and unambiguous, or, at the very least, is clear enough to rely upon as one's *crux interpretum*. The Protestant Reformers were guided by the principle that passages which are clear need to be relied upon to interpret those which are less clear.[12] The problem is that 1 Timothy 2 has proved notoriously difficult to interpret. It is anything but clear, as will be demonstrated below. The principle of being guided by what is clearer would reasonably discourage us from beginning with 1 Timothy 2.

A **third** doubtful assumption is that the author of 1 Timothy was alluding to Genesis in order to ground his teaching in the created nature of men and women, or, as evangelical complementarians like to put it, in a God-given 'order of creation.' Women and men, although similar in some ways, are also different, and God, taking wise account of these differences, assigns particular roles to men and women which are most suited to them. Included among these roles is leadership, a role reserved for men, and submission, a joyful privilege reserved for women and children, certainly within the home. Women and men thus complement each other in what is essentially a patriarchal arrangement. Patriarchy, according to this way of understanding things, is built into the very fabric of creation.

The problem is that this way of understanding doesn't find strong support from the text of Genesis 1-3. Though it is undoubtedly true that women and men do complement each other in a host of delightful and sometimes surprising ways (my wife, Judy, is more technical and practical than me, for example), a close look at Genesis 1-3 reveals an emphasis not on male-female differences, or complementarity, but on similarity and equality.

In the Bible's first reference to males and females, they are jointly and equally given authority over God's creation:

> God created man in his own image, in the image of God he created them,

---

12   See, for example, *The Westminster Confession,* Chapter I, 9, where this principle is spelled out.

male and female he created them. God blessed them, and said to them, 'Be fruitful and multiply, and fill the earth and subdue it; and have dominion over [every living creature].' Gen 1:27, 28.

The emphasis here is upon the fundamental equality of men and women as God's vice-regents tasked with the responsibility of ruling over the rest of the created order. They each bear the image of God.[13] The equality of the sexes is reinforced in the second creation account of Genesis 2 and 3, where the emphasis is upon the similarity, not complementarity, of men and women. After creating the first man, God declares, 'It is not good that the man should be alone; I will make a helper suitable for him,' 2:18. It has often been pointed out that the word translated 'helper' (Heb. *ezer*) does not denote inferiority of rank or value. In numerous Biblical passages, God is described using this word (e.g. Exod. 18:4; Deut. 33:7, 26, 29; 1 Sam. 7:12; Ps. 33:20; Dan. 11:34). What is required, in this context, is a helper of suitable nature and dignity to overcome the man's aloneness. The animals paraded before him don't quite fit the bill. They are certainly different from him, but the problem is that they are not sufficiently similar. And so, God creates a woman from the man's rib. She most certainly fits the bill. The man exclaims, 'This at last is bone of my bones and flesh of my flesh,' Gen. 2:23. James V. Brownson notes that this language is always used in Scripture of kinship.[14] The woman is his kin.

Kinship is also on view in verse 24, where the institution of marriage is reflected upon:

Therefore a man leaves his father and his mother and clings to his wife, and they become one flesh.

Some have suggested that what is on view here is the sexual union of the man and his wife. Some go even further to suggest that, in this union, the originally androgynous, then separated, first individual is reunited. So argues Robert A. J. Gagnon:

Only a being made from 'adam can and ought to become someone with whom

---

13   Some have suggested that the image of God is only fully represented in the union of males and females, a problematic suggestion, especially given its implications for singleness, including the singleness of Jesus.

14   James V. Brownson, *Bible, Gender, Sexuality: Reframing the Church's Debate on Same-Sex Relationships,* Grand Rapids: Wm. B. Eerdmans, 2013, 30.

'adam longs to reunite in sexual intercourse and marriage, a reunion that not only provides companionship but restores 'adam to his original wholeness.[15]

So also John R. W. Stott:

Out of the undifferentiated humanity of Adam, males and females emerged. And Adam awoke from his deep sleep to behold before him a reflection of himself, a complement to himself, indeed a very part of himself.'[16]

This view, although understandably attractive to those wanting to emphasize male-female complementarity, faces formidable exegetical difficulties, to which Brownson insightfully draws attention.[17] Not least of these difficulties is the likelihood that the one flesh union described in Genesis 2:24 is a kinship, rather than a sexual union. Brownson points out that in Ancient Near Eastern societies, men don't generally leave their parents to be joined to their wives. 'Leaving' in Genesis 2:24 thus most sensibly 'connotes the dissolution of one primary kinship tie and the creation of another.'[18]

Consequently, a complementarian reading of Genesis 1-3, is, at best, doubtful. As Brownson persuasively argues, '[the] primary movement of the text (from Genesis 1:27 into Genesis 2) is not from unity to differentiation, but from the isolation of an individual to the deep blessing of shared kinship and community.'[19] Understanding the verses in these terms helps to elucidate the meaning of the curse pronounced against Eve in Genesis 3:16:

To the woman [God] said, 'I will greatly increase your pangs in childbirth, in pain you shall bring forth children, yet your desire shall be for your husband, and he shall rule over you.'

Complementarians typically argue that the 'desire' spoken of here is the desire to overthrow or undermine the God-given authority or leadership of men.[20] However, as seen, the over-riding emphasis of Genesis 1-3 is

---

15   D. O. Via and Robert A. J. Gagnon, *Homosexuality and the Bible: Two Views*, Minneapolis: Fortress, 2003, 61.

16   John R. W. Stott, *Same-Sex Partnerships? A Christian Perspective*, Grand Rapids: F. H. Revell, 1998, 33.

17   *Bible, Gender, Sexuality*, 22-38.

18   *Bible, Gender, Sexuality*, 33.

19   *Bible, Gender, Sexuality*, 30.

20   It is often helpfully pointed out that the Hebrew words for 'desire' and 'rule' are again used together in Genesis 4:7, where the desire is a desire for mastery. Complementarians

on equality and similarity. Men and women are together given dominion (authority) over the created order. Nothing is said, or even implied,[21] about male authority or headship until the entirely negative assessment of post-fall relationships in Genesis 3. A few years ago, I preached on this third chapter of Genesis and offered the following suggestion about the meaning of verse 16:

> Verse 16 is predictive of what would be a perpetual struggle between husbands and wives, men and women. Women would, for their part, crave certain things from their menfolk, like love and intimacy, and empowerment. Men, for their part, would respond by being bossy, by assuming authority, by flexing their superior physical strength to rule over their wives, to *make* them submit, to *force* them to cease from their incessant demands. It is a picture of struggle, of alienation between men and women, of the battle of the sexes.

Patriarchy is thus introduced, or its presence accounted for, in Genesis 3:16. It is absent in the earlier idealised descriptions of human origins. This, at the very least, is a sensible interpretation of these verses and chapters. And it makes more likely an interpretation of 1 Timothy 2 which sees the writer's prohibitions as occasional and temporary in their application. In support of such an interpretation, Philip B. Payne notes that the form of the phrase which is used to introduce the prohibition on women teaching and usurping authority is one St Paul normally uses when indicating his own personal advice for a situation which is not universal.[22] In other words,

---

typically argue that the desire and rulership in 3:16 is a corruption of an earlier more healthy patriarchy.

21   Some do argue that various details in Genesis 2 imply male headship or leadership, such as the man naming the animals and then Eve. However, none of the proposed implications are necessary, and alternative implications can sensibly be drawn. For example, with respect to naming, in Genesis 1 joint authority over the natural order is granted to men and women, suggesting that we should not draw too many implications from the description of Adam (then single and lonely) naming the animals and then Eve, who would become his delightful companion and co-ruler.

22   Philip B. Payne, in *Man and Woman, One in Christ: An exegetical and theological study of Paul's letters,* Grand Rapids: Zondervan, 2009, 320. The Greek word, epitrepo, translated, 'I do not permit' – 1 Timothy 2:12. John Toews notes that the use of epitrepo in the Septuagint is almost always related to a specific and limited situation rather than a broad or universal one, John E. Toews, 'Women in Church Leadership: 1 Timothy 2:11-15, a Reconsideration,' in *The Bible and the Church: Essays in Honor of Dr David Ewert,* (ed.) A. J. Dueck, H. J. Giesbert and V. G. Shillington, Hillsboro, Kansas, Kindred, 1983.

this is not an instruction for all time, but a prohibition designed to meet a particular and temporary situation.

Further confirmation of the occasional nature of the prohibition on women teaching or having authority over men is found in the use of the Greek word *authentein*. This word does not occur elsewhere in the New Testament, and is not one of the normal words used by St Paul to mean 'to have authority.'[23] It has within its semantic range ideas of control or domination, and can even mean 'to murder' or 'to assert absolute sway.' It appears to be a very strong word, which is why all early Latin, Coptic and Syriac versions of this phrase translate the word as 'to domineer.' Marcus Barth translates it with the King James Version as 'to usurp authority.' This is certainly not something anyone should do, but the fact that it has been prohibited here implies women were usurping or illegitimately assuming authority over men, in all likelihood the male elders of that church. The verse, as it stands, does not prohibit the acceptable use of authority by women in that or any other congregation. At the very least, it leaves open the possibility of a non-abusive use of authority by women, which, quite possibly, was already being exercised in that congregation by female elders.[24]

The appeal to Genesis can also sensibly be understood as illustrating the quite specific and locally relevant instructions being given by the author. It might be helpful to again include the relevant verses:

> For Adam was formed first, then Eve; and Adam was not deceived, but the woman was deceived and became a transgressor. Yet she will be saved through childbearing, provided they continue in faith and love and holiness, with modesty, 1 Timothy 2:13-15.

It could be that the author of these words, whether St Paul or someone else, was reminding his readers of the dignity and special privilege that

---

23   Linda L. Belleville points out that had the author of 1 Timothy wanted to refer to the ordinary exercise of authority, he could have picked any number of words. She notes that within the semantic domain of 'exercise authority,' biblical lexicographers J. P. Louw and Eugene Nida have twelve entries, and of 'rule,' 'govern' forty-seven entries. Yet the author picked none of these, she suggests because *authentein* carried a nuance that was particularly suited to the Ephesian situation,' 'Teaching and Usurping Authority: 1 Timothy 2:11-15,' in *Discovering Biblical Equality: Complementarity without hierarchy,* Ronald W. Pierce and Rebecca Merrill Groothuis (eds.), Downers Grove: InterVarsity Press, 2004, 211.

24   For a fascinating discussion of references to female elders in 1 Timothy (sometimes hidden by translation decisions), see Bailey, *Women in the New Testament,* 4, 5.

Adam enjoyed by virtue of him being the first-created human. Women were not therefore to disrespect that dignity by forcefully assuming the role of teacher. It could also be that the writer is simply drawing attention to Adam's chronological priority. Adam was created first and therefore was the direct recipient of God's command and warning that he must not eat of the fruit of the tree in the middle of the garden, or else he would die. It was thus Adam's responsibility to 'teach' his wife; to pass on this crucial knowledge. The text of Genesis 3 suggests he didn't, or, at least, didn't do so adequately. Eve misrepresents God's command, telling the serpent they weren't even to 'touch' the fruit. The inadequately-instructed Eve was thus deceived. The story of Adam and Eve is thus being used illustratively to address a particular dysfunctional situation which is described and implied in the surrounding verses and chapters of I Timothy.

This is a possible, and, in fact, highly credible interpretation of 1 Timothy 2, especially given the wider New Testament context. But even if it is not the best interpretation, even if one concludes, after carefully weighing up all the relevant evidence, that some form of patriarchy is being assumed by the author of these words, even this is not a decisive reason for accepting these instructions, because of one further doubtful assumption.

This **fourth** doubtful assumption is that the biblical writers' understanding of the world needs to be our understanding of the world. As we have seen, those who wrote the Bible held to all sorts of cosmological and anthropological assumptions which we no longer feel obliged to accept. Patriarchy is one of those. It may well be the case that patriarchy is not dispensed with or fully jettisoned by the Biblical writers. However, this does not mean that we need to retain patriarchy. It is possible, and I would suggest, very sensible, to pick up the threads of a gradual loosening of patriarchal assumptions as the Bible progresses, and to then walk in the direction of those threads until patriarchy dies the death it probably deserves to die.

The point of the above discussion is that the case against the ordination of women to positions of authority in the church is not strong. It is built upon a succession of doubtful assumptions, all of which can reasonably be challenged. It will take courage to admit this. It will take courage for the leaders of churches who currently prevent women from exercising authority to allow the stained glass ceiling to be broken, and to thus give up their long-held monopoly on power. This will take great courage, but that is not to say it won't happen - one day.

Being honest about homosexuality

Honesty and courage is also urgently required, but sadly in short supply, when it comes to the now centuries long mistreatment of our lesbian, gay, bi-sexual, transgender and intersex sisters and brothers. It has not only been Christians, of course, who have been guilty of the misunderstanding and mistreatment meted out to people whose gender does not neatly fit the categories of male and female. Up until the last twenty years or so, most people in Australia and throughout the world have participated in the abuse, as people of alternative sexualities have been bashed, brutalised, murdered, ostracised, and ridiculed - simply for being who they are.

One of the perhaps understandable reasons for at least some of the mistreatment is ignorance about the nature and causes of sexual variations, including homosexuality. Speaking for myself, I was incredibly ignorant about these things for most of my life. The scientific community has taken its time to do the necessary research to gain what is still an incomplete picture about why a small percentage of the human population appears to be wired differently from the rest of the population. We are still learning, and have much still to learn. But having said that, we are learning, and as we learn, we all need to have the courage to be honest about the following.

Being honest about the harm done by the church

There is no doubt that Christians and the Christian church have contributed to harm done to those who don't fit the male-female duality. We and our teaching have done so in a number of ways. We have done so by insisting that there are only males and females. And the reason often given is that the Bible teaches that God made us male and female, Adam and Eve, not Adam and Steve. By denying that there is any other form of sexual being, we have contributed to, and, in our western and Christian cultures, have been largely responsible for, the stigmatizing of LGBTI people as defective and/or debauched. I have lost count of how many times I have heard Christians say that homosexuality is sinful. If you are homosexual, you are sinful, and, if not sinful, defective, and that is because there are only two legitimate, God-created genders. To assert that there is another or others is to contradict God, so the argument goes, and if you live out your claimed alternative disposition, you are doubly sinful.

Christians have contributed to misunderstanding and abuse by also not being willing to talk about this issue. Nigel Chapman, in an excellent article entitled 'Evangelical Churches and Same Sex Attraction' notes that same-sex sexual activity has been a taboo subject ever since Leviticus described such behaviour as abhorrent and detestable. Christian (and Jewish and Islamic) teaching has certainly contributed to the distaste, fear and loathing which people have felt towards those of non-standard sexual orientation. We need to be honest about that. As Christians, we need to admit that we have failed people like Matthew whose story was told earlier in this book. Matthew took years to summon up the courage to talk about his sexuality, largely because it was a taboo subject within his church and community, something people did not want to talk about or face up to.

A 2010 La Trobe University study entitled *Writing Themselves In #3,*[25] includes reports of experiences very similar to Matthew's, including the following:

> I go to a private Christian school and whilst I have not had to withstand any openly blatant homophobia from my teachers and administrators, they have done nothing about the bashings, have lectured me repeatedly on the sins of my actions, and assured me that I'm going to hell, and I've had to sit and listen as people verbally abuse me. (Adrian, 16 years)

> My mother threw me out of the house and said, 'Don't come back till you give your heart to Jesus.' (Christie, 16 years)

> I have had multiple thoughts of suicide. I have acted and failed on those thoughts a few times. I am never able to actively harm myself (i.e. cut myself), but I've wanted to many times. Any gay person who says they have never even thought about suicide is lying. Not being able to act on any of your desires, having to actively hide your true self, often having to pretend to hate the very thing you are. All of these things equate to a deep feeling that you don't deserve to live, or failing that, a deep desire to end the suffering. On a happier note, coming out has turned my life around. All of those things mentioned are starting to become a thing of the past. (Christopher, 20 years)

---

25   The study involved 3,000 same-sex attracted and gender-questioning 14-21 year old Australians.

In the 2010 survey, 4% of the participants mentioned religious involvement. Sadly, they were more likely than others to report feeling unsafe at home, more likely to report thoughts of self-harm and suicide, and more likely to carry out self-harm, though their reported rate of attempted suicide was the same as for those who did not mention religious involvement.[26]

We Christians need to have the courage to admit that we and our understandings have contributed to the misery and deaths of LGBTI people. We also need to repent for having walked by on the other side of the road in fear of being contaminated by the blood still flowing from the wounds of our sisters and brothers lying beside the road.

It takes courage to be like Jesus, who never seemed to worry about getting his hands dirty. My home city of Sydney hosts a gay and lesbian *Mardi Gras* every year, and Christians have not been noted for their attendance, except on the sidelines holding up banners to condemn the march. However, a couple of years ago, a brave clergyman decided to invite his fellow clergy to join him in a very public act of apology on behalf of Christians and Christian churches. He sought to marshal 100 Reverends (100 Revs) to join the march, dressed up in clergy gear if they had it. He didn't quite get 100, but those who marched were brave. In terms of their understanding of homosexuality and its implications, the clergy and church workers who marched differed from each other. Some were conservative. Some were more liberal in their beliefs, but all were willing to publically say sorry for their own and other Christians' mistreatment and misunderstanding of LGBTI people.

Being honest about the near impossibility of change

What has become increasingly clear is that homosexuality is best understood as an orientation, which, in most people, is not amenable to change. For some years now, Christians have believed that if they pray long enough, and engage in therapy for long enough, and believe in the healing power of God strongly enough, sexual orientation can change. All the emerging evidence suggests that this is simply not the case.

---

26 For example, in 2009 the American Psychological Association (http://bit.ly/1wJY6BX) and the U.K. Royal College of Psychiatrists ((http://bit.ly/Zj2n4k) warned against sexual orientation-change efforts as harmful. See also: http://www.glhv.org.au/files/wti3_web_sml.pdf

Among professional psychologists, it is generally accepted that efforts to change sexual orientation are neither effective nor safe.[27] Even Christian researchers, who have sometimes claimed instances of conversion from homosexual to heterosexual orientation, are quick to admit such cases are rare. Moreover, movements set up to assist gay and lesbian people to get rid of unwanted sexual desires and behaviour are now disbanding at a rapid rate, in large part because of the mostly fruitless results of reorientation efforts. Alan Chambers, the founder of one such organisation, Exodus International, recently acknowledged this failure publically. In June 2012, at the organisation's 38th annual meeting, Chambers renounced some of the movement's core beliefs, including that homosexuality can be cured. Regarding 'reparative therapy' he said that such therapy offers false hope to gays, and can be harmful. He recommended that Exodus move beyond its slogan that *Change is possible*. Upon closing the organisation in 2013, he stated that '99.9% of people' did not experience orientation change, and offered the following apology:

> We have told them that they should feel ashamed or that they should try to change these things that we have realised we *cannot change* ... I believe that causes all sorts of trauma and I know that there are people who have taken their life because they felt so ashamed of who they are, felt like God couldn't love them as they are, and that's something that will haunt me until the day I die.

A few years earlier, John Smid, the executive director of *Love in Action*, a flagship ex-gay ministry of Exodus International, noted for its claim that it could stop people from being same-sex attracted, expressed similar disquiet with the slogan that 'change is possible.' *Love in Action's* residential program was shut down in 2007. John Smid, who recently married his male partner, no longer believes it is possible to change someone's sexual orientation. In his words:

> One cannot repent of something that is unchangeable. I have gone through a tremendous amount of grief over the many years that I spoke of change, re-pentance, reorientation and such, when, barring some kind of miracle, none of this can occur with homosexuality. Actually, I've never met a man who

---

27   Nigel Chapman, 'Evangelical Churches and Same-Sex Orientation, 2 November, 2013, *chapman.id.au/files/EvangelicalChurchesAndSameSexOrientation.pdf*

experienced a change from homosexual to heterosexual.[28]

Being honest about the challenge of celibacy

According to *Writing Themselves In #3*, 60% of same-sex attracted youth were aware of this attraction by age thirteen, which means that during their adolescent years, teenagers who are gay will have a lot to cope with. Not only will they be going through an extraordinarily potent time of life, sexually, they will also be tormented by teaching that they are sinful or defective and need to be cured. They also face the discouraging prospect that, unless they are cured, sex is out for them permanently, and not just sex, but intimacy and romance and a family of their own. That is a terrible burden for young shoulders to bear.

Even if one comes to the conclusion that this is what must be, one needs to be honest and brave enough to acknowledge how hard it will be, and how hard it has been for countless of our LGBTI sons and daughters. It won't be good enough to simply say that this is no greater a challenge than faced by heterosexual teenagers, who also feel constrained by the belief that if they do not marry, they will be required to remain celibate for the rest of their lives. It isn't the same. As teenagers, they will always have had held out to them the possibility of marriage, and will have been encouraged to remain celibate for the sake of their future spouse.

Being honest about the current state of research

Although there is still much we don't know about homosexuality, there is much we do know. Research is increasingly suggesting a biological basis for homosexuality, as well as biological differences between heterosexual and homosexual people.[29] There are, it seems,[30] multiple biological pathways, which variously determine male and female sexuality.[31] Efforts to find a 'gay gene' have morphed into more sophisticated research, now guided by

---

28   http://thinkprogress.org/lgbt/2011/10/11/340335/former-ex-gay-ministry-leader-comes-out-recants-previous-teachings/

29   I. Savic and P. Lindstrom, (2008) 'PET and MRI show differences in cerebral asymmetry and functional connectivity between homosexual and heterosexual subjects', *Proceedings of the National Academy of Sciences*, Vol 105 (27), 9407.

30   I am indebted to a friend, Natalie Cooper, who has meticulously drawn together relevant material to assist me in this short section.

31   Kunzig, R. (2008) 'Finding the Switch', *Psychology Today*, Vol 41 (3), pp 88–93.

an understanding that most heritable traits are polygenic. For example, eye colour is determined by up to fifteen genes.[32] Moreover, genes may or may not be expressed, or show up as physiological traits, depending on environmental factors which either activate or deactivate genes. These epigenetic factors explain why monozygotic twins, arising from a single fertilized ovum, are not 100% concordant for traits that are known to be biologically governed.[33] They are also likely to explain why it is that the more times a woman becomes pregnant with a son, the likelihood that each subsequent son will be gay increases.[34]

Studies such as these are showing up all sorts of interesting facts, generating still further studies to help us better understand this complex subject. Significant differences have been found to exist in the brains of homosexual and heterosexual people. Homosexual men and women display features of the opposite sex with respect to connectivity between the amygdala and other areas of the brain. Cerebral symmetry differences also exist,[35] which cannot be attributed to behavior, because they are present in the foetus.[36] These and other brain differences are matched by, and perhaps have contributed to, other observed differences, including the ratio of limb length to trunk length, which has been found to be shifted in gender a-typical directions, as have gait and voice qualities. Homosexual men and women

---

32   D. White and M. Rabago-Smith (2011), 'Genotype-phenotype associations and human eye color,' *Journal of Human Genetics;* Vol. 56; 5 - 7.

33   For example, twins do not share an identical prenatal environment; the timing of zygote split determines whether they have a common or separate placenta, and also whether they inhabit one or separate amniotic sacs. See further, Singh, S.M., et al. (2002) 'Epigenetic contributors to the discordance of monozygotic twins', *Clinical Genetics* 62, 97-103. Czyz, W., et al (2012), 'Genetic, environmental and stochastic factors in monozygotic twin discordance with a focus on epigenetic differences', *BMC Medicine*, 10:93.

34   A. Bogaert and R. Blanchard, 'Homosexuality in men and number of older brothers', *American Journal of Psychiatry*, 153 (1996), 27-31; R. Blanchard & P. Klassen (April 1997) 'H-Y antigen and homosexuality in men', *Journal of Theoretical Biology*, 185 (3), 373-378. Blanchard and Klasson reported that each additional older brother increases the odds of the son being gay by 33%. Kathy Baldock, in *Walking the Bridgeless Canyon: Repairing the breach between the Church and the LGBT Community*, Reno, NY: Canyonwalker Press, 2014, notes that the 'strongest theory behind this observation holds that the mother produces testosterone-blocking antibodies in response to carrying a male foetus. These testosterone blockers stay in her body and influence subsequent foetal sons, but not daughters', 272.

35   That is, the relative size of the left and right hemisphere of their brains.

36   *Savic and Lindstron*, cited above.

have also been shown to be gender-shifted in a variety of male-favouring visuospatial traits such as mental rotation, targeting and navigation, as well as female-favouring tasks such as verbal fluency (both sexes) and object location memory (gay men only).

This is just a brief sampling of an expanding field of research findings. We need to be honest about these results. It would be dishonest to suggest that there has been no or little progress in our understanding of homosexuality, and that we therefore don't need to take notice of still-inconclusive research. More than enough is already known to rule out the notion, once commonly urged by Christians, that homosexuality is a matter of choice. It would be dishonest to persist in this misunderstanding, as it would be to use language in describing homosexuality which perpetuates this notion. It is not uncommon for Christians to use the words gay and lesbian to refer to behavior, such as the 'gay lifestyle,' and to mute the now common understanding of homosexuality as inbuilt. This leads to still further dishonesty with ministries claiming that people have been 'freed from' or 'cured of' their gayness simply because they have ceased sexual activity or entered into a mixed-gender marriage, even though they may still be same-sex attracted.

It is being dishonest to persist with discredited theories, such as that homosexuality is caused by dysfunctional families, consisting of absent fathers and over-protective mothers, for example.[37] It is being dishonest to fail to mention that 'environmental' factors, now commonly believed to be influential in the development of homosexuality, are generally not such things as family dynamics, teenage sexual experimentation, rape or other trauma, but are rather, and much more influentially, pre-natal or post-natal factors which impact upon biology, such as hormones and prenatal nutrition. People who deliberately and/or carelessly fail to clear up possible misunderstanding around this terminology are being deceptive.

It would be dishonest, or at least careless, to refer to or cite favourable research findings without checking the quality of the research or whether it has been confirmed or disconfirmed by other or more recent research. The great temptation for all of us, regardless of our convictions and beliefs, is to latch onto research or claims which support our particular point of

---

37   For a detailed summary of a range of once-favoured, but now disconfirmed psychosocial theories, see *Born Gay*, 29–42.

view. It is therefore imperative, especially if we are putting our thoughts into the public domain, to check our sources, or to check with those who have greater expertise than we do ourselves. This wasn't done, it seems, in the case of the Sydney Doctrine Commission Report into Human Sexuality, released in March 2015. The report makes a number of statements about the possibility of change:

> There is little consensus about whether all same-sex attraction is unchange-able. The evidence suggests that there is a spectrum of both permanence and degree of same-sex attraction, and so consequently varying degrees of change are possible. Despite the rhetoric claiming any attempt to encourage some-one to change their sexual orientation is impossible and cruel, the evidence simply does not support this. The reality is that God normally changes people incrementally, not with an instantaneous bolt of healing. He calls his children to the (often) painful pursuit of holiness and, by doing so, gradually changes them.[38]

> [It] is also important to challenge the view that it is wrong to encourage a same-sex attracted believer to seek to change their orientation, and also the belief that change is impossible. If such an orientation is not 'according to na-ture', but part of the broken-ness of our disordered world, then reorientation is clearly the ideal. Moreover, by the grace of God, radical change has been experienced by many – albeit often slowly.[39]

In making these claims, the report's authors acknowledge their reliance upon studies by Spitzer (2003)[40] and Jones and Yarhouse (2007),[41] which are referenced without comment. In his paper, Spitzer claimed that 'reparative' therapy, including aversive conditioning and spiritual intervention, can change sexual orientation. He reached this conclusion after one-time telephone interviews with 200 self-selected individuals who claimed they had become heterosexual after therapy. Peer commentary at the time highlighted the fact that Spitzer relied upon testimonies about thoughts and *behaviour which had* occurred on average twelve years prior to the

---

38   *Human Sexuality and the Same-Sex Marriage Debate*, 94.

39   *Human Sexuality and the Same-Sex Marriage Debate*, 95-96.

40   R. L. Spitzer, (2003) 'Can some gay men and lesbians change their sexual orientation? 200 participants reporting a change from homosexual to heterosexual orientation', *Archives of Sexual Behaviour* 32:5, 403–417.

41   S. L. Jones and M. Yarhouse, (2007), Ex-Gays: A longitudinal study of religiously motivated change in sexual orientation, Downers Grove: IVP, 2007.

interview, and that no follow-up interviews were conducted, with no third-party (for example, spousal) interviews taking place.[42] Finally, Spitzer's selection criteria excluded those who had tried to change their orientation without success. The Doctrine Commission's authors failed to mention that in May 2012, Spitzer retracted the findings of his 2003 work; stating that the study's 'fatal flaw' was the lack of a valid way to measure orientation change; and that claims of change were 'unproven.'[43] He apologized for any misunderstanding he might have caused:

> I apologize to any gay person who wasted time and energy undergoing some form of reparative therapy because they believed that I had proven that reparative therapy works with some 'highly motivated' individuals.[44]

The Commission's citing of the Jones and Yarhouse study is equally troubling. The study, published in book form, was not submitted for publication to any peer-reviewed scientific journal, a perplexing failure given the book's claim that 38% of participants reported some degree of successful orientation change.[45] The study was conducted with self-selecting participants of Exodus-run groups. It relied exclusively upon self-reporting by participants, without feedback from others. Study results were compromised by a drop-out rate of 36% (from 98 original participants), and by the fact that results from men and women were collated and analyzed together, as well as by the fact that at least some of the reported changes can be accounted for in terms of subtle changes in bi-sexual focus.[46] Moreover, success in the

---

42   G. Herek, (2003) 'Evaluating Interventions to Alter Sexual Orientation: Methodological and Ethical Considerations' in *Peer Commentaries on Spitzer*. Accessed at: http://psychology.ucdavis.edu/faculty_sites/ rainbow/html/Herek_2003_SpitzerComment.pdf

43   R. L. Spitzer, (2012) 'Spitzer Reassess His 2003 Study of Reparative Therapy of Homosexuality' (Letter to the Editor) *Archives of Sexual Behaviour* 41:757.

44   *Archives of Sexual Behaviour* 41:757.

45   The authors may have been reluctant to do so, given that their work was funded by Exodus International, an organization committed to the belief that orientation change is possible. According to their study, 15% of participants reported substantial reductions in homosexual attraction and substantial conversion to heterosexual attraction and functioning, sufficient to allow them to enter into a heterosexual relationship. A further 23% similarly reported significant reductions in homosexual attraction, but not so significant that they would countenance entering an opposite-sex relationship.

46   It is widely acknowledged that female sexuality is more fluid than male sexuality, meaning that the reporting of substantial change by female participants is likely to skew results.

process of change was determined by whether participants *reported* [my emphasis] that they *felt* their change to be successful, and could *report* substantial reductions in homosexual attraction and substantial conversion to heterosexual attraction functioning, including the embracement of chastity, all of which, without objective checks, is highly subjective,[47] and is hardly the basis for any confidence that significant orientation change is possible.

That Sydney's Doctrine Commission could quote this report in support of its claim that change is possible, and for many actual though slow, is disturbing, especially given that in 2009, Jones and Yarhouse published a follow-up paper in which they acknowledged significant methodological deficiencies in their earlier work, including a lack of rigor and an inadequate sample size.[48] In an update study published in 2011, Jones and Yarhouse defended their earlier conclusion that orientation change is possible, but they also acknowledged that people would do well to not be too optimistic about the likelihood of change.[49] Notably, there were no reported instances of participants moving from a homosexual to a heterosexual orientation, no instance of someone replacing same-sex attraction with heterosexual attraction.[50] At best, the study provided some evidence of some change in that direction.[51] What Jones and Yarhouse did emphasize, however, was that most of the reported change occurred early in the change process. In their own words, 'these findings go against the common argument that change of

---

47   R. L. Bassett, ed., (2009), 'Book Review: Ex-Gays? A Longitudinal Study of Religiously Mediated Change in Sexual Orientation' *Journal of Psychology and Christianity* Vol 28 (2), 182 – 183.

48   Jones, S. & M. Yarhouse, (2009) 'Ex Gays? An Extended Longitudinal Study of Attempted Religiously Mediated Change in Sexual Orientation.'

49   A Longitudinal Study of Attempted Religiously Mediated Sexual Orientation Change", *Journal of Sex and Marital Therapy*, 37:5, 2011, 424.

50   Giving credence to suggestions that many of the reported instances of change may well be accounted for in terms of changes along a bisexual continuum.

51   As the authors honestly point out: 'These results do not prove that categorical change in sexual orientation is possible for everyone or anyone, but rather that meaningful shifts along a continuum that constitute real changes appear possible for some … The authors urge caution in projecting success rates from these findings, as they are likely overly optimistic estimates of anticipated success.' 427.

orientation is gradual and occurs over an extended period of time,'[52] which is exactly what the Doctrine Commission claimed is the case.[53]

Being honest about one's fears and doubts

It is unsettling, in fact deeply unsettling, to have one's beliefs questioned, as I have just done in raising questions about the Doctrine Commission report. In thinking about how the authors could be so careless in their unsubstantiated and misleading claims, it occurred to me that such carelessness probably has a lot to do with our tendency, mentioned earlier, of latching onto arguments and evidence which support our prejudices and pre-understandings. This tendency is especially likely in cases where our beliefs are dear to us, or where disturbing them might have large repercussions, which clearly is the case with the topic of homosexuality, or the associated, and even more emotive topic of same-sex marriage.

It takes courage to admit uncertainties, especially in environments which trade in certainty. The truth is that there are lots of things we don't know for certain. I would like to finish this chapter with some comments by Pope Francis, made during an interview in August 2013 with Father Antonio Spadaro. The interview was conducted in Italian, but translated into English. Spadaro reminded the Pope of some words he had written earlier that year in an encyclical entitled 'Lumen Fidei'. He had said that in order to see reality one must look with a gaze of faith. To fully understand, one must begin with faith, which is what St Augustine had said. Pope Francis agreed and elaborated in terms of the need for a quiet and contemplative spirit, which discerns God in all things, but not in such a way as can be proven. Moreover, mistakes can be made. In Pope Francis's own (translated) words:

> Yes, in this quest to seek and find God in all things there is still an area of un-certainty. There must be. If a person says that he met God with total certainty and is not touched by a margin of uncertainty, then this is not good. For me, this is an important key. If one has the answers to all the questions – that is proof that God is not with him. It means that he is a false prophet using religion for himself. The great leaders of the people of God, like Moses, have always left room for doubt. You must leave room for the Lord, not for our

---

52   *Ex-gays? An Extended Longitudinal Study*, 7.

53   To again quote: 'Moreover, by the grace of God, *radical* [my emphasis] change has been experienced by many – albeit often slowly,' *Human Sexuality and the Same-Sex Marriage Debate*, 96.

certainties; we must be humble. Uncertainty is in every true discernment that is open to finding confirmation in spiritual consolation.

The risk in seeking and finding God in all things, then, is the willingness to explain too much, to say with human certainty and arrogance: 'God is here.' We will find only a god that fits our measure. The correct attitude is that of St. Augustine: seek God to find him, and find God to keep searching for God forever.

Pope Francis goes on, in the interview, to question doctrinal certainties, a truly brave thing to do for a Roman Catholic Pope. As journalist Kyle Cupp pointed out in an article in the New York Times, dated May 26, 2014:

[The Catholic Church is] an institution that has devoted centuries to hammering out and polishing an authoritative system of doctrines concerning who God is and what God expects. It claims to have been founded by Jesus Christ and to be guided infallibly by the Holy Spirit. It has warned of eternal damnation if its authority and precepts are ignored or rejected. In other words: If Catholicism is true, you don't want to be in doubt about its teachings.

Despite this, Pope Francis was honest and brave enough to suggest that even in its doctrines the church needs to move forward, and to not slavishly hold to the past:

Because God is first. God is always first and makes the first move. God is a bit like the almond flower of your Sicily, Antonio, which always blooms first. We read it in the Prophets. God is encountered walking, along the path.

If the Christian is a restorationist, a legalist, if he wants everything clear and safe, then he will find nothing. Tradition and memory of the past must help us to have the courage to open up new areas to God. Those who today always look for disciplinarian solutions, those who long for an exaggerated doctrinal 'security,' those who stubbornly try to recover a past that no longer exists – they have a static and inward-directed view of things. In this way, faith becomes an ideology among other ideologies.

One may or may not disagree with these words of Pope Francis. But they are brave, and they are honest; and it is bravery and honesty such as this that can make Christianity attractive once again to those who are now inclined to not give it a second thought.

CHAPTER SEVEN

The Exhilarating Risk of Inquisitiveness

One of the good things about being uncertain or not overconfident in one's beliefs is that you develop a thirst to know more. You won't worry about being wrong in this or that belief. In fact, you will think it likely you are wrong in some and probably many of your beliefs. You therefore welcome the correction of others, and are happy to be guided towards better conclusions. Uncertainty and the desire to know more is a good thing. It is also realistic, because we are limited in our understandings.

Uncertainty is also productive. For children, a lack of knowledge is the engine room of discovery. They are happily lacking in knowledge, because it motivates them to find out more. They are, by nature, inquisitive and wanting to learn. Sadly, youthful inquisitiveness is often stifled. At some point in their lives, and on some subjects, people are discouraged from the creative quest to know and discover more. This is especially sad when it happens within communities of faith. One would have hoped that the quest to know more, and to find out what is true, would be nurtured and encouraged within faith communities, but it too often is not.

There are all sorts of reasons for this. One of the quite understandable reasons is that matters of faith are hugely important. They represent the core of what many people believe. And so, inquisitiveness can quickly become threatening, and be seen as needing to be restricted, and kept within safe boundaries. But there is another reason why inquisitiveness is likely to be seen as risky, and that is that these core beliefs are often considered fixed and unchallengeable.

Roger Olson helpfully articulates two models of evangelical theology, with this helpfulness not restricted to evangelicalism. The first is the fortress model. People who follow this model believe that all the important questions about God have been answered. They are therefore suspicious of new discoveries or alterations to what they consider to be the received tradition. The task of theology is thus to articulate and defend this tradition, which, for evangelicals, is believed to be derived directly from the pages of the Bible. Nothing new will be of significance. It will already have been said, though it may need to be re-articulated in terms which are understandable to a contemporary audience.

The fortress model is a good descriptor of the current state of Sydney Anglican evangelicalism. People who express even slightly different points of view from the dominant Sydney line on women or Biblical authority or homosexuality quickly come under suspicion. To even suggest there might be a different way of thinking about these issues will get you into trouble. A big part of the reason for that is the conviction that the truth about these matters is already well enough known. God is a good communicator, and the truth extracted from the Scriptures will always be the truth. The job of the Christian is to exegete that truth, and then to defend it, but not to question it.

The stakes are raised even higher by construing contentious issues as gospel issues. If it is the case that issues, such as those mentioned above, are joined at the hip to the centre or core of evangelical theology, the gospel, then they are matters of the first importance, and no quarter can be given. The walls of one's theological fortress must remain intact and strong, no matter how persuasive the attacks upon it might appear.

The big problem with this model is that many of the issues currently being debated in the church are anything but clear and fixed, as I have sought to show in this book. There are a host of good questions currently being asked, about literalism, about inerrancy, about homosexuality and patriarchy, about Adam and Eve and the Exodus, and even about how the gospel should best be understood. Pretty much everything about Christianity is being questioned at the moment, and efforts to stifle healthy debate are not only likely to be abusive, they won't help in the process of finding good answers to those questions.

But there is another approach open to evangelicals and to others, which Olson dubs the pilgrimage model.[1] Rather than viewing Scripture as a not-yet-systematized collection of propositional truths which the church has gone about mining, organising and defending, one can see it rather as a drama, the interpretation of which is more an art than a science. This approach sees the Scriptures as an unfolding story, not as a text book from which theologies for all time can be lifted. The full humanity of this drama can also be acknowledged as the Bible's characters (real, mythical and/or legendary) struggle, just as we do, to understand God and their place in the world. This story is God's gift to us as we are drawn into it, and as we continue to live it. N. T. Wright compares the Bible and tradition to an unfinished play with us as its actors. In this, the fourth act of the play,[2] we are called upon to improvise as participants in what is a continuing drama.[3]

This second model makes good sense. We are not forced by it to turn the Bible into anything other than what it is, an ancient text. We don't need to insist that all of its stories be taken as factually accurate. We are not required to embrace each and every one of the assumptions which impregnate its stories. We think differently. We would tell these stories differently. Stories, by their nature, are malleable and adaptable, able to be told differently in every age. And we now have our own stories to live and tell, as we continue the long, challenging and hope-filled pilgrimage begun so promisingly within the pages of the Bible.

What this model does is to leave room for questions. The Bible itself is filled with questions, is built upon questions as the Biblical writers strove to make best sense of their experience of life and of God. And we have questions as well, some of them new, some of them old. Almost twenty centuries of theological reflection has produced a succession of possible answers, some better than others, some enlightening, some obfuscating, none complete or final. And that, too, means that questions are inevitable and necessary.

We should not be afraid to ask questions. We must not let ourselves be bullied into silent acquiescence to beliefs, especially to systems of belief,

---

1   Roger E. Olson, *How to be an Evangelical without being Conservative*, Grand Rapids: Zondervan, 2008, 147.

2   Following on from the Old and New Testaments and post-apostolic tradition.

3   See further, N. T. Wright, 'How can the Bible be authoritative,' *Vox Evangelica*, 1991, 21, 7–32.

which have been built with pillars and beams no longer strong enough to prevent them from collapsing. Some of them are collapsing, or, at the very least, are in urgent need of renovation.

But what I find especially attractive about this model is that it leaves room for inquisitiveness, which is not so readily supplied by the fortress model. I love the word inquisitive. The *Oxford English Dictionary* defines it as 'eagerly seeking knowledge.' There is an innate joyfulness and freedom associated with inquisitiveness. One doesn't know in advance what one will find, but the assumption is that it will be worth finding. Inquisitiveness and trust go hand in hand. Inquisitiveness is nurtured in environments where people feel safe. It ought to come naturally to Christians who believe in a generous and good-hearted heavenly Father, who loves to give good gifts to his children, including the gift of rationality. Inquisitiveness sets out on the quest to know and understand in the confident belief that truth will be its own reward. From a Christian point of view, we seek after truth in the comforting knowledge that all truth derives from God, who is Truth.

We don't need to be fearful, therefore, even though there is some risk in being inquisitive. The major risk involved is the risk of remaining open to possibilities that may turn out to be unsettling or threatening. But surely it is better to face the truth, however threatening, than to run away from it or put our heads in the sand. Thomas Paine once remarked, 'it is error only, and not truth, that shrinks from inquiry.'

It is important that we keep asking questions, because only then are we likely to progress in our understanding. Questions have a habit of generating even more questions which can guide us to some form of resolution, often in the form of a theory, which, if it is a good theory, will make good sense of all the relevant data. Inquisitiveness is often activated when some bits of data don't neatly fit the prevailing or favoured theory. This happens in science. It also happens in theology. Inquisitiveness is provoked, in theology and science, when cognitive dissonance occurs. The overcoming of cognitive dissonance becomes the engine room of further discovery, and, hopefully, better theories.

Throughout this book, we have been teasing away at a number of issues, two of which are worth thinking about in terms of cognitive dissonance.

Women leading and teaching men

Cognitive dissonance sometimes strikes unexpectedly. I was chatting once with a former student of mine from Moore Theological College who is currently the rector of one of Sydney's Anglican parishes. He said to me that he had once happily embraced the common Sydney position that women should not teach or have authority over men in the context of church meetings. He had been persuaded that 1 Timothy 2, in combination with other passages, was enough to bar women from engaging in such activities.

But he said that one day he was accosted by the wife of an assistant minister who had newly joined the parish from theological college. She was upset that the male leader of one of the church's Bible study groups had allowed his wife to lead the study on just one occasion when he was out of town. This, the young wife said, was in violation of the Bible's clear prohibition of such behaviour. My friend, somewhat taken aback by this, thought to himself, possibly for the first time, 'There is something not quite right about this.' And as he thought about it, he concluded it was the aesthetics of this hard-line reaction that finally got to him. It violated his sense of what was good and beautiful. It seemed ugly. And it prompted him to re-think his theology.

Cognitive dissonance can do that. One thing which has bothered me about the case against women leading or teaching men in church is that those who argue this way prove more than they need. As noted in earlier chapters, advocates typically argue that the instructions in 1 Timothy 2 are grounded in the created order, and that is why they are permanent in their application. Women shouldn't lead or teach men because they weren't created to do this. But if that is the case, then they also shouldn't lead corporations or countries, or be in charge at any level of any mixed-gender organisation. They weren't created to lead. Nor were they created to teach mixed groups of people, and so we shouldn't have them teaching in our colleges or universities. Such activity is in violation of the God-mandated order of creation.

To even talk in these terms is laughable, and most now recognize this. However, what this acknowledgement means is that those arguing the case against the ordination of women to teaching and leadership positions in the church must find a convincing reason for restricting the relevance of these verses to churches. I am yet to hear such a reason.

But the cognitive dissonance doesn't end there. We now know that women do teach and lead just as competently as men do, no doubt with subtle differences because men and women are not identical, and, at the level of generalisation, are likely to prefer different styles of leadership and teaching. But they are superb leaders and teachers. At the time of writing this chapter, Hillary Clinton had just launched her campaign to become the President of the United States. If she succeeds, as she probably will, she will be one of the most powerful people on the planet, joining the ranks of other impressive female leaders, including Angela Merkel, who has been the Chancellor of Germany since 2005, and who years before that was a research scientist with a doctorate in physical chemistry.

In our own Australian setting, we have recently been graced by the extraordinary talents of our first female Prime Minister, Julia Gillard, who more than capably fought her way to the top of a male-dominated profession.[4] One of my most highly regarded politicians is Tanya Plibersek, currently deputy Federal Opposition leader, a person of sharp intellect and extraordinary skills as a debater and public speaker. But if Tanya was an Anglican, and wanted to progress through the ranks of the Sydney Anglican Church, she wouldn't be allowed to progress beyond being a deacon, and wouldn't be allowed to preach to mixed-gender congregations in most of Sydney's Anglican churches. For almost all non-church-going Australians, this situation appears ludicrous. For many church-going Australians, it also appears ludicrous. For those who don't think it is ludicrous, it ought to at least provide some cause for a re-think.

Women clearly are more than able to lead and preach, in some ways more able and more suitable than men, as the following tongue-in-cheek piece suggests:

10 reasons why men shouldn't be ordained

1. A man's place is in the army.
2. The pastoral duties of men who have children might distract them from the responsibility of being a parent.

---

4   Julia has not been alone in breaking through the political glass ceiling. With the exception of South Australia, every state of Australia has had a female Premier, in order of time, Carmen Lawrence, Joan Kirner, Anna Bligh, Kristina Keneally, Lara Giddings and Annastacia Palaszczuk.

3. The physique of men indicates they are more suited to such tasks as chopping down trees and wrestling mountain lions. It would be 'unnatural' for them to do ministerial tasks.

4. Man was created before woman, obviously as a prototype. Thus, they represent an experiment, rather than the crowning achievement of creation.

5. Men are too emotional to be priests or pastors. Their conduct at football and basketball games demonstrates this.

6. Some men are handsome, and this will distract female worshippers.

7. Pastors need to nurture their congregations. But this is not a traditional male role. Throughout history, women have been recognized as not only more skilled than men at nurturing, but also more fervently attracted to it. This makes them the obvious choice for ordination.

8. Men are prone to violence. No really masculine man wants to settle disputes except by fighting about them. Thus they would be poor role models as well as dangerously unstable in positions of leadership.

9. The New Testament tells us that Jesus was betrayed by a man. His lack of faith and ensuing punishment remind us of the subordinated position that all men should take.

10. Men can still be involved in church activities, even without being ordained. They can sweep sidewalks, repair the church roof, and perhaps even lead the song service on Father's Day. By confining themselves to such traditional male roles, they can still be vitally important in the life of the church.[5]

The tenth good reason why men should not be ordained is particularly telling. No matter how nicely things are dressed up by those opposing women's ordination, such efforts are still likely to sound patronizing. This too is likely to create cognitive dissonance for those still thinking they just can't get past 1 Timothy 2, and what they have been taught it says and implies.

---

5   This list was compiled by the late Dr David M. Scholer, a former New Testament professor at Fuller Theological Seminary.

I was chatting by e-mail to a friend, a fellow clergyman, who admitted to me, 'I have no idea why God would restrict the clearly very capable ministries of women.' He could not supply a credible (to himself) reason for any gender-based restrictions of role or ministry. His sole reason for following the party line was that this is how he believes the New Testament 'determines it.' And a big part of the reason for that, possibly for him, but certainly for many, is teaching from elsewhere in the New Testament on the 'headship' of men. In the letter to the Ephesians, husbands are described as the 'head' of their wives, with wives instructed to submit to their husbands:

> Submit to one another out of reverence for Christ. Wives, submit yourselves to your husbands as you do to the Lord. For the husband is the head of the wife as Christ is the head of the church, his body, of which he is the Saviour. Now, as the church submits to Christ, so also wives should submit to their husbands in everything. Husbands, love your wives, just as Christ loved the church and gave himself up for her to make her holy, cleansing her by the washing of water though the word, to present her to himself as a radiant church, without stain or wrinkle or any other blemish, but holy and blameless. In the same way, husbands ought to love their wives as their own bodies. He who loves his wife loves himself. After all, no one ever hated their own body, but they feed and care for their body, just as Christ does the church – for we are members of his body. 'For this reason a man will leave his father and mother and be united to his wife, and the two will become one flesh.' This is a profound mystery – but I am talking about Christ and the church. However, each one of you must love his wife as he loves himself, and the wife must respect her husband.[6]

Without going into too much detail, the argument is often mounted that what should happen in marriage, as mandated in passages such as this, provides the model and ultimate rationale for what happens in church. Just as husbands are to be the heads of their homes, with headship interpreted in authoritarian terms,[7] so they should also exercise headship in church, which can usefully be described as a family, the church family. The argument makes good sense, but it is not without problems and cognitive dissonance producing implications.

---

6   Ephesians 5:21-33 NIV.

7   There is on-going and vigorous debate about whether headship implies authority, with other meanings of the word, including 'source,' also suggested as making good sense of the New Testament's headship passages.

A first big problem with the appeal to male headship is that it isn't certain, and it might not even be likely, that the author of Ephesians, whether St Paul or someone else, was mandating patriarchy for all time. He may simply have been assuming patriarchy as the ubiquitous social custom it was, and regulating it according to Christian or gospel principles. That is how one of evangelicalism's finest New Testament scholars, Ben Witherington III, has extensively argued. He acknowledges that the language of headship is used in various of the New Testament's household codes, such as in Ephesians 5, but he argues that the intention of these instructions was (1) to place more and more strictures on the head of the household to limit his power and the way he relates to his wife, children and slaves, and (2) to make the head of the household aware that women, children and slaves are, in fact, persons created in God's image, not chattel or property. Summing up, he suggests, 'Paul is working to place the leaven of the Gospel into pre-existing relationships and change them.'[8]

The second big problem is that when patriarchy is regulated according to gospel principles, when husbands love their wives as Christ loved the church, and when wives willingly submit to their husbands, patriarchy has a habit of withering away and dying.[9] Patriarchy gives power to husbands, but when that power is exercised in the very best interests of their wives, issues of power and authority evaporate. In the contemporary world, where power is no longer typically invested in husbands, marriages very often become egalitarian, in practice, if not in theory. I remember listening to an interview with Archbishop Glenn Davies, just after he had been elected Anglican archbishop of Sydney, and the interviewers appeared quizzical about the widely held view amongst Sydney Anglicans that women are expected to submit to their husbands. Archbishop Davies responded by noting that in all of the many years of his marriage to Dianne Davies, he had not even once felt the need to pull rank and tell her what to do. That, at least, is my memory of his words. Not once did he use his God-given

---

8   Ben Witherington, *Patheos* blog, 2 June 2015: http://wp.production.patheos.com/blogs/bibleandculture/files/2015/03/bwiii2.jpg

9   It ought to be noted that Ephesians 5:21 mandates mutual submission, in which case husbands are to submit to their wives, in some sense and to some degree, as well, just as wives are, without doubt, expected to love their husbands. Understood in these terms, this passage represents a clever subversion of patriarchy, especially when considering that the humble, self-giving love of Christ is presented as the model for husbands (and wives).

authority in the context of their obviously very egalitarian marriage. A good thing I thought, but I was left wondering what submission means in practical terms; and what, if anything, is left of patriarchy, which the archbishop clearly felt he needed to up-hold for Biblical reasons.

Just maybe, as suggested above, patriarchy is not mandated in the Bible. Just maybe, the gospel has blown it out of the water, and, if so, a major reason for preventing women from being ordained priest, bishop and Archbishop is similarly blown out of the water. If what happens in the home is our guide to what happens in church, then women ought to be given exactly the same opportunities as men within the life of Christian congregations. Patriarchy has long since passed its use-by-date, and the Christian gospel has significantly contributed to this.

But, of course, there are some who are still emotionally and theologically wedded to patriarchy, who won't give it away without a fight. Among those are some who are aware that for patriarchy to continue it must have at least some practical implications. There is no point in asserting patriarchy if one lives like an egalitarian, as I think most Christians now do. Preventing women from teaching or leading men in church is one big step in the direction of giving the concept practical bite. But in the home, which is believed to be the conceptual heartland of the concept, it is somewhat harder, although not too hard for those who are diligent in finding practical ways to express their commitment to patriarchy.

I once had a chat with someone who had done just that. In his marriage, he makes all the decisions, except in those cases where he delegates authority to his wife. But, he assured me, he is the ultimate authority for every decision. And the weight of that authority lay heavily upon him. He feared he might act unwisely or wouldn't be the diligent and loving head of his wife and family as the Scriptures expect him to be.

The point is that patriarchy can work, and has done throughout human history and across most human cultures. It is also likely to be softened and made to work better if gospel principles of love and respect are followed. It is not the worst of human institutions. However, as a generalisation, patriarchal marriages are more likely to be abusive than are egalitarian marriages. Those who argue for the retention of patriarchy often argue that patriarchy is a God-given institution for our good. Therefore, if we retain patriarchy and regulate it by gospel principles, we will have the best possible outcome for our marriages, families and society.

The sobering fact is that this is simply not the case, creating yet another instance of cognitive dissonance for those with ears to hear. Dr Alan Craddock, retired senior lecturer in psychology from Sydney University, who taught pastoral psychology at Moore Theological College for many years, has drawn my attention to a number of studies[10] which have consistently suggested that egalitarian relationships have higher levels of couple satisfaction and lower rates of conflict and violence. If those research findings are accurate, then, once again, we are given reason to jettison patriarchy. As noted above, either the custom is meaningless, because of being so heavily and happily regulated by gospel imperatives, or, if we make it meaningful by giving unequal power and authority to males, this will increase the likelihood of abuse, abuse which has always accompanied patriarchy throughout its long history.

On the fraught issue of homosexuality

There was a time in my experience, and in the experience of most Christians, when there was no cognitive dissonance whatsoever on the now vexed issue of homosexuality. I believed, along with almost everyone else, that there was nothing to be uncertain about. There was no conceivable reason for the bells of cognitive dissonance to start ringing. The Bible's teaching on

---

10   Antill, J., Cotton, S. and Tindale, S. (1983), 'Egalitarian or Traditional: Correlates of the perception of an ideal marriage', *Australian Journal of Psychology*, 35, 245-257; Bowen, G.L. (1989), 'Marital sex role incongruence and marital adjustment', *Journal of Family Issues*, 10, 409-415; Bowen, G.L. and Orthner, D.K. (1983), 'Sex role congruency and marital quality', *Journal of Marriage and the Family*, 45, 223-230; Brown, N. (2002), 'Happy marriages. 20 Years of Research at Pennsylvania State University', 23 (1): Online at www.rps.psu.edu/0201/ happy.html; Coleman, D. H. and Straus, M. A. (1988), 'Marital power, conflict, and violence in a nationally representative sample of American couples', *Violence and Victims*, 1, 141–157; Craddock, A.E. (1980), 'The effect of incongruent marital role expectations upon couples' degree of role consensus in the first year of marriage', *Australian Journal of Psychology*, 32,117-125; Craddock, A.E. (1983), 'Correlations between marital role expectations and relationship satisfaction among engaged couples', *Australian Journal of Sex, Marriage and Family*, 4, 33-46; Craddock, A. E. (1998), 'Attitudinal and structural differences between satisfied and dissatisfied married and cohabiting couples', Australian Journal of Psychology, 50, 83-88; Li, J. T. and Caldwell, R. A. (1987), 'Magnitude and directional effects of marital sex role incongruence on marital adjustment', *Journal of Family Issues*, 8, 97-110; Olson, D. H. and Olson, A. (2000), *Empowering Couples: Building On Your Strengths*, Minneapolis: Life Innovations.

this topic was clear, plain and consistent, and people were being perverse to suggest otherwise. Leviticus 18:22 is surely as clear as clear can be:

> You shall not lie with a male as with a woman; it is an abomination. NRSV

And if that doesn't seem clear enough, then read on until you get to Leviticus 20:13:

> If a man lies with a male as with a woman, both of them have committed an abomination; they shall be put to death; their blood is upon them. NRSV

In case we hadn't quite realised the seriousness of this prohibition, Leviticus 20 treats male to male intercourse as a capital offence. Both verses describe this activity as 'an abomination,' which is a strong word of disapproval, the root meaning of which is 'to abhor' or 'detest.' This is detestable behaviour in God's sight according to the author or authors of Leviticus. It is hard to imagine anything more straightforward than these verses. Moreover, so clear-cut are they that subsequent Biblical authors appear to assume their on-going purchase for Jewish and then Christian behaviour. Men should not have sex with men. Almost certainly, these two verses lay influentially in the background to St Paul's negative evaluation of same-sex sexual activity in Romans 1.

St Paul argues, from verse 18, that human beings, although they have always known God, have tended to suppress that knowledge, resulting in the widespread idolatry of Gentile nations, which, in turn, has been the fertile breeding ground for all kinds of immoral behaviour, including sex between men. Once again, it is hard to get around the import of St Paul's negative evaluation of this sort of sex, which he appears to consider as evidence of the judgement of God; of God giving people over to the sorry consequences of their idolatrous choices:

> Therefore God gave them up in the lusts of their hearts to impurity, to the degrading of their bodies among themselves, because they exchanged the truth of God for a lie and worshipped and served the creature rather than the Creator, who is blessed forever! Amen. For this reason God gave them up to degrading passions. Their women exchanged natural intercourse for unnatural, and in the same way also the men, giving up natural intercourse with women, were consumed with passion for one another. Men committed shameless acts with men and received in their own persons the due penalty for their error. Romans 1:24-27 NRSV

Where, one might ask, is there room for cognitive dissonance? St Paul's meaning is clear enough. Any scope for being inquisitive on this matter is surely ruled out by the fact that theologians and exegetes, Jewish and Christian, have been in almost universal agreement throughout all of their combined histories: sex between people of the same gender, and certainly between men, is wrong and is abhorrent to God. It seems simple. It appears to be straightforward. A Christian theologian and former colleague of mine summed up the situation in these terms, 'God's wrath is being revealed from heaven ... because of homosexuality.' That, he believes, is the clear and unambiguous message of Romans 1. Where is there room for being inquisitive?

Surprisingly, there is room, in fact, lots of it and increasingly so. What might at first sight appear straightforward is anything but, once you begin to dig a little deeper. Looking more closely at what St Paul wrote in Romans 1, he is describing a process, a very particular process with its own internal dynamics. At the outset of this process is the knowledge of God which St Paul believed was accessible to every human being (1:19-20). Paul appears to have had in mind some, perhaps intuitive knowledge of God, which is then suppressed and distorted. Human beings, although they know God, create idols which they worship instead of God. This perverse choice then results in a corruption in their thinking, which becomes foolish and darkened (1:21-22). God then ratifies their distorted and distorting choices by giving them over to foolish and perverse lifestyles, which they themselves have chosen. Included among these perverse life choices is the choice to 'exchange' natural for unnatural sexual relationships,[11] which St Paul sees is a direct consequence of their decision to 'exchange' the true knowledge of God for a lie.

What is being described is a process; a process of progressive degeneration resulting from the evil and wilful choices of human beings. St Paul's analysis makes good sense, and we can certainly find examples of what he describes throughout human history and into the present. However, his description appears to have almost nothing to do with homosexuality as understood

---

11   Sarah Harris and Michael Bird suggest that for St Paul, the 'quintessential example of "dishonourable passions" is women and men doing what is sexually unnatural with each other and committing shameful sexual acts', 'Paul's Jewish view of sexuality in Romans 1:26-27', in Michael Bird and Gordon Preece (eds), Sexegesis: An Evangelical Response to Five Uneasy Pieces, Sydney: Anglican Youth Works, 2012, 89.

and experienced in contemporary culture, and certainly within the cultures of Christian congregations. St Paul appears to be talking about something other than what we understand to be the case about homosexuality.

The best way to illustrate this is by referring again to the experience of Matthew, whose story is briefly told in chapters five and six; and whose parents' account of his story is told in the Introduction. Matthew grew up in a loving and nurturing Christian home. He believed in the Christian God from infancy. He didn't choose to be gay. His discovery that he was gay was entirely unwelcome; so unwelcome that he prayed for years that God would change him, that God would heal him of this affliction which so disturbed him that he self-harmed and was often suicidal. Rather than choosing to walk away from God, Matthew threw himself into Christian ministry. I had the privilege of reading Matthew's diary, which he kept through those years. It is filled with references to his love for God and Christ; filled with the painful struggles of one who desperately wanted to keep on loving and serving God. Eventually, he came to embrace his gayness and to distance himself from a Christianity which considered him and/or his behaviour as sinful and perverse.

St Paul's words appear to be irrelevant to Matthew's experience, and to the experiences of scores of devout homosexual Christians like him. So irrelevant do they appear that some have argued that Romans 1 does not address the issue of homosexuality, at least not directly. To further explore this cognitive-dissonance-producing possibility, it might be helpful to probe St Paul's words a little further. There are some beliefs and assumptions he appears to hold which may help to explain why his words appear to so miss the mark for homosexual Christians.

A first likely assumption is that all human beings are heterosexual. They have been created by God as either male or female. St Paul didn't have the benefit of the distinctions we now make between heterosexual and homosexual,[12] and so to even talk in these terms is anachronistic. However, there is every good reason to think that St Paul would have accepted the simple duality, male and female, with nothing in-between or other.

---

12   It was a Hungarian writer and journalist, Karl Maria Kertbeny (1824-1882), who, in 1869, coined the term 'homosexual' in his campaign against the German sodomy laws. The term 'homosexuality' was coined in the late 19th century by a German psychologist, Karoly Maria Benkert.

A second assumption, which St Paul makes explicit, is that sex between men is unnatural. It goes against nature in some sense. Paul describes such activity as *para physin* or 'contrary to nature.' He does not say what he means by this, however, and this has invited all sorts of speculation about his meaning. Robert Gagnon suggests he had in mind the 'unnatural' use of the sex organs.[13] James V. Brownson argues at length that this is unlikely to have been St Paul's understanding.[14] The use of the phrase *para physin* elsewhere in his writings suggests another possibility. In 1 Corinthians 11:7, St Paul asks, 'does not nature itself teach you that if a man has long hair it is a disgrace to him?' Some notion of propriety or rightness appears to lie behind St Paul's use of nature here. This isn't what men do, in other words. St Paul had any number of contemporary allies in describing same-sex sexual relationships as unnatural. Plato, for example, agreed that such sexual activity is 'contrary to nature.'[15] Pseudo-Lucian referred to 'a sacred law of necessity that each should retain its own nature ... that neither should the female grow unnaturally masculine nor the male be unbecomingly soft.'[16] Pseudo-Phocylides, roughly contemporary with St Paul, enjoined, 'Do not transgress with unlawful sex the limits set by nature. For even animals are not pleased by intercourse of male with male. And let women not imitate the sexual role of men.'[17]

A third likely assumption is that because same-gender sex is unnatural, it is also immoral and perverse. Various scholars have pointed out that Romans 1 reflects, sometimes word for word, the writings of contemporary Stoic philosophers, including Seneca, who believed that an understanding of nature was the key to ethics; and that if something was contrary to nature it was wrong.[18] St Paul appears to have concurred. It is likely he also had

---

13   Robert Gagnon, *The Bible and Homosexual Practice: Texts and Hermeneutics,* Nashville: Abingdon, 2001, 254.

14   *Bible, Gender, Sexuality,* 232-244.

15   Plato, *Laws* 1.2 (636 BC) cited in Bird and Harris, *Paul's Jewish View of Sexuality in Romans 1: 26-27,* 91.

16   Ps.-Lucian, *Erotes* 19, quoted in *Paul's Jewish view of sexuality in Romans 1:26-27,* 92.

17   Ps.-Phocylides, Sentences, 190-93, quoted in *Paul's Jewish view of sexuality in Romans 1:26-27,* 92.

18   Note, however, that what was depicted as wrong (or contrary to nature) was passionate and uncontrolled sex (reflected in Paul's description), with sexual behaviour needing to be cool-headed and rational.

in mind his own Hebrew Scriptures with its descriptions of God creating creatures into various kinds, with clearly defined characteristics. Every kind, including humankind, was created to behave in certain well-defined ways, appropriate to their kind. For human beings to choose to act in ways that violated their created natures was perverse and immoral; immoral because perverse, but also immoral because choosing to engage in such behaviour represented an act of deliberate rebellion against God the Creator.

These three likely assumptions: one, that all people are heterosexual; two, that homosexual behaviour is unnatural; and three, that such behaviour is immoral, appear to make good sense of what St Paul writes in Romans 1, so much sense, in fact, that most Christians down through the years have embraced all three of these assumptions.

The problem is that none of these three assumptions is generally accepted today, certainly in secular Australia. Even amongst Christians they have begun to be questioned. Something akin to what has happened with the story of Noah is now occurring. The story of Noah once made perfectly good sense as a straightforward description of what took place in the not-too-distant past. It was a credible story given ancient and pre-modern cosmological assumptions, as was the story of Adam and Eve. However, once those ancient and pre-modern assumptions are shed, as they now have been by most people, those stories are no longer quite so credible as descriptions of actual events. Much the same is now happening with the issue of homosexuality.

People still do try, valiantly and understandably, to harmonize Paul's words with emerging understandings of homosexuality, although not with any great success. Our assumptions about why people would even want to have sex with people of their own gender are changing, informed by emerging scientific understandings. Discoveries in the areas of biology and genetics have precipitated a significant re-think on this issue, as have the brave testimonies of increasing numbers of LGBTI people.

Information emerging from contemporary research is new. None of the biblical writers would have been aware of this information, certainly not in these terms. Robert A. J. Gagnon, of Pittsburgh Theological Seminary, marshals evidence to show that people in the ancient world were aware of entrenched homoerotic tendencies known to be resistant to change,[19] which, perhaps uncomfortably for the conservative Gagnon, is evidence for the existence and persistence of entrenched homosexual preferences throughout history. However, what is new is our growing understanding of the genetic and biological origins of these homosexual tendencies. The ancients lacked the conceptual wherewithal to differentiate, as we now can, between a homosexual and a heterosexual. As Richard B. Hays has pointed out: 'The idea that some individuals have an inherent disposition towards same-sex erotic attraction and are therefore constitutionally "gay" is a modern idea of which there is no trace either in the NT or in any other Jewish or Christian writings in the ancient world.'[20] This understandable lack means that there is conceptual room to move in plotting new ways forward and in understanding the Biblical prohibition against same-gender sex.

In light of this new information, it might be helpful to look more closely at each of the three assumptions which are likely to have informed St Paul's words in Romans 1. As for the first likely assumption, that God created human beings to be heterosexual males or females, this doesn't appear to be the case, or to put it differently, the reality is more complex.

One useful way to highlight this complexity is to utilise and then clarify two complementary words, sex and gender. These words are sometimes used interchangeably. However, it is helpful to differentiate them. Sex is biological, and includes physical attributes such as sex chromosomes, sex hormones, internal reproductive structures, and external genitalia. We can usually determine the sex of our children at birth by simply glancing in the right direction. Gender is the more complex interrelationship between these physical traits and one's internal sense of self of being male or female, or both or neither, as well as how one presents and behaves in the light of that perception. In the case of someone who is transgender, their gender expression and identity does not match their assigned sex.

---

19   R. A. J. Gagnon, 'The Faulty Orientation Argument of Anglican Archbishop Harper of Ireland' in *Fulcrum: Renewing the Evangelical Centre*, at http://www.fulcrum-anglican.org. uk/page.cfm?ID=325, see also R.A.J. Gagnon, 'Does the Bible Regard Same-Sex Intercourse as Intrinsically Sinful' in R.E. Saltzman (ed), *Christian Sexuality: Normative and Pastoral Principles*, 2003, 106-55.

20   Richard B. Hays, 'Relations Natural and Unnatural: A Response to John Boswell's Exegesis of Romans 1', *Journal of Religious Ethics* 14/1 (1986), 200.

Complications also exist at the level of sex. Our sex is normally determined by the twenty-third of our twenty-three pairs of chromosomes, with a male designated as XY in genetics, and the female as XX. However, in one out of 1,666 instances, a number of possible variations occur, such as XXY, XO (the O denotes that neither an X nor a Y is present), XXX, XXYY, and XXXY. The twenty-third chromosome, in these instances, is not male or female, but a third sex, intersex. Thus, to use Genesis-type language, God created male, female and intersex.[21]

When people are born who grow up to be lesbian or gay, their sex is as easy to determine as anyone else's. However, in a largely heterosexual world, their gender eventually and inevitably comes under question because their sense of who they are sexually is informed by some uncommon internal realities. These unusual internal realities are now captured by the terms homosexual and homosexuality. A quick scan of on-line dictionaries came up with the following definitions of homosexuality:

> Sexual attraction to or sexual relations with members of the same sex.[22]

> Sexual orientation to or sexual activity with persons of the same sex.[23]

Wikipedia elaborates in these terms:

> Romantic or sexual attraction or behaviour between members of the same sex or gender. As an orientation, homosexuality refers to an enduring pattern of, or disposition to, experience sexual, affectionate, or romantic attractions primarily or exclusively to people of the same sex; it also refers to an individual's sense of personal and social identity based on those attractions, behaviors expressing them, and membership in a community of others who share them.

The word 'orientation' is critical here. Homosexual individuals are oriented or attracted to people of their own sex. Nigel Chapman describes this

---

21   The word intersex is used to refer to variations in sex characteristics involving chromosomes, gonads or genitals that do not allow a person to be distinctly identified as male or female. See further, Kathy Baldock, *Walking the Bridgeless Canyon: Repairing the breach between the Church and the LGBT Community*, Reno, NY: Canyonwalker Press, 2014, 190-191.

22   *Collins English Dictionary – Complete and Unabridged*, HarperCollins, 1991, 1994, 1998, 2000, 2003.

23   *The American Heritage Dictionary of the English Language*, Houghton Mifflin, 2000, 2009.

orientation as 'permanent, involuntary and exclusive.' This is what it is to be homosexual,[24] and somewhere between 1% and 5% of the Australian population fall into this category,[25] matching figures elsewhere in the world.

Homosexuality is just one of many examples of gender diversity reflected in an expansion of labels which themselves are only generalisations to make conceptual sense of a reality which is even more complex, with every individual likely to be at least slightly different from every other individual. People can now identify as lesbian, gay, bisexual, or transgender, conveniently short-handed to LGBT, with the letters IQ sometimes added for intersex and queer, so LGBTIQ. Such is the diversity of gender and sexuality in human populations that the concept of a gender spectrum has been suggested in order to represent this complexity. This spectrum seeks to take account of variations in anatomy, biology, gender expression and gender identity.

The point is that not everyone is heterosexual. Not everyone can neatly or conveniently be categorised by the simply binary concept of male or female. The reality is otherwise.

The second of St Paul's likely, in fact certain, assumptions was that same-gender sex is, in some sense, unnatural. This also is an assumption we are likely to question. As mentioned above, it is not absolutely certain what St Paul meant by 'nature' or 'natural,' but if he meant something along the lines of what people generally think is acceptable, as he appears to have meant in talking about the unnaturalness of men having long hair, then what people generally think has changed, quite radically and quickly. Many, in fact most, people in Australia think that sexual relations between men who are gay are acceptable, in fact, exactly what one would expect.

---

24 David Myers, an evangelical Christian who teaches at Hope College in Michigan, helpfully compares sexual orientation to handedness. 'Most people are one way, some the other. A very few are ambidextrous. Regardless, the way one is endures,' *Psychology*, 10th edition, New York: Worth Publishers, 2013, 428.

25 Gordon Preece in his introduction to *Sexegesis* (p. 11) draws on J. Harvey's 2003 study *Sex in Australia*, in suggesting that 97.4% of Australian men are heterosexual, 97.7% of women are heterosexual, 1.6% of men are exclusively gay and 0.9% of women are exclusively lesbian, the balance being largely bisexual. Higher figures in the range of 3-5% are widely used in other literature.

If St Paul was thinking more in terms of what human beings created by God were meant to do to express their created natures, this only makes sense if one also assumes, as St Paul probably did, that human beings are created heterosexual, and, in that case, the only natural thing to do is to have sex with someone of the opposite sex. But if St Paul was wrong on assumption one, assumption two begins to look shaky.

The concept of what is natural is likely to have been different for St Paul than it is for us, but I would suggest that they are not altogether different. We are blessed with a growing understanding of how nature works. The human genome project is now cooperating with other scientific disciplines to give us new ways of understanding human nature and its biological origins. We now know that many other animal species have sub-sections of their populations that are same-sex attracted. We are not alone as a species in this. From a contemporary perspective, homosexuality is entirely natural.[26]

St Paul's third likely assumption, that because same-gender sex is unnatural, it is also immoral and perverse is also one that we are now likely to question. The nexus between what is unnatural and what is immoral is a complicated and important one. It is fraught with all sorts of pitfalls. For example, a paedophile might argue that what he wants to do is 'natural' to him; it is how he is hardwired. It is his 'orientation.' It is natural and therefore not immoral for him. The kleptomaniac or arsonist or masochist or sadist might argue likewise, which is a problem for all those who argue from nature to morality. Those who argue that way need, ultimately, to rely on a larger picture not only of what is natural, but of what is good for humankind. Integral to that process is the development of an anthropology, both a real and an idealised view of humankind. This is how human beings can be, and ideally should be. The Bible provides significant guidance in this, certainly for Christians. Human beings are depicted as responsible for their actions. They are honoured by their high place in the purposes of God. They are described as being created in the image and likeness of God with responsibility to care for the earth and for each other, to the glory of

---

26   As is now widely accepted, certainly within the medical and psychological fraternity. In the past 25 years, the American Psychological Association, the American Psychiatric Association, and the American Medical Association have changed their definition of homosexuality to that of a 'normal variant' (like being left-handed) rather than as a disease.

God. This noble and ennobling description of humankind can guide our thinking and actions, as it did St Paul's.[27]

Consequently, just because something feels right, or we find ourselves inclined towards it, is neither a necessary nor a sufficient reason to do it. A decision as to what is right or wrong needs to be made in the light of one's metaphysic, which includes one's beliefs about God and humankind. It can also be made by observing human conduct over time. Some things that humans do will damage them. Trying to fly when you can't will harm you. Not sleeping for extended periods of time will harm you. Being always angry and revengeful will harm you, and, in all likelihood, others. Having sex with children will harm them and you, as will stealing or cruelty. We can go some distance towards working out what is good for human beings by observing over time the consequences of their actions, both individually and as a society.

And in this process, we will encounter things which we will describe as perverse, actions which so run up against our vision of what is pure, good and right that we will describe it as perverse. If it is the case that all human beings are heterosexual, and that the only healthy way of living is as a man or as a woman, then having sex with someone of your own gender can sensibly be described as perverse. But as we have seen, things are not that simple. Nature itself is more complicated, and therefore decisions about what is moral or immoral, perverse or pure, are also likely to be more complicated. We will need to do some serious rethinking here.

Rethinking on this issue will be scary for some. Some people have made up their minds already. They have established their careers and reputations by resisting any revisions to traditional understandings. So it won't be easy, and it almost certainly will be risky, but it might also be honest. Cognitive dissonance is happening on this issue. It is not just in the papers, or on radio and television, or on-line. It is happening as our children, neighbours and work-mates challenge us to think again. It is happening in the wake of decisions by governments around the world to legislate in favour of same-sex marriage.

---

27   Brownson helpfully notes that St Paul's discussion of what is 'natural' would not have been limited to individual tendencies or desires, but included awareness of larger social and cosmic dimensions, as was the case with Stoic philosophers with whom he was finding common ground in Romans 1. See further, *Bible, Gender, Sexuality*, 228-237.

Same-sex marriage

While writing this book, the US Supreme Court ruled, on June 26, 2015, that the right to same-sex marriage was derivable from the equal protection provisions of the US Constitution, putting an end to efforts by a minority of US States to prevent same-sex marriages happening within their borders. The US has followed Ireland and a growing number of mostly Western nations in legislating in favour of same-sex marriage. There is every chance that by the time this book is published, or shortly thereafter, same-sex marriage will be legal throughout Australia as well.

The pressure of these changes and prospective changes has, in itself, precipitated a re-think by some, as has the fact that increasing numbers of Christians are expressing support for same-sex marriage. Theologians of all stripes, including generally conservative Roman Catholic theologians, are re-envisaging homosexuality and its implications.[28] A cacophony of conversations, most of them heated, but some of them productive, are occurring inside and outside of Christian communities. Although it is true that the sheer pace of change has tended to polarise people into warring camps - conservatives versus progressives - it is also true that people are genuinely wanting to know; wanting to do what is right; wanting to hear both sides of the question.

When people do listen, I find that something very interesting and significant happens. One of the things you may have noticed is that Christians are less and less likely to publically chastise gay people for their 'sin,' or to refer to homosexual intercourse as an 'abomination,' or as abhorrent, or as deserving of death or hellfire. Part of the reason, no doubt, for this increasing silence (or silencing) of Christians is fear, fear of being ridiculed, fear of being called a fundamentalist or a bigot or a homophobe or worse. But another big part of the reason is that we have begun to get to know our LGBTI neighbours and work-mates; have begun to see how much they love and care for each other, how normal they are, but also how special,

---

28   Almost daily there are reports of this or that Roman Catholic Bishop or theologian opening doors, sometimes only by a crack, sometimes more widely, to new discussions around how the Roman Catholic Church needs to rethink the gender issue, along with all the theological and pastoral issues involved. A special Synod on the family, convened by Pope Francis in October 2015, was notable for sometimes passionately expressed differences of opinion on marriage, divorce and gender, with a significant minority of participants willing to countenance reform and rethinking on these issues.

with talents and sensitivities seemingly all part of the wonderful package that is them. They are not defective; they didn't choose the way they are; their homosexuality didn't come about because of their rejection of God, or because they had embraced idolatry, or because they have let their illicit passions get out of control. It is just the way they are, and our society, and Christians also, increasingly acknowledge and celebrate this specialness.[29]

But what this has done is to create a problem for Bible-believing Christians. How can they explain, even to themselves, their discomfort with gay sex and opposition to same-sex marriage? I once visited a book-reading group that had just finished reading *A Restless Faith*. At one point in our discussion, we discussed same-sex marriage. One of the participants, who wasn't in favour of same-sex marriage, commented that when discussing this issue with his children, who simply couldn't see anything wrong with same-sex marriage, he was struck by how unconvincing his own arguments were, not just to his children, but to himself. *He* didn't find them compelling.

That is telling. There are, as far as I have observed, four main arguments used by Christian opponents of same-sex marriage. They are: (1) it will harm participating individuals; (2) it will harm society; (3) it will be a slippery-slide to other evils; and (4) it violates Bible-based and long-held definitions of marriage.

Each of the arguments is ultimately grounded in the conviction that the Bible prohibits sex between people of the same gender, and so, naturally, same-sex marriage is wrong. Marriage essentially involves having sex. And because Christians are now more inclined not to see same-sex orientation as sinful, the focus has shifted to the sex act itself, which, in any case, is what the Bible explicitly prohibits – men having sex with men. Christians therefore look for reasons why the Bible prohibits sex between men. Some have suggested health reasons, though there is emerging evidence that the health of gay people improves when they can marry.[30] Some argue that the

---

29   As a result of processes such as these, Australian Christians are increasingly changing their minds about homosexuality and same-sex marriage. A Galaxy poll (2009-2012) found that 53% of Australian Christians were in favour of same-sex marriage. A 2014 Crosby Textor poll found that support had increased to just under 60%; with Anglicans and Uniting Church adherents at 57% and Roman Catholics at 67%.

30   'Sex practices National Survey of Sexual Health and Behaviour,' Indiana University, 2010, http://www.nationalsexstudy.indiana.edu/graph.html.

relevant body parts do not fit together naturally or healthily when men have sex with each other, though this argument fails to rule out lesbianism.[31] What it would also rule out, perhaps uncomfortably, is oral sex, enjoyed by many people, including Christians, as it would anal sex enjoyed by many heterosexual couples. Evidently, one quarter of all heterosexual women under the age of forty (in the US at least) participate in anal sex. Not all gay couples engage in anal sex. It is not a requirement for same-sex intimacy or marriage. However, a reason it is engaged in by people of varying sexualities is that it brings pleasure including orgasm.[32]

There are a host of arguments being advanced about the social harm likely to eventuate if same-sex marriage becomes common practice. They have varying degrees of strength, though too many of them are alarmist and involve scare-mongering, especially given that same-sex unions have been around for a long time. Same-sex marriage itself has been institutionalized and become commonplace in countries such as my birthplace of Canada,[33] without obvious social damage, in fact, the opposite.[34] Some of the arguments currently being proposed are fear-driven obfuscations, including arguments to the effect that religious freedoms will be lost, or that polygamy or bestiality will be next on the agenda of God-and-Christian-

---

31   For a thorough and fascinating discussion of this and other arguments, see R. D. Weekly, *Homosexianity: Letting Truth Win The Devastating War Between Scripture, Faith & Sexual Orientation,* Createspace, 2009.

32   As pointed out by Kathy Baldock, '[all] men, gay or straight, have a prostate, a walnut-sized gland located between the bladder and the penis and just in front of the rectum, an area of the body with an abundance of nerve endings. Stimulation of the prostate gland with a finger or the penis inserted into the rectum via the anus can be highly pleasurable and can lead to orgasm. It can be a safe practice between partners in loving sexual exchanges, caring for each other by using lubricants and condoms,' *Walking the Bridgeless Canyon,* 216, 217.

33   Since 2001, when The Netherlands legalised same-sex marriage, twenty countries have followed suit, in the following order: Caribbean Netherlands, Belgium, Spain, Canada, South Africa, Norway, Sweden, Portugal, Iceland, Argentina, Denmark, Uruguay, New Zealand, France, England, Wales, Luxembourg, Scotland, Finland, Ireland and the United States.

34   A 2009 study, for example, which considered the social impact of same-sex marriage in two locations where it has been legal for over a decade, the Netherlands and Massachusetts, detailed a range of positive benefits, including enhanced feelings of security, safety and acceptance for involved couples and children. M. V. Badgett, N. Goldberg and C. Ramos, *What happens When Gay People Get Married: What Happens When Societies Legalise Same-Sex Marriage,* New York: New York University Press, 2009.

hating activists. For example, James Dobson, high profile advocate for the family in the US, reportedly asked in a radio interview in 2013, 'How about group marriage? Or marriage between daddies and little girls? Or a marriage between a man and his donkey? Anything allegedly linked to civil rights will be doable, and the legal underpinnings of marriage will be destroyed.' Slippery slope arguments, like this one, bring no credit to those who urge them. Any and every social change must be carefully considered as to its impacts and likely contribution to the common good.

The now most common argument mounted against same-sex marriage is the definition argument. In short, for same-sex marriage to go ahead, marriage itself will need to be re-defined, which of course is true. A redefinition process has already begun in those countries which have accepted same-sex marriage. Many Christians are disturbed by this. On the very same day that the US Supreme Court brought down its ruling in favour of same-sex marriage, a coalition of evangelical leaders, including D. A. Carson, David Platt, J. P. Moreland, J. I. Packer, Kevin De Young, Mark Dever, R. Albert Mohler, Randy Alcorn and Ron Sider published a declaration entitled, *Here We Stand: An Evangelical Declaration on Marriage*. Central to this document was protest over the redefinition of marriage, which the signatories believed had been defined once and for all in the Bible. As they put it:

> The Bible clearly teaches the enduring truth that marriage consists of one man and one woman. From Genesis to Revelation, the authority of Scripture witnesses to the nature of biblical marriage as uniquely bound to the complementarity of man and woman. This truth is not negotiable. The Lord Jesus himself said that marriage is from the beginning (Matt. 19:4-6), so no human institution has the authority to redefine marriage any more than a human institution has the authority to redefine the gospel, which marriage mysteriously reflects (Eph. 5:32).[35]

The argument has some obvious weaknesses. The Bible doesn't actually teach that 'marriage consists of one man and one woman.' It recognises and legitimises a variety of marriage customs, including polygamy and levirate marriages. It isn't therefore of the essence of Biblical marriage that just two people are involved. As is often pointed out, many of the Bible's heroes had

---

35   http:///.christianitytoday.com/ct/2015/june-web-only/here-we-stand-evangelical-declaration-on-marriage.html?start=3

more than one wife, some, like Solomon, far too many.[36] And he was known to be a wise king![37] Polygamy is not a custom I would encourage, nor does the Bible, but it was, nevertheless, a Biblically-accepted marriage variation, originally devised, no doubt, for the protection of women, and, in the case of levirate marriages, for the protection of widows. Social circumstances at the time dictated the need for such variations. They may not have been ideal, but the marriages involved were still marriages.

Moreover, marriage customs have changed. Biblical marriages were patriarchal, with husbands having ownership of their wives and children, who had next to no rights. Marriages have been like that for millennia, reaching back into pre-history, with pair bonding initially devised as a way of organising and controlling sexual conduct, while providing a stable structure for child-rearing. The first recorded evidence of marriage contracts and ceremonies dates to 4,000 years ago, in Mesopotamia. In the ancient world, marriage served primarily as a means of preserving power, with kings and other members of the ruling class marrying off daughters to forge alliances, acquire land, and produce legitimate heirs. Even among the lower classes, women had little say over whom they married, with the purpose of marriage being to produce heirs.[38] Issues of love, intimacy or mutuality hardly entered into the equation.

The idea that there can be no change to what we find in the Bible is flawed, flawed because within the Bible itself earlier customs are critiqued and modified. As for the reference to complementarity, it was noted earlier that gender complementarity is not what is emphasised in Genesis 1-3. What is emphasized is mutuality, fellowship and kinship, all of which can be found and enjoyed within same-sex marriages.

The appeal to Jesus' words in Matthew 19:4-6 is also misplaced:

> Some Pharisees came to him, and to test him they asked, 'Is it lawful for a man to divorce his wife for any cause?' He answered, 'Have you not read that the one who made them at the beginning made them male and female,' and said, "For this reason a man shall leave his father and mother and joined to his wife, and the two shall become one flesh"? So they are no longer two, but one flesh.

---

36   To be precise, 700 wives and 300 concubines.

37   At least early in his reign.

38   http://theweek.com/articles/475141/how-marriage-changed-over-centuries

Therefore what God has joined together, let no one separate,' 19:3-6.

These words cannot reasonably be taken to exclude the possibility of change or exceptions. Jesus acknowledged as much in the immediately following verses by mentioning divorce, legislated for, he said, because of people's hardness of heart. Divorce is less than ideal, but it remains actual, and in some cases unavoidable. Jesus, no doubt, was referring to what he believed was God's ideal for marriage, but the description of an ideal does not in any way rule out variations or exceptions such as existed within the Bible itself. The idea that people of the same sex could marry is unlikely to have crossed Jesus' or his listeners' minds, but it is now our issue, with which we need to deal.

There are some who argue that the possibility of having children, or, at least, a broad orientation towards having and caring for children is of the essence of marriage.[39] I am not persuaded. It is clearly not *essential* for a marriage that children come or were intended. There are any number of sensible and responsible exceptions. The imminent end of the age might be one St Paul may have urged. But even if one grants that marriages do well to be oriented to the care of children, many same-sex marriages are so oriented.

Arguments about the importance of having a mum and a dad, and thus the influence of a variety of gender role models do have merit, but are at least partially countered by the fact that gay and lesbian parents do expose their children to gender diversity, simply by virtue of the fact that they are gay and lesbian, not to mention the obvious importance of having children brought up within communities or 'villages,' rather than in often insular nuclear families, with even more isolation happening in the case of single parents. Same-sex couples have an advantage over single-parent families, by virtue of having two parents and not one. And children are clearly the beneficiaries of this. Since same-sex marriage came into effect, and even beforehand, numerous studies have been conducted to gauge the impact on children of being brought up by parents who are gay. Overwhelmingly,

---

39   Rev. Dr John Dickson, for example, has argued that the inherent power to create and nurture their own children is the reason that this relationship attracts the unique status and title of marriage, and that because gay people simply cannot meet this requirement their relationships can never rightly be called marriage. To be consistent, he even argues that couples who don't intend to have children should not get married, which, to me, seems odd, given that an equally important purpose of marriage, in fact its defining ethos, is the sexually expressed union of two individuals lovingly committed to each other for life.

and with few exceptions, those studies have concluded that these children are not worse off than those brought up by their biological mothers and fathers.[40] Moreover, same-sex marriages come surprisingly close to the idealised description of marriage articulated by Jesus. As Nigel Chapman helpfully spells out:

> Same-sex marriage fulfils every aspect of the biblical ideal of marriage that is actually possible for a same-sex oriented person to fulfil; a life-long union of sexual and romantic intimacy, of care and companionship, of faithful monogamy, and the possibility of raising a family. The only aspects of the ideal that are missing from this picture are the ones precluded by a constitutional incapacity for heterosexual attraction, whether sexual or romantic.[41]

Leading American evangelical ethicist, David P. Gushee, concurs. While lamenting the disastrous weakening of marriage customs in the US, he notes that gay and lesbian couples are, in many cases, embracing his own preferred model of marriage, a covenantal model, which he articulates in these terms:

> Christianity has historically said: God's plan for sexual ethics requires a man and a woman to make a binding lifetime marriage covenant with each other (before God, church and state, representing civil society) and to remain faithful to the promises of that covenant, including fidelity and exclusivity, until one partner dies a natural death.[42]

---

40 More than 100 studies have been conducted into the outcomes for children of having same-sex or heterosexual parents. Some of the earlier studies had limited sample sizes and methodological short-comings which later studies have sought to avoid. And, without doubt, more studies are needed as time goes by, as children grow up, and as societies adjust to the new reality of same-sex marriages, but the strong indications so far are that children are not damaged simply by virtue of the gender of their parents. See further an ABC Fact Check dated 29 July 2015: http://www.abc.net.au/news/2015-07-24/same-sex-parenting-fact-or-fiction/6616352 See also the following meta-studies: T. J. Biblarz and J. Stacey, 'Does the gender of parents matter? *Journal of Marriage and Family*, Volume 72, Issue 1, February 2010, 3–22; J. Adams and R. Light, 'Scientific consensus, the law and same sex parenting outcomes,' *Social Science Research*, Volume 53, September 2015, 300-310; Alicia L. Fedewa, Whitney W. Black & Soyeon Ahn (2015) Children and Adolescents With Same-Gender Parents: A Meta-Analytic Approach in Assessing Outcomes, *Journal of GLBT Family Studies*, 11:1, 1-34.

41 Blog post entitled, 'Forty-Five Questions for Evangelicals Supporting Marriage Equality', dated 2 July 2015.

42 David P. Gushee, *Changing Our Mind: a call from America's leading evangelical ethics scholar for full acceptance of LGBT Christians in the Church*, 2nd edition, Canton, Michigan:

Gays and lesbians cannot fulfil the one man and one woman aspect of this ideal, but they can fulfil all other aspects. Gushee, who once thought otherwise, cannot now think of any conclusive reason (Biblical or otherwise) to prevent gay and lesbian couples from entering into marriage so understood.[43] Many, like Gushee, are finding that the reasons proposed against it are not convincing. Moreover, efforts to exclude gays and lesbians increasingly appear mean and un-Christ-like, in part because of the perceived weakness of arguments against same-sex marriage. There is also the sense of a profound unfairness involved in preventing well-intentioned gay and lesbian people from entering what is rightly considered a cherished institution, which was reflected in the reasoning of the majority of the Supreme Court judges in their landmark decision in the US, as evidenced by the following portion of their judgement:

> No union is more profound than marriage, for it embodies the highest ideals of love, fidelity, devotion, sacrifice, and family. In forming a marital union, two people become something greater than once they were. As some of the petitioners in these cases demonstrate, marriage embodies a love that may endure even past death. It would misunderstand these men and women to say they disrespect the idea of marriage. Their plea is that they do respect it, respect it so deeply that they seek to find its fulfilment for themselves. Their hope is not to be condemned to live in loneliness, excluded from one of civilisation's oldest institutions. They ask for equal dignity in the eyes of the law. The Constitution grants them that right.

There were many Christians who applauded the Supreme Court for its decision, and who agree that withholding marriage from our LGBTI sons and daughters would be unfair, and therefore unloving. Thoughts such as these contributed to a change of mind for Matthew's father, whose story is told in the Introduction to this book. Between when he first wrote his story and when this book was about to be published, he changed his mind, and is now in favour of same-sex marriage. To reproduce just some of the words of his more recent letter:

> I am thrilled to report that there has been a change in my heart. It has come with much contemplation of Scripture and with the guidance of the Peace of

---

Read the Spirit Books, 2015, 102. Gushee contrasts the covenantal model or ethic with two others that have become prominent in the US, with damaging effects: the mutual consent ethic and the loving relationship ethic. See further, *Changing Our Mind*, 102-104.

43   *Changing Our Mind*, 105.

Christ in my heart. It was brought into focus by a very interesting book, *Torn: Rescuing the Gospel from the Gay Vs Christian Debate*,[44] and by my lessening reliance on the attitudes, statement and positions of the Church.

I now consider that my previous position, of believing that gay marriage was outside the will of God, was in error.

Influential in this father's change of mind were considerations of the love of God, which he didn't see being displayed in the attitude of some of his fellow Christians. He reflected that if *he* had been the recipient of these attitudes, he also may have stopped going to church as his son has done. He noted that Justin Lee's experience, sensitively recounted in *Torn*, was very similar to his son's experience, and also noted Jesus' prioritizing of people and love over law, as well as the freedom of the church to leave behind customs such as circumcision and head coverings for women, even though St Paul appeared to employ culture-independent arguments for this latter practice.[45] These and other considerations, including the post-New Testament rejection of slavery, the constant imperative to love, and the importance of being led by the Spirit of Christ in thinking through issues, brought about a massive change in this father's thinking and attitudes, so much so that, in his words, 'I now fully and whole-heartedly believe that gay marriage *is* accepted by God and *is* part of the church living out Christ in the world.'

Something very similar happened in the thinking and experience of Tony Campolo, the well-known and highly respected evangelical preacher and activist who, for close on 60 years (he is now 80), has been one of evangelicalism's leading voices, similar in stature and reputation to Rev. Billy Graham (now 96). Campolo released a statement on 8 June 2015 entitled 'For the Record.' In it he described his change of mind about same-sex marriage. Following are some of his words:

---

44   Justin Lee, *Torn: Rescuing the Gospel from the Gay Vs Christian Debate*, New York: Jericho Books, 2012.

45   Adherence to the Sabbath commandment could also have been mentioned, set aside even though it was one of the 10 commandments. That its meaning was in some ways fulfilled by the coming of the Christ does not, in itself, justify its complete jettisoning or effective replacement by Sunday. Clearly the church felt at some liberty to set non-ceremonial requirements aside to accommodate new circumstances and needs; felt at liberty to realise underlying principles in new ways.

It has taken countless hours of prayer, study, conversation and emotional turmoil to bring me to the place where I am finally ready to call for the full acceptance of Christian gay couples into the Church.

For me, the most important part of that process was answering a more fundamental question: What is the point of marriage in the first place? For some Christians, in a tradition that traces back to St. Augustine, the sole purpose of marriage is procreation, which obviously negates the legitimacy of same-sex unions. Others of us, however, recognize a more spiritual dimension of marriage, which is of supreme importance. We believe that God intends married partners to help actualize in each other the 'fruits of the spirit,' which are love, joy, peace, patience, kindness, goodness, faithfulness, gentleness and self-control, often citing the Apostle Paul's comparison of marriage to Christ's sanctifying relationship with the Church. This doesn't mean that unmarried people cannot achieve the highest levels of spiritual actualization – our Savior himself was single, after all – but only that the institution of marriage should always be primarily about spiritual growth.

In my own life, my wife Peggy has been easily the greatest encourager of my relationship with Jesus. She has been my prayer partner and, more than anyone else, she has discerned my shortcomings and helped me try to overcome them.

One reason I am changing my position on this issue is that, through Peggy, I have come to know so many gay Christian couples whose relationships work in much the same way as our own. Our friendships with these couples have helped me understand how important it is for the exclusion and disapproval of their unions by the Christian community to end. We in the Church should actively support such families. Furthermore, we should be doing all we can to reach, comfort and include all those precious children of God who have been wrongly led to believe that they are mistakes or just not good enough for God, simply because they are not straight.

As a social scientist, I have concluded that sexual orientation is almost never a choice and I have seen how damaging it can be to try to 'cure' someone from being gay. As a Christian, my responsibility is not to condemn or reject gay people, but rather to love and embrace them, and to endeavour to draw them into the fellowship of the Church. When we sing the old invitation hymn, 'Just as I am,' I want us to mean it, and I want my gay and lesbian brothers and sisters to know it is true for them too.

Rest assured that I have already heard – and in some cases made – every kind of biblical argument against gay marriage, including those of Dr Ronald Sider, my esteemed friend and colleague at Eastern University. Obviously, people of good will can and do read the scriptures very differently when it comes to controversial issues, and I am painfully aware that there are ways I could be wrong about this one.

However, I am old enough to remember when we in the Church made strong biblical cases for keeping women out of teaching roles in the Church, and when divorced and remarried people often were excluded from fellowship altogether on the basis of scripture. Not long before that, some Christians even made biblical cases supporting slavery. Many of those people were sincere believers, but most of us now agree that they were wrong. I am afraid we are making the same kind of mistake again, which is why I am speaking out.[46]

The experience of Campolo and of Matthew's father may not be yours. It may be that you are still persuaded by those who argue that same-sex marriage is not likely to be a good thing, either for those who participate in it or those affected by it. Fair enough. It may be that you have gone through a very similar journey to the one Campolo and this father travelled, and have still concluded that you cannot, in good conscience, support same-sex marriage. Again, fair enough. However, I suspect that along this journey bells of cognitive dissonance will have begun to ring, and perhaps are still ringing. If they are, my advice, and the advice of this chapter, is: do not silence those bells. Let them keep ringing until they silence themselves.

---

46   http://tonycampolo.org/for-the-record-tony-campolo-releases-a-new-statement/#.
VZzoLxuqqko

CHAPTER EIGHT

The Inescapable Need for Appropriation

People are understandably wary of disrupting long-held traditions, especially when those traditions seem so patently grounded in sacred Scripture. They feel they have no alternative but to make the best of those increasingly uncomfortable parts of Scripture which not only fly in the face of contemporary scholarship and culture, but which also sit uneasily with their own evolving understandings and experience. Many are concluding that their only alternatives are either to stick with the faith of their younger years or give it away altogether.

Happily, those are not the only choices available to 21st century Christians. There is at least one other way, which, perhaps surprisingly, is as deeply rooted in Biblical religion as are more common approaches such as literalism or inerrancy. It is the way of appropriation.

To appropriate is to adapt. It is to make use of something that maybe doesn't quite meet your immediate needs or speak directly to your current circumstances, but which, perhaps with slight modification, can be usefully and relevantly used by you. We are often and inevitably involved in appropriation. We go to see a movie, and although the location, storyline and experiences of the movie's characters can be very different from anything we have experienced, we can still imagine ourselves into the story and take away all sorts of lessons and challenges which are entirely relevant. We thereby appropriate the movie's story, hopefully for our benefit and enrichment.

Appropriation is just as important and necessary when we read the Bible. The Bible's stories are all ancient and set in mostly Middle Eastern contexts which are very different from what most of us are used to. We need, therefore, to be sensitively aware of those differences as we seek to draw lessons from those stories or to hear the voice of God speaking to us through them. It is the same with the Bible's many injunctions and even its theology. They are all set within, and applied to, ancient contexts which draw on ancient conceptualities, some of which are no longer comfortably held, some of which have been superseded by new understandings.

The need for appropriation is therefore constant and complicated, but it also needs to be critical; critical in the sense of discerning, critical in the sense of keeping our wits about us as we come to this ancient text with our modern, and, in all likelihood, postmodern beliefs and convictions, not all of which are likely to be helpful or long-lived, most of which are likely to be affected by our finiteness, foolishness and constant tendency to get things wrong. To be critical is to be self-critical, whilst also making responsible use of all the intellectual tools at our disposal as we seek to better understand the Bible, the world and ourselves.

Someone who has written extensively on the notion of appropriation is the French philosopher Paul Ricoeur (1913-2005). For Ricoeur, appropriation is the process of making one's own what is initially alien. It was, for him, the final stage of a three-part hermeneutical process.[1] Ricoeur's hermeneutical arc, as it is sometimes called, begins with a first or naïve understanding, a 'first naïveté,' which generally occurs when one first encounters a text, like the Bible. One's initial response to any text will be determined by the mix of beliefs and prejudices one brings with one to the reading of the text. Ancient readers will bring ancient beliefs and prejudices. Modern readers will bring modern beliefs and prejudices. The first stage of Ricoeur's arc is non-reflective or pre-contemplative. It is like one's first impression of someone we have just met.

But first naïveté gives way, and has given way historically, to a second stage of Ricoeur's hermeneutical arc, which is critical engagement. We begin to subject the text to critical analysis. We take a step back from the text. Ricoeur refers to this as distanciation. We analyse the text as if it were a specimen to be put under the microscope of critical analysis. We make use of all the critical tools now at our disposal in the wake of the scientific and

---

1   For an early articulation of this process, see Paul Ricoeur, *The Symbolism of Evil*, Boston: Beacon Press, 1967.

historiographical revolutions arising out of the European Enlightenment. In the case of our study of the Bible, we can helpfully draw on the burgeoning results of textual criticism, literary criticism, genre criticism, redaction criticism, historical criticism, rhetorical criticism and narrative criticism, the now large and growing family of disciplines associated with the historical-critical method.

To subject the text of the Bible to this level of critical analysis is not necessarily disrespectful. Nor will it inevitably be dismissive of the text. In fact, at its best, it is the opposite. Ricoeur was aware of the danger of using texts abusively and self-servingly, and as instruments of ego, a danger for all readers of the Bible, liberal and conservative alike. He was aware of the danger of deciding in advance what one will find in the text, of letting one's pre-understandings domesticate the text, of being reductionistic in one's approach to the text, thereby evacuating it of contemporary relevance. One of the reasons that distanciation is necessary is because of the need to put ego, ideology and prejudice aside, to better listen to the text and be taught by it.

Critical analysis, no matter how respectful and responsive, will, however, also create challenges as older ways of understanding the text are shown to be inadequate. We can no longer sensibly read the Bible without noticing the presence of myth and legend, without coming to realise that the development of the Bible's storyline and associated theology was frequently advanced by the employment of stories, which, if they aren't fiction, are heavily fictionalised. To read these stories as narratives of sober fact is, more often than not, to misread them, is not to respect them for what they are. It is to read into them prejudices we now need to set aside.

Moreover, there is no way back to a first naïveté. There can be no sensible return to pre-modern, or even to pre-postmodern ways of understanding the Bible. We simply cannot turn the clock back. But that doesn't mean there isn't a way forward. And the way forward, for Ricoeur, is the way of appropriation, which he describes in terms of the need for a 'second naïveté,' a coming back to the text to be challenged and transformed by it.

To enter a second naïveté one must move beyond the endlessly critical and suspicious hermeneutic of the Enlightenment to re-engage earlier texts, including the ancient text of the Bible.[2] Not that being critical and suspicious doesn't have its place, but one need not forever remain at a distance, forever suspicious. One can become attentive to what the Bible might have to say to oneself, can listen for the still, small voice of God speaking to us through its pages.

Appropriation involves personalising what one encounters in the text of the Bible. The constant challenge of interpretation is the need to overcome the distance between the past to which the text belongs and the interpreter. To overcome this distance, the interpreter appropriates the meaning of the text to himself or herself. What is foreign is transformed to become familiar and one's own. The object of interpretation, according to Ricoeur, is to come to a deeper and more complete understanding of oneself, to come to 'self-understanding by means of understanding others.'[3]

Aiding this process of appropriation and self-understanding is the realisation that the meaning of texts is never fixed or invariable. In the subtle and ever evolving interplay between interpreter and text, texts have a life of their own somewhat independent of the intentions and understandings of the original authors. Texts are able to speak with renewed and renewing insight into each new situation and to each new reader. A big part of the reason for this is that texts have an essentially open-ended character. They imply or foreshadow or prefigure new worlds of possibility.[4] In the case of the Bible, one is introduced to the world of divine encounter, which one can choose to inhabit, thus becoming a recipient of divine encounter oneself.

I have found Ricoeur's model of hermeneutics to be hugely helpful, and have tried to appropriate it for my own use as I continue to read and be challenged by the Bible. It is a more dynamic model than the one I grew up with, largely because of its open-endedness. It also allows me to

---

2   Ricoeur took issue with hermeneutical approaches, such as those represented by Freud, Marx and Nietzsche, for being both suspicious and reductionistic in their approach to mythical or symbolic consciousness. See, for example, in Paul Ricoeur, *Freud and Philosophy: An Essay on Interpretation,* (New Haven and London: Yale University Press, 1970), 32-36, and Paul Ricoeur, 'The Critique of Religion,' in *The Philosophy of Paul Ricoeur: An Anthology of his Work,* Boston: Beacon Press, 1978, 213-222.

3   Paul Ricoeur, 'Existence and Hermeneutics,' *The Conflict of Interpretations: Essays in Hermeneutics,* edited by Don Ihde, Evanston: Northwestern University Press, 1974, 16-17.

4   Paul Ricoeur, 'Phenomenology and Hermeneutics,' *From Text to Action: Essays in Hermeneutics, 11,* Evanston, Illinois: Northwestern University Press, 17.

be respectful and honest about what I find in the Bible. It allows me to fully acknowledge the ancientness of this text, while leaving ample room to appropriate its many insights and convictions, on the way to a deeper understanding of myself, the world and of God. It also isn't very different from the interpretative methods employed by Jesus and those who wrote the Bible. They too were first-class appropriators.

Appropriation as practiced by Jesus and the Biblical writers

Some people assume that their way of reading the Bible is the only way, and that it was the way Jesus and his apostles read their Scriptures. But neither assumption is warranted. Over the years, there have been many ways in which the Bible has been read and interpreted by Christians,[5] and the way Jesus and his apostles read and interpreted their Bibles is not the way we read ours.

Jesus, the apostles, and the authors of the New Testament employed interpretive methods current at the time they lived, that time being the Second Temple period of Jewish history, the period between the completion of Jerusalem's Second Temple in 516 BCE and its destruction by the Romans in 70 CE. These interpretive methods included typology and *pesher midrash*,[6] which was an exegetical practice used at Qumran. By this method, Old Testament texts were read and interpreted in the light of contemporary events, which were seen to be their eschatological fulfilment. The meaning of older texts was not self-evident. One had to go searching. One also had to wait for events that would fulfil those ancient texts.

---

5   Origen (185-254 CE) developed a three-fold hermeneutic involving attention to the literal, moral and allegorical senses of Biblical texts. John Cassian (360-435) added a fourth, the analogical or mystical sense, which is their eschatological significance. None of these interpreters used the grammatical-historical method which, more recently, has been the favoured approach, certainly among Protestant evangelicals.

6   *Pesher,* meaning solution or deciphering, *midrash* meaning exegesis or interpretation. For more information, see Richard B. Hays and Joel B. Green, 'The Use of the Old Testament by New Testament Writers', in Joel B. Green, *Hearing the New Testament: Strategies of Interpretation,* Grand Rapids: Eerdmans, 1995, 222-238, as well as E. Earle Ellis's excellent monograph, *The Old Testament in Early Christianity,* Tubingen: J.C.B. Mohr, 1991. A recent publication which wrestles with the implications of *pesher midrash* for an evangelical hermeneutic is, Peter Enns, *Inspiration and Incarnation: Evangelicals and the Problem of the Old Testament* (2005).

Like the Qumran community, Christians developed their own *pesher* exegesis, scouring the Torah and the Prophets for prophetic references to Jesus.[7] Sometimes, what they found appears strange and unconvincing to us, because their way of reading texts, and drawing meaning from texts, was very different from the way we read and understand texts. For example, the writer of Matthew's Gospel draws attention to a number of details in the life of Jesus that were thought by him 'to fulfil what had been spoken by the prophet[s].'[8] Without going into detail, and volumes have been written on this, the original intended meaning of the Old Testament texts cited was almost certainly not the same as the meaning gleaned from those passages by the writer of Matthew's Gospel. To us, it appears he was reading into texts things which weren't originally there. This strangeness of interpretation has generated any number of creative attempts to understand Matthew and his method. Some of those efforts have been designed to argue that Matthew's interpretive technique is consistent with, if not a case of, the grammatical-historical method favoured by evangelical Protestants. I haven't found such approaches convincing.

The writer of Matthew's Gospel was an ancient exegete following ancient hermeneutical approaches available to him at the time. He would sometimes take a very literal approach, and, at other times, a metaphorical or typological approach. There was no one approach that ruled out others, but rather an interweaving and blending of interpretive approaches, unified for him and for the other New Testament writers by a Christological reading of the Old Testament texts.[9] Despite efforts to argue otherwise, he wasn't using the grammatical-historical approach, an approach which emerged much later in history. Even his literalism was different from the literalism of many contemporary Christians. Dale Martin notes that although the

---

7   Some scholars have sought to distance the New Testament writers from the techniques of *pesher midrash*. However, it is non-controversial that the New Testament writers did, at the very least, employ *pesher*-like techniques of interpretation.

8   Included among passages where such fulfilment formulae are used are: Mt. 1:22-23 (Is. 7:14); Mt. 2:15 (Hs. 11:1), Mt. 2:17-18 (Jr. 31:15); Mt. 4:14-16 (Is. 8:23-9:1); Mt. 8:17 (Is. 53:4), Mt. 12:17-21 (Is. 42:1-4), Mt. 13:35 (Ps. 78:2) Mt. 21:4-5 (Is. 62:11; Zch. 9:9), Mt. 27:9-10 (Zch. 11:12-13; Jr. 18:3, 59:6-9).

9   R. Longenecker, *Biblical Exegesis in the Apostolic Period*, (Grand Rapids: Eerdmans, 1975), 103. Note that Biblical texts were often modified, or particular versions preferred, because they suited the interpreter better, as in Matthew's use of the LXX with its more favourable (to his point) translation of Isaiah 7:14.

Biblical writers did, at times, take a literal approach to the Bible, they weren't, as modern interpreters have attempted, trying to discover the original intended meaning of the text. 'They rather taught that the real author of Scripture … was God or the Holy Spirit,' and, because of that, they could be expected to find meanings intended by God, but not by the original human authors.[10]

There are a few things worth noting from this short description of interpretive methods used by Jesus and those who wrote the New Testament. The first is that there is no way that we, as 21st century Christians, can continue to employ 1st century interpretive methods. We no longer use *pesher midrash*, and we are wary about reading things into texts that probably weren't in the minds of the original authors. We have developed a whole new raft of interpretive strategies, which isn't a bad thing, unless we think we should read our Bibles the way Jesus and his apostles did.[11]

Secondly, although we cannot turn back the hermeneutical clock, we are, in broad terms, doing just what Jesus and his apostles did. We, like them, are making use of interpretive strategies available to us. We come to the text of the Bible with the benefit of almost two millennia of research and study. There has never been a literary work subjected to more critical scrutiny, much of which has illuminated our understanding of the text and context of the Bible. The Bible has been looked at from almost every angle imaginable, and that has meant that we have come to understand the Bible in new and fresh ways.

Thirdly, we have no choice but to be influenced by our current understandings and beliefs. We could try to put them out of our heads, but we wouldn't succeed. We cannot return to a first naïveté.

To give one short and simple example, I was often puzzled, in my younger years, by references to stars falling from the sky, in the Olivet Discourse in Matthew 24:29, for example. The end of the ages would be ushered in by the stars of heaven crashing onto the earth. I wondered what those references

---

10   D. Martin, Pedagogy of the Bible: An Analysis and Proposal, Louisville: Westminster John Knox Press, 2008, 43.

11   It is, I think, an uncomfortable thing for many conservative Christians that they don't, or can't, employ the same hermeneutical methods as Jesus did. They are comfortable to quote verses that appear to support an inerrantist hermeneutic, drawing on Jesus' authority to do so, but then fail to follow his way of reading texts.

could mean, given that stars simply cannot do that. I remember at one stage thinking that this was just apocalyptic hyperbole, and conjectured that what would happen would be something like being interrupted in one's watching of a movie by the jamming of the movie reel, with the image first stopping, then melting away by the heat of the projector. Reality itself would do something like that. That was as good a solution as I could come up with until I realised that the ancients believed that stars could fall to the earth. Stars were small enough, and not that far above the earth, embedded within a firmament, and so were able to be dislodged by the cataclysmic events of the eschaton. The point of the illustration is that we cannot help but bring with us to the reading of the Bible our own often well-formed and warranted beliefs and convictions.

Fourthly, although we can't avoid bringing our current beliefs and convictions to the reading of the text of the Bible, we can be careful and scrupulous about how we come to those beliefs. We will need to be honest and cautious, and aware of the insidious and ever-present tendency to give in to lesser motives of self-protection and self-promotion; of the danger of embracing beliefs, or stubbornly holding onto beliefs, largely because they enable us to join, or not be ejected from, the tribe from which we draw our significance and security.

Fifthly, in coming to the text of the Bible formed by our hopefully well-formed and honestly-held beliefs and hermeneutical methods, we are doing just what Jesus and the Biblical writers were doing. We are seeking to appropriate those ancient texts for our present benefit. The New Testament itself is a work of appropriation. Armed with their now ancient pre-understandings, the authors of the New Testament were seeking to explain, in their terms, the meaning of the encounter they had had with Jesus.[12] That is what we seek to do as well.

In what remains of this chapter, I'd like to give some examples of what appropriation might look like when applied to some of the issues previously raised in this book, as well as one or two others.

---

12   As Peter Gomes notes: the New Testament itself 'is the product of an early and radical hermeneutic,' with the 'first hermeneutical task of the disciples [being] to reconcile the transforming event of Jesus' resurrection with the body of Scripture' they had inherited, *The Good Book: Reading the Bible with Mind and Heart*, New York, HarperOne, 1996, 30.

Adam and Eve

St Paul's understanding of Genesis has decisively and understandably shaped the way Christians have understood that book's seminal stories. The following words from his letter to the Romans have been immensely influential:

> Therefore, just as sin came into the world through one man, and death came through sin, so death spread to all because all sinned. Romans 5:12 NRSV

It is possible, though it is hard to know how likely, that St Paul did not intend these words to be taken literally, and also, therefore, that he did not understand the early stories of Genesis to be literal accounts of Adam and Eve's tragic choice to disobey God. It may be that St Paul was unconcerned with the distinction we often make, and in modern times have become obsessed with, between fact and fiction, and was simply alluding to a story that can as easily be taken metaphorically as literally. Maybe.

Speaking for myself, I have long been of the opinion that the author of Genesis 2 and 3, which contains the story of Adam's poor choice and resulting death sentence, did not intend this story to be taken literally, but was instead reflecting on the experience of his people, the Israelites, who, at the time of writing, had already had a long history, reaching back to their occupation of the land of promise, and, more recently, of being ejected from that land at the time of the Exile of 587 BCE.[13] The writer was, I think, projecting his people's story backwards into what he would have thought was a likely story of human beginnings. He was doing theology by way of mythology, which was the ancient way. He was also constructing

---

13   During most of the 20th century, the dominant belief among Biblical scholars was that the Torah, which includes Genesis, was composed by the intertwining of four originally separate documents (the documentary hypothesis). Those four documents or sources were identified as: the Jahwist (or Yahwist), within which God is characteristically referred to as Yahweh; the Deuteronomist, the author or authors of Deuteronomy, Joshua, Judges, Samuel and Kings; the Elohist, within which God is characteristically described as Elohim; and the Priestly source (JDEP). The documentary hypothesis has fallen into some disfavour recently, with a complicated array of alternative proposals broadly divided between 'fragmentary' and 'supplementary' models. Most scholars agree that a variety of differently-dated sources were brought together by the final redactors of the Hebrew Scriptures. Genesis 2 and 3 is commonly attributed to the Yahwist (J) source, with an increasingly common view among scholars that it was composed in the aftermath of the Judean Exile of the early 6th century BCE.

an anthropology, a way of understanding himself and his people, in relation to God, other peoples, and the world. The dates, the location, and the characters of the story are reflective of the world he knew. He would have had little knowledge of Africa, and none of China or the Americas or Australia. His story, so clever and profound in every way, was constructed of details one would expect from someone writing at that time and in that part of the world, whilst also representing a quite radical statement of an emergent monotheism.

Whether or not St Paul was a literalist at this point is not something about which we can be certain, but what has become obvious over the last few centuries is that literalism is misleading and unworkable, certainly as applied to these early chapters of the Bible. Moreover, emerging understandings of our world, and of human occupation of the world, are necessarily precipitating a profound re-think of our inherited theologies, not likely to be an easy task, as George Emeleus, a retired physicist and theologian, points out:

> In theology … contemporary understandings of the cosmos present immense challenges to how we imagine God to be, and how we imagine God to be present and active within it. It is one thing to be open to belief in 'something which our minds cannot grasp' and which nevertheless pervades all that we are aware of [as Einstein suggested]. It is quite another to re-imagine the God of religious traditions in ways coherent with contemporary scientific cosmology, and to interpret those traditions in ways which may be clearly recognized as important and life-changing.[14]

Emeleus is right. The challenge of rethinking one's theology in the light of contemporary understandings is immense, made all the more challenging by the fact that large swathes of Christian theology appear inextricably linked to literalistic readings of texts such as Genesis 2-3 and Romans 5. Systematic and Biblical theologies have been built around the notion of humans 'falling' into sin at a particular point in time. If this is not true to fact, as seems likely, the implications are many and far-reaching, as Jack Mahoney, Emeritus Professor of Moral and Social theology at the University of London, points out:

> Darwin's scientific advance has served to explain individual death as a regular

---

14   George Emeleus, 'Uncertainty in Science and belief in God,' *Uniting Church Studies*, Vol 18, No 2, December 2012, Faith and Atheism.

evolutionary phenomenon affecting all living things in nature, long predating humanity, and, in the process, it has thrown into question the need for the whole Judeo-Christian intellectual construct of fall and redemption, whose purpose, I have argued, was to explain the origin of death as a penalty for human sin, with the corollary of continuing human sinfulness and debilitating moral frailty. It has also rendered unnecessary the need for that primordial sin, with the resulting fallen condition of human nature, to be atoned for in some way and to be redeemed by the sacrifice of an incarnate God who became human precisely for that purpose. Indeed, for practical purposes and in the interests of argumentative clarity, it may now be possible and useful to categorise the originally Israelite hypothesis of a primordial fall and progression to a subsequent cosmic restitution as instances of speculative Biblical theology, emerging from and tied to Israelite culture.[15]

These are radical thoughts, and whether one agrees with them or not, they highlight the pressing need to re-think and re-articulate one's theology in the light of new understandings. To hold out against these understandings and to keep insisting on literalism, because it is the basis of so many dearly-held doctrines, is the way of death, or, less dramatically, the route to intellectual obscurity and irrelevance. We need to go back to these ancient texts and re-examine them in the light of what we now know and/or reasonably believe.[16]

It won't be a comfortable process, I am guessing. It won't simply be a matter of rethinking one's approach to the Bible's early stories, because those early stories, and the assumptions underlying them, permeate the rest of the Bible, becoming the theological building blocks for all the Bible's major doctrines, including Christology. This is, I am sure, one of the reasons conservative Christians have fought so hard to resist any questioning of the Biblical stories, or of any small part of the Bible, because the truth is that the Bible is profoundly interconnected. To question one part will involve questioning other parts, creating fear that the whole building will come crashing down.

---

15 J. Mahoney, *Christianity in Evolution: An Exploration*, Washington: Georgetown University Press, 2011, 143.

16 For a good example of two people who have done that with promising results, a theologian and a scientist, see Gregory J. Laughery, George Diepstra, *From Evolution to Eden: Making Sense of Early Genesis*, Destinee, 2015.

It is an understandable fear, but it is also a fear that is sure to be realised if nothing is done, if Christians keep on insisting on literal readings of texts which cannot now reasonably be read that way. As I see it, we face a simple choice, the choice to keep on holding out against contemporary understandings and new discoveries, perhaps only giving in when it is absolutely necessary, at the significant cost of being inconsistent, or, we do essentially what the Biblical writers did, we subject earlier texts (in our case the whole of the Bible) to a systematic re-think. I personally don't have the wherewithal or the necessary expertise to do this. I will have to leave that to others, but what I can do is to illustrate what re-appropriation might look like.

Noah

How do we appropriate the story of Noah, given that we can no longer reasonably believe that what it describes happened? I don't think the answer is too difficult once we have a closer look at the story, once we move beyond first naïveté to critical engagement. In fact, not taking the story literally helps in the process of coming to understand it. And there are hints in the text that it shouldn't be taken literally.

In Genesis 6:4, is the following enigmatic verse:

> The Nephilim were on the earth in those days – and also afterward – when the sons of God went in to the daughters of humans, who bore children to them. They were the heroes that were of old, warriors of renown.

The Nephilim, apparently, were giants. This bit of the Noah story reads like a legend, which it most probably is, although myth might be a better category given the reference to the sons of God, in all likelihood angels, having sex with human beings. This, in itself, suggests we do well not to take this story literally. But there is another detail which suggests the same. The Nephilim are described as being on the earth in those days (possibly as the off-spring of angels having sex with women), but the text indicates that they were also on the earth 'afterward,' in other words, after Noah's flood. This is not easily reconciled with the words of Genesis 7:23:

> Every living thing on the face of the earth was wiped out: men and animals and the creatures that move along the ground and the birds of the air were wiped from the earth. Only Noah was left, and those with him in the ark.

There are other indications in the text that the Noah story cannot be taken literally, and also that it probably wasn't intended to be so taken. For example, there are contradictory descriptions of how many of each kind of animal were taken onto the ark.[17] There are contradictory details about when the flood began[18] and about the length of the flood.[19] Noah is also described as sending out three doves, one after the other (8:8-12), or just one bird, a raven (8:7).

None of these contradictions or other problems mentioned above is a problem if one doesn't feel compelled to take the story literally. It seems that the composer of this narrative brought together two slightly different flood stories and melded them together, without any obvious concern about reconciling the details. He was more concerned, it seems, with getting his message across than with specific details.

What should we make of this ancient narrative? We need, at first, to try to think our way back into the thought world of the author or composer of this graphic and powerful story. What seems likely is that he was drawing on a number of existing flood stories, possibly including the *Epic of Gilgamesh* and the *Atrahasis Epic*, both dating to around the turn of the second millennium BCE. The story taps into some primordial fears, particularly the fear of drowning, which he depicts in terms reminiscent of Genesis 1, where God is depicted as establishing order over an otherwise chaotic and watery world. Water and chaos are identified. God establishes order by separating the water from the land, creating fixed boundaries to keep the water above the heavens from cascading onto the earth; keeping the waters under the earth from surging to engulf the earth, returning it to its original chaotic state.

God is the God of order, and that order extends to the circumstances of human life. There are God-created boundaries to acceptable human behaviour which must be respected; and not breached. A big part of the reason for the catastrophic flood is found in the first few verses of Genesis 6.

---

17   Noah is commanded to gather seven pairs of clean animals (7:2) or only two of each animal (6:19-20; 7:8, 16).

18   The flood is said to start seven days after Noah enters the ark (7:7, 10) and on the day Noah entered the ark (7:11-13).

19   Forty days and forty nights (7:4, 12, 8:6) or one hundred and fifty days (7:24, 8:3).

When people began to multiply on the face of the ground, and daughters were born to them, [2] the sons of God saw that they were fair; and they took wives for themselves of all that they chose. [3] Then the LORD said, "My spirit shall not abide in mortals forever, for they are flesh; their days shall be one hundred twenty years." [4] The Nephilim were on the earth in those days—and also afterward—when the sons of God went in to the daughters of humans, who bore children to them. These were the heroes that were of old, warriors of renown. [5] The LORD saw that the wickedness of humankind was great in the earth, and that every inclination of the thoughts of their hearts was only evil continually. [6] And the LORD was sorry that he had made humankind on the earth, and it grieved him to his heart.

It was because of this boundary-breaching wickedness, and especially angels having sex with humans, that God decided to open up the windows above and the springs below, to allow the waters of chaos to submerge the earth, returning it to its pre-ordered state.

What can we take away from a story like this? How can it be appropriated for contemporary use? Quite easily, I think. We don't see the world the way the ancient writer did, but we can identify with notions of chaos, both within our own circumstances when everything seems to be swirling out of control, and within our inner experience which can so quickly become disordered by fear or desire, or by behaviour which we sense will see us unravel. We are all well aware of behaviour which breaches sensible and protective boundaries, unfaithfulness between partners, sex with children or animals. We know from painful experience when those sensible and protective boundaries are breached, and we can share the anger and disappointment of God, and wonder with God whether it would have been better for us to have not existed, given the terrible messes we make, and the damage we inflict upon each other. We resonate with the desire for justice; and the hope for a better world and a fresh start. The story of Noah can continue speaking to us down through the ages.

Avoiding chaos

A question which exercised the minds of those who wrote the Bible was how to avoid being overwhelmed by chaos. Not how to avoid death, an unavoidable given,[20] but how to move through life safely and peacefully. They lived in a dangerous world, as do we. One of the major answers to

---

20   Though it too required explanation.

the question of how to avoid chaos was: obey God; follow the ways of God; keep the commandments of God, and then you will have peace, protection and a long life, as will your descendants. The writers were well aware of the grace-full character of life itself, of the underpinning and pre-existing reality of grace, which was often represented in their writings. For example, the provision of a fruit-filled garden for Adam and Eve, and God's provision of clothing for them even after their disobedience, God's pre-warning of Noah and his contemporaries of an impending flood, the promise of blessing to Abraham, and the provision of a land for his descendants. God's commandments were always set within a context of generosity and grace, but the commandments were meant to be kept, in order that peace, prosperity and long life would follow.

The writer of Deuteronomy articulated this vision of life in clear and unambiguous terms. In chapter 11 of his book, which creates the vision for the Deuteronomic history which follows, the people of Israel are presented with the choice of blessing or curse (26-28). If they love God and keep his commandments, they will be successful in their conquest of the land (8); will have long life (9); they will be blessed with a fertile land watered by spring and autumn rains, which will always arrive on time (13-15). Larger and mightier nations will be driven out and kept at bay (22-25).

It is a simple vision. Do good and good will come to you; do evil and evil will befall you. It provided a way of making sense of Israelite history, but it didn't make complete sense. The experience of Israel, and of individual Israelites did not always match this simple formula; in fact, it often didn't, creating a contrary stream of Biblical reflection.[21] The Book of Job explores a different scenario; the experience of the righteous sufferer; the person who suffers because he is righteous. The author of Ecclesiastes is disturbingly honest in expressing his doubts about whether the Deuteronomic vision of life is adequate or accurate. He observes:

> In my vain life I have seen everything; there are righteous people who perish in their righteousness, and there are wicked people who prolong their life in their evil doing, 7:15.

> There is a vanity that takes place on earth, that there are righteous people who are treated according to the conduct of the wicked, and there are wicked peo-

---

21 See, for example, Jeremiah 12:1-2; Job 21:7-26.

ple who are treated according to the conduct of the righteous, 8:14.

> Again I saw all the oppressions that are practiced under the sun. Look, the tears of the oppressed – with no one to comfort them! On the side of their oppressors there was power – with no one to comfort them, 4:1.

How does one appropriate passages such as these? We are more likely, I think, to identify with Ecclesiastes or Job. We are certainly well aware of how unjust the world is, and of how limited is the insight that good behaviour is the key to a long and peaceful life. We also look at these passage through the lens of the constant mistreatment of prophets and visionaries, including Jesus, the supremely righteous sufferer.

Complicating matters, for the earlier Biblical writers, was that they did not believe in life after death, at least in life after death understood positively. For most of the period during which the Hebrew Scriptures were being written, people believed that to die was *almost* to become non-existent. The place of the dead was a cold, dark, miserable place called Sheol occupied by the semi-conscious or unconscious souls of the dead. And so, the writer of Psalm 6 can write, 'In death there is no remembrance of you; in Sheol who can give you praise?'[22] The writer of Ecclesiastes put it this way:

> The living know that they will die, but the dead know nothing; they have no more reward, and even the memory of them is lost. Their love and their hate and their envy have already perished; never again will they have any share in all that happens under the sun … Whatever your hand finds to do, do with all your might; for there is no work or thought or knowledge or wisdom in Sheol, to which you are going.[23]

The idea that there might be a life after death like this life, and, what's more, a full-bodied and fully conscious life, only emerged at the very end of the Old Testament period, and into the Inter-Testamental period.[24]

As 21st century Christians, what do we make of that? How do we appropriate teaching that we recognise is inaccurate or not yet fully enlightened? The simple answer is: we understand it in those terms. We recognise that we are blessed with increased knowledge, which gives us renewed hope. Not that

---

22   Psalm 6:5

23   Ecclesiastes 9:5f, 10.

24   For a detailed study of the emergence of the idea of resurrection, see N. T. Wright, *The Resurrection of the Son of God*, Minneapolis: Fortress Press, 2003.

the problem of evil and suffering is thereby solved. It isn't. In fact, as Jewish theologians embraced the idea of a blessed and fulsome life after death, to be enjoyed by the righteous, they also embraced the idea of post-death punishment for the unrighteous. This solution to the problem of an unjust world created its own new set of ethical problems. This has certainly been the case for very restrictive doctrines about who will be saved and who will be lost, especially if those who miss out are believed to be doomed to eternal conscious torment. Solutions can also become problems. However, the point is that appropriation will sometimes involve recognizing the inaccuracy of earlier-held beliefs.

Slavery

I've heard people say, 'The Bible might not be scientifically accurate, but in matters of morals or ethics, it is faultless.' I don't think this is borne out by what we read in the Bible. The Bible contains practices which are morally objectionable. Some of these practices are enshrined in legislation purporting to come directly from God. For example, Exodus 21 contains the following instructions about how the Israelites were to treat their slaves:

> If you buy a Hebrew servant, he is to serve you for six years. But in the seventh year, he shall go free, without paying anything. If he comes alone, he is to go free alone; but if he has a wife when he comes, she is to go with him. If his master gives him a wife and she bears him sons or daughters, the woman and her children shall belong to her master, and only the man shall go free, (Ex 21:2-4).

> If a man sells his daughter as a servant, she is not to go free as menservants do. If she does not please the master who has selected her for himself, he must let her be redeemed. He has no right to sell her to foreigners, because he has broken faith with her. If he selects her for his son, he must grant her the rights of a daughter. If he marries another woman, he must not deprive the first one of her food, clothing and marital rights. If he does not provide her with these three things, she is to go free, without any payment of money, (21:7-11).

> When a slave owner strikes a male or female slave with a rod and the slave dies immediately, the owner shall be punished. But if the slave survives a day or two, there is no punishment, for the slave is the owner's property, (21:20-21).

These commandments, introduced as direct instructions from God, offend our sensitivities at a number of levels. We are likely to believe that slavery is morally objectionable, in large part because of a number of objectionable assumptions which underlie the above instructions. Slaves are considered the property of slave owners. They own the slaves, and, because they are property, slaves have fewer rights than free individuals. Slave owners escape sanction, even if they beat their slaves mercilessly; even if their slaves die as a result of this mistreatment, unless they die just a day or two after being beaten. The children of slaves are considered the property of their masters.

Some may argue that these instructions are enlightened by the standards of the day, and that may be true, but we no longer believe that such behaviour and such an institution is acceptable, even though the Bible nowhere condemns slavery.

How do we appropriate these verses from the Jewish Bible? We rightly say that slavery and the assumptions which underlie it are inconsistent with the high view of humankind found elsewhere in the Bible, and expressed supremely by Jesus. These commandments are no longer relevant. However, they remind us that certain things that are said and even commanded in the Bible cannot now be accepted as morally adequate.

Women and men

It was not just slaves who were considered to be the property of others. Throughout the Biblical period, women and children were also considered the property of their husbands and fathers, reflecting contemporary practice. A man could sell his daughter into slavery, for example, or to become a concubine of some other man. If a man wanted to marry a woman, he had to pay a bride price to that woman's father. Thereafter, the wife would become the husband's property, and she would be expected to refer to him as her 'master' or 'lord', in much the same way as a slave would address his master or lord.

This idea of women being the possession of men was enshrined in Old Testament law. For example, if a virgin was raped, the rapist was required to pay a fine, not to her, but to her father whose possession she was.

Patriarchy gave authority and therefore power to men, power which they could choose to misuse if they wished, with very few legislative constraints. This unequal distribution of power may well have had some justification in terms of the protection of women and children, who, at various times in their lives, were in need of greater protection. However, it could also, and easily, be abused, not just in individual cases, but also systemically in legislation which almost inevitably favoured those with greater power. This is true of Old Testament legislation, which clearly and disturbingly favoured men. Women needed to prove their virginity before marriage.[25] Men didn't. If a woman was found to be a non-virgin upon marriage, she was to be stoned to death,[26] but no such penalty applied to a man. If a wife was suspected of adultery, she had to go through an elaborate ritual to prove her innocence,[27] but men had no such test. A man could divorce his wife relatively easily.[28] No such right existed for the wife.

How do we, as 21st century Christians, appropriate these unfair legislative requirements? We can do no better than Jesus or St Paul. Both were revolutionary in their respectful treatment of women and children. Jesus gave the power to divorce to women.[29] St Paul mandated that a wife had as much authority over her husband's body as he had over hers.[30] Though it is uncertain whether St Paul intended patriarchy to be dismantled, simply by following the example of his Master, he lay the groundwork for its eventual dissolution. As has been argued previously, we have no good reason to retain patriarchy, and every good reason to jettison it. We certainly have no good reason to retain the Biblically-accepted practice of women being the property of their husbands, especially given the increased risk of abuse, a risk that will always be present and potent while-ever a power differential between a wife and her husband is retained.

Homosexuality

The Bible doesn't say anything about homosexuality, or, at least, not directly. As has been noted earlier, the terms homosexual and homosexuality are recent, as are the conceptualities involved. The idea that a small sub-section of all human populations is sexually and romantically attracted to people of

---

25   Deut. 22:13-19

26   Deut. 22:20-21

27   Numbers 5:11-31. In a case where marital infidelity was proved, a wife was always stoned (presumably because she belonged to another man), whereas the husband was only stoned if his infidelity involved another man's wife, (Lev 20:10, Deut. 22:22-24).

28   Deut. 21:10-14, 22:19, 29:1-4.

29   Mark 10:12

30   I Corinthians 7:4

the same gender, with an orientation which is permanent, involuntary and exclusive, is relatively new. However, the Bible does have things to say which are certainly relevant to a contemporary discussion of homosexuality. It prohibits sex between people of the same gender, for example.

How do we appropriate those bits of the Bible which touch on this topic? The best answer, in my opinion, is to do exactly what we have done with the earlier examples. We begin by initially taking at face value what we read in the Bible. We then move on from first impressions and/or inherited understandings to critical examination of the relevant texts. We take a step back from our passions and prejudices to embark on as disinterested an investigation as we are capable of.

That is not an easy task. Although the Book of Leviticus is unambiguous in its prohibition of men having sex with men, it does not supply a reason for this prohibition, other than that the behaviour is an abomination. We are required to read between the lines to see if we can discover a likely reason or rationale for this prohibition.

There are some clues, the first of which is that this activity is described as an abomination. The use of this word suggests that this is something which is seriously bad, and, in most of the hundred or so instances where it is used, that is what it denotes. Included among abominable activities are: idolatry,[31] harlotry,[32] murder,[33] adultery,[34] child sacrifice,[35] temple prostitution,[36] cheating by using rigged weights,[37] dishonesty,[38] perjury,[39] usury,[40] and oppressing the poor and needy.[41] Not all of these offences are in the top drawer of abhorrent actions. At least some of them we are likely

---

31   Deuteronomy 7:25, Isaiah 44:19

32   Ezekiel 16:22

33   Ez. 18:10

34   Ez. 18:11

35   Jeremiah 32:35

36   I Kings 14:24

37   Deut. 25:13-19

38   Proverbs 12:22

39   Jeremiah 7:9

40   Ez. 18:13

41   Ez. 18:12

to be guilty of, but they certainly do qualify as immoral actions, with the interesting possible exception of usury. However, the Hebrew word for abomination used in Leviticus 18 and 20 is also used of behaviour which we would consider to be anything but immoral, in fact, the opposite. Deuteronomy 14 contains a list of clean and unclean animals, and describes the eating of unclean animals as an abomination. Among the unclean animals are seafood that lacks fins or scales, which would include oysters, shrimps, crabs, lobsters, clams and mussels. Eating them constitutes an abomination, according to Deuteronomy 14, as does eating camels, hares, badgers, pigs, and a long list of birds, as does eating all insects, apart from locusts, crickets and grasshoppers.[42]

These prohibitions seem so very strange to us, and have sometimes been used as ammunition to mock Christians who claim that the Bible's depiction of same-sex intercourse as an abomination is enough, in itself, to condemn the practice forever. It is not. We do need to carefully consider what is meant by the use of this term. A clue to why sex between men is considered an abomination is to be found, perhaps surprisingly, in the notion of things being 'unclean.' Gordon Wenham notes that the word 'clean,' as used in Leviticus, means 'pure,' but more broadly, it approximates our notion of normality. Cleanness is the normal condition of things, animals and people.

Deuteronomy 14 and Leviticus 11 divides the animal kingdom into the clean and the unclean. Clean animals are those who travel in a manner that is appropriate to their class, in the normal way. Fish with scales and fins are clean, but those without these normal aids to propulsion are unclean. The idea of normality underlies the ban on priests with any abnormality ministering at the altar.[43] Wenham's suggestion does not account for all instances of clean and unclean animals. Apparently, there are other factors involved as well. For example, many of the birds which are considered 'unclean' appear to be unclean because of their propensity to come in contact with blood or dead animals. Others appear to be unclean because they don't neatly fit into appropriate categories. Pigs are unclean because they have a cloven foot like cattle, but don't chew their cud. The categorical boundaries separating animals into various 'kinds' is somewhat blurred in the case of animals considered unclean.

---

42   Deut. 14:3-21

43   G. Wenham, *The Book of Leviticus,* London: Hodder and Stoughton, 1979, 20.

These possibilities suggest a reason why the author (or authors) of Leviticus believed that men having sex with men is unacceptable. It is not acceptable because it is not normal, or, in St Paul's terms, is unnatural. That is why Leviticus 18:22 and 20:13 describes it as 'an abomination.' The actual wording of Leviticus 18:22 supports this interpretation. Literally, the verse reads, 'And with (or at) a male you shall not lie the lyings of a woman: it is an abomination.'

The choice of Hebrew words suggests something that is done to a person or at a person; not so much 'with' as 'at.' The action envisaged is penetrative sex. The word 'to lie with' has the same connotation as it has for us. It means having sexual intercourse. The writer could have written 'a male shouldn't lie with a male– full stop,' but he added 'with the lyings of a woman,'[44] probably to make it crystal clear that what is on view here is a male having sex with a male in the same manner as he would have sex with a woman; though with an obvious anatomical variation involved.

Why is such behaviour considered to be so abhorrent? Put very simply, the likely answer is, this isn't what men do. It isn't what men are supposed to do. It is not normal. It is not how they were created. When God created, he set in place various protective boundaries which are not meant to be breached, which are not meant to be blurred. They are there to protect us, to prevent a slide back into chaos. The food laws are a visual aid to remind us of this, and to guide us in matters of greater moral significance, such as same-gender sex.

That this explanation is likely is further supported by the surrounding prohibitions in Leviticus 18 and 20. Also prohibited in these two chapters are:

- having sex with one's next of kin (18:7-18)
- having sex with one's wife when she is menstruating (18:19)
- having sex with one's neighbour's wife (18:20)
- having sex with an animal (18:23)

44   The phrase 'the lying of a male' (*miskav zakhar*) is found in the Book of Numbers. Women who know the lyings of a man are experienced in intercourse. The lyings of a woman is likely to mean what a man experiences in intercourse with a woman, that is, the engulfment of the penis, Rabbi Steven Greenberg, *Wrestling with God & Men,* Wisconsin: Wisconsin Press, 2004, 80.

- having sex with one's neighbour's wife (20:10)
- having sex with one's father's wife (20:11)
- having sex with one's daughter-in-law (20:12)
- having sex with a mother and her daughter (20:14)
- men having sex with animals (20:15)
- women having sex with animals (20:16)

A few things to notice from these lists: (1) almost all the prohibitions are addressed to men, reflecting the patriarchal nature of the society into which these instructions were given; and (2) they are mostly addressed to those understood to be the likely initiators, the ones with the overwhelming power and responsibility in relationships of these sorts. Perhaps the most obvious characteristic of the bulk of these prohibited actions is that they breach boundaries which sensibly should not be breached. A human being should not have sex with an animal, nor with a daughter-in-law, nor with a neighbour's spouse, because such actions violate boundaries which have been sensibly put in place to protect all those involved, including especially the most vulnerable and powerless.

We can resonate with this. We can see how relevant and important this is. We recognise the importance of boundaries, and of the need to protect the vulnerable. In my work as a parole officer, I am constantly reminded of the terrible and long-term impact of paedophilia and rape, not to mention unfaithfulness and other forms of terrible abuse. We can, I think, appreciate and appropriate the deep concerns which underlie these chapters from Leviticus.

We are also likely to resonate with St Paul's distaste for sexually perverse behaviour. He was right to condemn it. St Paul would have known about drinking parties, called symposia, where male and female slaves were brought in as part of the entertainment offered. He would have known of the frequent sexual abuse of girls and boys in the households of Roman citizens, of the trade in young boys who were captured, imported, sold and then prostituted into sexual slavery.[45] He would have known how acceptable it was in Greek and Roman society for a man to have sex with a woman, and then, for variety, to have a younger man to take the role of a woman for him.

---

45   As noted in chapter 3, this heinous trade may well have been in the mind of the author of the vice list in 1 Timothy 1:8-11.

St Paul's critique of Gentile perversity and immorality was well-informed and well-targeted. As New Testament scholar, James Brownson, points out, 'male-male sex in the ancient world was episodic. It was mainly young boys with older men or male slaves and masters. It was not mutual. These were not relationships, they were not marriage and they were not meant to turn into marriage.' Moreover, these activities were viewed as heterosexual 'sexual excess' akin to gluttony.[46] St Paul certainly had plenty of ammunition to construct his critique. However, the question remains as to whether what he wrote has any direct relevance to the issues we are now struggling with arising from emerging contemporary understandings of homosexuality.

We have new information to feed into our reading of these ancient texts. With this new information, and drawing on earlier methods of Biblical interpretation, including hermeneutical practices found within the Scriptures themselves, we have the wherewithal to make promising progress on this issue. New information makes a significant difference to how we understand and appropriate Biblical texts, as has been the case with the Adam and Noah stories. It is just the same on this issue. As suggested earlier in the book, sexual and gender boundaries are not so fixed as once was thought. It isn't the case that there are only males and females. People cannot neatly be divided into heterosexual males and heterosexual females. The very use of the term heterosexual implies the existence of variations, which, as we now recognize, have long existed and have nothing or little to do with what people choose, have nothing or little to do with perversity, but almost everything to do with how things simply are among humans and many animals.

What is increasingly seen as perverse is the inflexible attitude of many Christians, who, because they stubbornly resist or deny advances in understanding on this issue, are continuing to cause hurt and damage to people of varying sexualities. One could also argue that by insisting that homosexual Christians must remain sexually abstinent for life, thus imposing celibacy as an unbreakable life-sentence, we are making it more likely that people will express their sexualities in underhand, unhealthy and perverted ways. We have thus contributed to perversity, in just the same way as the Roman Catholic Church has contributed to perversity and sexual abuse by insisting that all of its priests should remain abstinent.

---

46   For more information see, James Brownson, *Bible, Gender, Sexuality,* 2013.

Whether such insistence is consistent with a Christian's primary responsibility of love, for God and neighbour, will be the topic of the next chapter.

CHAPTER NINE

The Reliable Guidance of Love

I grew up thinking that what one believes, and, in particular, what one believes about Jesus, is more important than almost anything. Believing in Jesus was the key to eternal life. If you believed in Jesus, you would be saved. If you didn't, you'd be in big trouble. Believing was therefore extremely important. It had eternal consequences. I thought it was more important even than love, which, although a good thing, was never going to be enough to get one into heaven. Embedded in this thinking was a true insight, which is that God's favour comes to us as gift, not as something we deserve or have earned. Faith is akin to grateful acceptance, or trust.

Belief never seemed an onerous expectation as I was growing up, but I did, over time, come to see that the sort of belief expected of most Christians is more than simply grateful trust. It involves believing certain propositions, such as that we are unworthy, that Jesus is our Saviour, that he is the Son of God, that love is important once you are saved, and so on. None of these beliefs seemed unreasonable when taught to me as a child. In fact, they were part and parcel of the gospel I happily embraced from my earliest days.

But it wasn't too long before I realised that not everyone believes as I do about even these most basic propositions. Not everyone identified as a Christian, and even among Christians there were differences of opinion. Because I had grown up thinking beliefs were what counted, I categorized people as Christian or non-Christian depending on what they believed. Simply *saying* that one was a Christian wasn't enough, especially if the proof you offered was that you were a good person, or that you were trying hard to love God and neighbour. That was, in fact, enough to disqualify you from being a Christian, because, clearly, you didn't understand grace. There were all sorts of people I didn't think were Christian during my growing up (and even early adult) years. I didn't think Anglicans were Christian at one stage. I was a Methodist.[1] I didn't think Roman Catholics were, or people of Orthodox belief. None of these people understood grace the way I did. And it certainly didn't matter how loving they were. They didn't believe correctly.

Beliefs, of course, are important. They generate action and are important to one's health and well-being. They are sometimes worth fighting for. But I do now wonder if they have been overrated. One of the results of thinking that beliefs were so important was that I devoted myself to studying philosophy. I wanted to know what healthy beliefs looked like, and how one could sensibly form, retain, or discard them. I wanted to subject my Christian faith to critical scrutiny, while also wanting to commend faith as vigorously and scrupulously as I could. I fell in love with apologetics, which is about mounting a defence of key Christian beliefs.

What I discovered was revealing. In wanting to defend key Christian beliefs, it soon became obvious that, for some Christians, the list of key Christian beliefs is long, with a tendency to get longer. It wasn't just the doctrine of grace or the divinity of Jesus or the truth of the resurrection that needed to be defended and commended, it was the penal substitutionary atonement or the inerrancy of the Bible or the need for wives to submit to their husbands. These also needed to be argued for. For some Christians, everything is important.

The second big discovery was that some, in fact many, of the things Christians believe are simply not true. There are Christians who believe that the world is not much older than six thousand years. There are some, I understand, who still believe the world is flat. It soon became obvious to me that Christians around the world hold to an extraordinary variety of truthful and untruthful beliefs. Those who think that their beliefs are all, or even mostly, true are almost certainly wrong. Their belief system is likely to be peppered with untrue beliefs. If believing the right things is so very important to God, then it is strange to find so large a variety of truthful and untruthful, credible and incredible beliefs among Christians.

---

1   The Anglicans I knew had what I thought was a ritualistic faith. They had faith in their rituals, not in Jesus, I thought.

A third big discovery for me was that most of the beliefs Christians hold onto are not well-supported by good evidence. Some have no evidence whatsoever. For example, there is no evidence, outside of the Bible, that Adam and Eve existed or that there was an Exodus from Egypt of fleeing Israelite slaves. Not only is there little or no evidence for many of the Bible's stories, what evidence there is often runs in the opposite direction, making it even less likely that the stories are factual.

A fourth and even more alarming for me (at the time) discovery was that even beliefs as indisputably important as the resurrection of Jesus, or, more fundamentally still, the existence of God, are not so strongly supported by good evidence that one would be intellectually irresponsible not to believe them. The recently retired American philosopher Alvin Plantinga spent many years analysing arguments both for and against the existence of God. He himself devised and revised versions of arguments in favour of God's existence, and believed them to have merit.[2] He saw them as part of a cumulatively strong case for the existence of God. He himself believes in God. He is devoutly Christian. However, he also came to the conclusion that when you take account of all the arguments, both for and against God's existence, the very best you can say is that God's existence is slightly more probable than not. A reasonable thing to do in the light of this uncertain conclusion is to suspend belief and be agnostic. It is certainly not the case that one is compelled to believe in God, or that the evidence is so strong that you would be irrational or immoral not to believe in God.

The same applies to arguments in favour of distinctively Christian beliefs, such as belief in the resurrection of Jesus. Evidence for this event has often been relied upon by apologists, me included, as the linchpin of their case for the gospel's truth. But Plantinga is not persuaded. In his opinion, the historical case for the resurrection of Jesus is weak, too weak to rest one's belief on. Others are likely to disagree, but his conclusion was that even if one had a fine command of the vast literature on the historicity of the

---

2   Plantinga speaks positively of there being 'a whole host of good theistic arguments, all patiently waiting to be developed in penetrating and profound detail'. In this context, he mentions over 30 examples of such arguments. A. Plantinga, 'Christian Philosophy at the end of the 20th Century', in Sander Griffioen and Bert Balks (eds.), *Christian Philosophy at the Close of the 20th Century,* (Kampen: Uitgeverij Kok, 1995), 40, 41.

resurrection, one would 'presumably think it pretty speculative and chancy, its probability being either low or inscrutable.'[3]

It is not that Plantinga doesn't believe in the resurrection. He does. However, as with belief in God, Plantinga has been persuaded, after a lifetime of careful reflection, that the sorts of arguments and evidence that are typically presented to verify the truth of Christianity, including belief in the existence of God, are nowhere near strong enough to verify, or even to successfully defend, key Christian beliefs, let alone the dense superstructure of inherited Christian doctrines. Once again, if rightly believing certain things was so very important to God, one would expect that the evidence would be stronger; one would expect that the way would be made easier to come to these acceptable beliefs.

Perhaps having right beliefs is not as important to God as I grew up thinking. Maybe it is okay with God that we humans have a mixture of true and false beliefs; that we haven't got things all sewn up; that we don't have at our disposal an arsenal of irresistible proofs to enforce compliance with what we take to be God's will. Maybe the situation is more subtle, on purpose. What is interesting about Plantinga's arguments is that they also entail the conclusion that those who confidently proclaim that God does not exist are equally unwarranted in their beliefs. If the arguments both for and against God's existence are as evenly poised as Plantinga suggests, then atheistic overconfidence is as objectionable as theistic overconfidence.

In light of the limitations of arguments, Plantinga suggests a number of promising alternative belief forming mechanisms which are much more direct and experiential in nature than are arguments. People come to believe in God, and in the truth of the Christian gospel, Plantinga suggests, because of the impact of factors such as our observation of the beauty and splendour of nature. We are drawn to belief in God and to the truth and relevance of the major themes of the Christian gospel by factors which go beyond what is provided by arguments and evidence. These processes are not irrational, but are a function of non-argumentative aspects of our belief forming mechanisms. Put simply, there is more to life than we can rationally defend or commend by way of careful argument.

---

3   A. Plantinga, *Warranted Christian Belief,* Oxford: Oxford University Press, 2000, 276.

The truth is that we in the West have been much too concerned about what can be established by way of argument. We have been much too dismissive of the non-rational and the experiential. Christians, deeply affected by modernity's quest for rational certainty, have tended to reduce Christianity to a set of propositions that require rational justification; only to find that their justificatory efforts have fallen a long way short of the certainty for which they hoped, leading either to disillusionment and the current mass exodus from Christianity, or, just as alarmingly, to increasingly shrill claims of continuing certainty.

Maybe it is not so important that we are certain. Maybe the beliefs we come to are not as important to God as we might once have thought. Maybe there are other things that are more important. As I have thought about the strange mix of true and false beliefs that characterise the believing lives of Christians, myself included, I have been struck by something of an anomaly; a surprising and promising anomaly. Although there are lots of things in life about which we are uncertain, there are other things about which we can justifiably be confident.

One of those is that humility is a good thing. I am sure it is true that various historical and cultural factors play into our valuation of humility, not least the extraordinary and revolutionary humility of Jesus, who willingly embraced the humiliation of the cross, and who gave us the supreme example of humility. However, humility also makes sense as the entirely appropriate attitude of intellectually and morally weak individuals like us. There is so much we don't know. There are many things we think we do know that time will tell us we didn't know, or didn't know comprehensively, or with proper balance. We are not just prone to error, we race to it, and persist in it, because it suits us, protects us, promotes us. Humility makes very good sense. It has a way of keeping us in touch with reality.

But humility is more than simply acknowledging weakness and limitation, it also involves an attitude of self-forgetfulness in the presence of others. The humble person gives of themselves for the benefit of others, is not concerned about their own glory, which consists of humble self-forgetfulness. We are attracted, we are drawn to humility, and, in the Biblical story, discover that God is humble. Humility is a good thing. It is also integral to other virtues, which are equally attractive and manifestly good.

Compassion is the sister of humility. When we fully own up to the reality of our weakness and limitation, we are much more likely to be compassionate towards others; to not think of ourselves as better, but to empathise, to feel with the struggling other.

The mother of compassion and humility is love. The author of 1 John describes God as love. He writes that when we experience love, we experience God, for God is love (1 John 4:8, 12). St Paul highlighted faith and hope as important, but was convinced that the 'greatest of all is love,' I Corinthians 13:13. I don't know too many people in the world who would disagree with St Paul. There is no good reason to be uncertain about the importance of love. It is something the world has always believed.

Jesus provided a practical guideline for loving when he commanded that we 'do to others as we would have them do to us,' Luke 6:31. In saying this, he assumed, as a given, that we usually have a fairly good idea of what we don't like having done to us. Love demands that we don't do these things to others. This is a 'golden rule,' a rule that does not originate with Jesus. It has a much older ancestry.

Lorraine Parkinson, in *The World According to Jesus: his Blueprint for the Best Possible World*, recounts the story of the great Pharisee Hillel who died when Jesus was in his teens. He was somewhat more liberal than the conservative Jewish scholar, Pharisee Shammai, his contemporary. According to a well-known story, both scholars were approached by a Gentile who wished to convert to Judaism. The Gentile first approached Shammai and said to him, 'Teach me the whole of the Torah while I stand on one foot.' Shammai pushed him away with a stick. The same person approached Hillel, who said, 'That which is despicable to you, do not do to your fellow. This is the whole of the law and the rest is commentary. Go and study it.'[4] Jesus clearly agreed with Hillel.

Parkinson notes that there are several different versions of the Golden Rule, which was first articulated in the sixth century BCE by the Chinese philosopher, Confucius. It occurs in all major religions of the world,

---

4   L. Parkinson, *The World According to Jesus: his blueprint for the best possible world*, Richmond: Spectrum Publications, 2011, 165.

including Baha'i, Buddhism, Christianity, Confucianism, Hinduism, Islam, Judaism, Sikhism, Taoism and Zoroastrianism.[5]

The principles which underlie the Rule make intuitive sense. Generally speaking, the things we don't like done to us will hurt us or diminish or disrespect us, or, more seriously, will dehumanise or degrade us. Our, perhaps inbuilt, moral sense tells us this is wrong, and that we shouldn't do these things. The Rule can also be articulated in positive terms, as an encouragement to do what pleases, respects and enhances the human dignity of the people we encounter and have dealings with, which is to love them. 'Love is patient; love is kind; love is not envious or boastful or arrogant or rude. It does not insist on its own way; it is not irritable or resentful; it does not rejoice in wrongdoing, but rejoices in the truth. It bears all things, believes all things, hopes all things, endures all things,' 1 Corinthians 13:4-7.

We can recognise love when we see it. We know it is good. We hardly need to have it taught to us. Which brings us back to what God might expect of us. Although it is unlikely that God expects us to have a comprehensive and fully accurate set of beliefs, especially given that the Biblical writers weren't disabused of their erroneous cosmological, anthropological and even theological ideas, it is likely that God expects us to love.

Love is a good thing. It ought to guide us in what we do, but it can also guide us in what we think. Love is not simply the key to good practice, it is also a key to good thinking, and also good theology. St Augustine, the Bishop of Hippo in North Africa (354-430 CE), recognized this. For him, love was a key to Biblical interpretation.

Love as a guide to interpretation

St Augustine counselled that we rise above the Bible's details to discover the Biblical heartbeat. At the centre of that heartbeat is love: God's persistent and patient love for his creation; a love that both creates and recreates; a love that forgives and keeps forgiving; a love that restores and transforms; a love which does not give up on the created order, creating hope which is also the heartbeat of the Biblical narrative. It is 'faith, hope and love which persist, and the greatest of all is love,' 1 Corinthians 13:13.

---

5   *The World According to Jesus,* 165.

Understanding the Bible's heartbeat means that we resist the tendency to be distracted by contentious details. St Augustine was impatient with people in his day who spent their time disputing over this or that interpretation of some part of the Bible, thereby missing bigger points, including love:

> Let no one irritate me further by saying, 'Moses did not mean what you say. He meant what I say… They speak as they do not because they are men of God or because they have seen the heart of Moses, your servant … but simply because they are proud. They have no knowledge of the thoughts in his mind, but they are in love with their own opinions, not because they are true, but because they are their own. If this were not so, they would have equal respect for the opinion of others, *Confessions* 12.25.

St Augustine emphasised the clarity of the 'light that shines from the Lord our God,' which he contrasted to uncertainty about what a fellow human being might have meant by his words. In disputes about particular interpretations, we need to be humble, recognising the possibility of alternative interpretations, but, at the same time, we can be unified and agreed on what is clear, and among those clear things is the central importance of love:

> When so many meanings, all of them acceptable as true, can be extracted from the words that Moses wrote, do you not see how foolish it is to make a bold assertion that one in particular is the one he had in mind? Do you not see how foolish it is to enter into mischievous arguments which are an offence against that very charity for the sake of which he wrote every one of the words we are trying to explain? *Confessions* 12.25

Given that love is the Bible's central and most important theme and virtue, it is a betrayal of the Bible, and therefore of God, to insult others in the name of the Bible. We thereby 'make the Lord a liar,' *Confessions* 12.25. Karen Armstrong sums up St Augustine's thinking in these terms, 'Any interpretation of Scripture that spreads hatred and dissention was illegitimate; all exegesis must be guided by charity.'[6]

The need to have exegesis guided by love is important in all areas of dispute currently dividing Christians. It is not just that love ought to characterise the manner in which we disagree, along with our attitude to those with whom we disagree. It should also guide our interpretation of Biblical texts.

---

6   K. Armstrong, *The Bible*, New York: Grove Press, 2007, 125.

If the heartbeat of the Bible is love, because God is love, then we are obliged to interpret and appropriate Biblical texts in ways which are consistent with love. The love-guided nature of our attitudes and conclusions ought to be obvious.

I am afraid that for many people looking on, debates currently wracking the church don't appear to be very loving at all; either in the manner in which they are conducted, or in their conclusions. This certainly applies to debates over evolution and inerrancy and the leadership of women and same-sex marriage. Love is an early casualty of our many disputes as Christians. The watching world isn't impressed.

With respect to same-sex marriage, those looking on are especially mystified, because the sort of love for which Christians believe they ought to be known appears to be almost entirely absent in what Christians say, and in how they say it. I recognize that impressions are often misleading, and acknowledge that Christians opposed to same-sex marriage do believe they are being guided by love, and often are genuinely empathetic in their attitude to their LGBTI brothers and sisters, but that is not how it all too often comes across; and this is so not simply because of the distorted bias of unsympathetic media. People are genuinely perplexed by what appears (on the outside, but also on the inside) to be a lack of consistency with Christianity's deepest of all convictions, especially love.

It just doesn't seem right that Christians would speak so negatively and dismissively of a small and long-persecuted minority within our societies; should seem so anti-gay, so insistently against what might otherwise be seen as a generous expansion of the meaning of marriage to include a previously oppressed and misunderstood minority. Christians, in this, seem so un-Christ-like, so unlike their Master whose love had him bravely identifying with the outcasts of his society, oblivious to the impact on his reputation, oblivious to whether his associations might be interpreted as a condoning of immoral behaviour. Jesus loved. His contemporary followers are not so well known for their love.

Love must guide us in all we do, including our interpretation of Scripture. Dale Martin, an interpreter of great skill, who lectures in New Testament Studies at Yale University, emphasises the importance of love in Augustinian-like terms:

Any interpretation of scripture that hurts people, oppresses people, or destroys people cannot be the right interpretation, no matter how traditional, historical, or exegetically respectable. There can be no debate about the fact that the church's stand on homosexuality has caused oppression, loneliness, self-hatred, violence, sickness and suicide for millions of people. If the church wishes to continue with its traditional interpretation it must demonstrate, not just claim, that it is more loving to condemn homosexuality than to affirm homosexuals. Can the church show that same-sex loving relationships damage those involved in them? Can the church give compelling reasons to believe that it really would be better for all lesbian and gay Christians to live alone, without the joy of intimate touch, without hearing a lover's voice when they go to sleep or awake? Is it really better for lesbian and gay teenagers to despise themselves and endlessly pray that their very personalities be reconstructed so that they may experience romance like their straight friends? Is it really more loving for the church to continue the worship of 'heterosexual fulfilment' (a 'non-Biblical' concept, by the way) while consigning thousands of its members to a life of either celibacy or endless psychological manipulations that masquerade as 'healing'?

The burden of proof in the last twenty years has shifted. There are too many of us who are not sick, or inverted, or perverted, or even 'effeminate', but who just have a knack for falling in love with people of our own sex. When we have been damaged, it has not been due to our homosexuality, but to your and our denial of it. The burden of proof is now not on us, to show that we are not sick, but rather on those who insist that we would be better off getting back into the closet.[7]

Love's presence is obvious. There is a spirit of love, which is the Spirit of God, which is the Spirit of Christ. St Paul urged Christians to test the spirits to see if they are of God. Where love is absent, whether in our attitudes, behaviour, or in our exegesis, God is absent.

In the remaining pages of this chapter, I'd like to explore a little further what this spirit of love looks and feels like, with a special focus on epistemological issues, of how issues of belief and love line up. Love that is genuine and true has characteristics we are likely to notice when we see them.

---

7   Dale B. Martin, 'Arsenokoitēs and Malakos: Meanings and Consequences,' in Robert Brawley, (ed.), Biblical Ethics and Homosexuality: Listening to Scripture, Louiseville: Westminster, John Knox, 1996, 130, 131.

True love is humble and honest

St Augustine's words, quoted above, are worth re-quoting:

> When so many meanings, all of them acceptable as true, can be extracted from the words that Moses wrote, do you not see how foolish it is to make a bold assertion that one in particular is the one he had in mind? *Confessions* 12.25.

St Augustine was observing what we have come to understand more fully, and that is that texts are not so fixed in their meanings that only one acceptable interpretation of them is possible. This applies to the Bible as much as to any text. Ancient exegetes were aware of this. In fact, they made a virtue of the multiplicity of acceptable interpretations. They believed the Bible to be an inexhaustible depository of meanings and applications. Jewish Rabbis writing at or around the time of the New Testament liked to point out that King Solomon was able to devise three thousand parables to illustrate every single verse of the Torah, and could give a thousand and five interpretations of each of those parables – which meant that there were three million, fifteen thousand possible expositions of each unit of Scripture.[8]

Leaving aside the obvious hyperbole, the point is well made. Biblical texts, including all of the key Biblical texts involved in current disputes among Christians, are sensibly able to be interpreted in a range of different ways. We need to acknowledge this and be suitably humble in offering our suggested interpretations.

We need to be humble for all sorts of good reasons. Alvin Plantinga, a man of prodigious talent, once said that the more he studied epistemology the more complicated it got for him. The ocean of knowledge, even on this one subject, appeared to get bigger and deeper the further he waded into it. Even the cleverest of people knows only a fraction of what there is to know. But not only are we limited in brain power and capacity, we are also adept at getting things wrong, for all sorts of reasons, some of which I will explore later in this chapter.

Add to that the inbuilt limitations of our reasoning processes. In the matter of Biblical interpretation, what often happens is that we opt for one interpretation (among many) of a verse or passage, then combine it with

---

8   Armstrong, *The Bible*, 81.

one interpretation (among many) of another passage, and of another, and another, in the sensible process of trying to arrive at generalisations that will guide us towards further conclusions. This, essentially, is the process of systematic theology. But it is fraught. Suppose that where you choose to begin this process you make a poor decision, or even a reasonable decision, which will take you in one direction, when other directions were always possible. At every step along the way, you will be required to make decisions which have the potential to usher you towards wildly different conclusions from someone sensibly following another track of reasoning.

This can be well illustrated by reference to the vexed issue of homosexuality. Leviticus 18:22 prohibits men from 'lying with the lyings of a woman' with other men. We are not exactly sure what this means, but what seems likely is that the ancient legislator, believing himself to represent God's view on this, is forbidding sexual intercourse between men. If one were to be a complete literalist at this point one could point out that this does not prevent affection between men, or romance, or even erotic encounters, so long as intercourse is avoided. What this illustrates straight away is that we very quickly, naturally, and legitimately, draw inferences from verses like this. We are not strictly literalists. We go beyond the actual words to discern the spirit and larger import of what is said. We go looking for principles, and so we should. But it is at this level of inference that we can get into trouble. It is at this level of inference that other elaborations and explanations are possible. The track we begin walking down might not be the only track we can legitimately explore.

This verse from Leviticus, so deceptively simple on first reading, raises a raft of questions which are likely to take interpreters down different roads. For example, why did the ancient legislator not prohibit sexual activity between women? Why is it that there is no (or at most one) Biblical condemnation of women having sex with women?[9] Was it because, in the ancient mind, sex was identified with sexual intercourse; and therefore women were considered unable to have sex with each other, and so there wasn't the same

---

9   As noted in an earlier chapter, the only possible reference to women having sex with each other is in Romans 1:26. It is not at all certain that sexual relationships between women is on view in this verse. As pointed out by Brownson, for the first 300 years of church history the verse was understood to refer to non-coital or non-procreative forms of heterosexual intercourse, *Bible, Gender, Sexuality*, 225. For debate about this issue, see *Bible, Gender, Sexuality*, 160, note 20.

interest in them at this point? Another highly relevant question is: what exactly was it about this activity which was objectionable? Was it because it violated the marriage norm of Genesis 2? Was it because it was extra marital? These suggestions don't quite stack up with other legislation which appears to at least tolerate men having sex with their slaves or concubines. Is it because such activity involves one of the men taking the place of a woman, thus demeaning his masculinity, thereby upsetting a created order considered fixed? Perhaps. There are a number of reasonable possibilities, some more likely than others, but all of them able to become the building blocks of contrasting theologies and associated ethics.

An important question for today's Christians is: what do we do in the face of reasonable uncertainties? How do we decide which path to walk down, or, if we have decided to walk down one path, how do we think about those who have walked down another path? The simple and I think right answer is that we love and are guided by love. We love those with whom we differ as much as we hope they will love us. But we can also be guided by love in deciding which path to walk down, or to remain on. Love can and should be our guide in how we think, in how we exegete, in how we do our theologising, in how we accept, or set aside, conclusions. If our conclusions make it more likely that people will be hurt or oppressed, or that love for God or neighbour will be undermined, we will have good reason to go back to the drawing board to rethink our exegesis and theology.

Love can do that. James V. Brownson, whose skilful and careful exegetical work has hugely assisted me in the writing of this book, shares with his readers a powerful example of love's influence in this own thinking and rethinking. Five years prior to writing *Bible, Gender and Sexuality*, Brownson was a moderate traditionalist when it came to issues of homosexuality, but then something happened that radically altered his life, in his words:

> [My] eighteen-year-old son told my wife and me that he believed he was gay. I wish I could say that, since I had always been such a thoughtful and empathetic scholar, when I was faced with this case in my own family, I would simply find the conclusions I had already arrived at in my prior study on this subject to be adequate. But I must confess – to my regret and embarrassment – that this was not the case. I realized, in fact, that my former work had stayed at a level of abstraction that wasn't helpful when it came to the concrete and specific questions I faced with my son. Indeed, the answers that I thought I had

found seemed neither helpful nor relevant in the case of my son.

For example, I had made a sharp distinction in my earlier thinking between homosexual *orientation* (which my denomination had declared was not necessarily sinful) and homosexual *behaviour* (which, I had believed, was forbidden in Scripture). But in my son's case, the issue was not sexual activity; he was simply trying to understand his own emotional makeup and disposition. The traditionalist treatment of sexual orientation seemed shallow and unhelpful to my wife and me when we looked at our son. We found the neo-Freudian explanations for the familial origins of male homosexuality (absent father, dominant mother) to make little sense in the dynamics of our household. Moreover – and this was perhaps the most important thing – our own son's resolute good humor and good will, his natural leadership abilities and good grades in school, his physical strength and quickness (a black belt in Tae Kwon Do), and his easy-going nature all seemed clearly and self-evidently to say, 'There is nothing wrong here!' Or to put it more precisely, we considered him a normal and healthy high school senior, someone in need of the grace of God, as we all are, but not deeply troubled (apart from his anxiety about talking to us about his sexual orientation).[10]

Brownson didn't change his mind straight away, but his love for and experience with his son helped to guide him and now many others along a different path.

True love is courageous

Love that is humble and honest will also need to be courageous. It takes courage to admit your opinion might be wrong; that although you hold it to be true, the best you can often say is that it is likely or probable, or, from your point of view, the best possible explanation you've come across. In ten years' time you might think differently. It takes courage to admit this, especially when you are passionate about what you believe, especially if you think the issue you are arguing for is a matter of justice or fidelity to the Scriptures. The cause may be so important to you that you risk undermining it if you admit uncertainty, especially if you are one of the cause's leading spokespersons.

Sociologists have become aware of some pretty scary ways in which people can get caught up in habits of thought and action, which, over time, can undermine honesty and humility, and which can also have the effect of

---

10   *Bible, Gender, Sexuality*, 11, 12.

making it increasingly hard for people to be courageous. One such way of thinking and acting is captured by the notion of culpable ignorance.

Culpable ignorance

West's *Encyclopedia of American Law* defines culpable ignorance as 'the lack of knowledge or understanding that results from the omission of ordinary care to acquire such knowledge or understanding.'[11] Margaret Heffernan defined culpable ignorance in these terms, 'If there is knowledge that you could have had and should have had, but chose not to have, you are still responsible.'[12]

The associated legal concept of willful blindness originated in the 19th century.[13] The judge in the case of Regina v Sleep (1861) ruled that an accused person could not be convicted for possession of government property unless the jury found that either he knew the goods came from government stores or he had 'willfully shut his eyes to the fact.'[14]

In the early stages of writing this book, a high profile court case involving South African Olympic athlete Oscar Pistorius was coming to its conclusion. He was accused of murdering his girlfriend, but was found to be guilty of culpable homicide. His defense was that he believed an intruder had entered the apartment where he and his girlfriend were sleeping, and, believing they were in danger, had fired shots through the bathroom door, accidentally killing his girlfriend. The judge in the case accepted that there was reasonable doubt about whether Pistorius intended to kill his girlfriend, but found him guilty of negligence; of not taking steps that he reasonably could be expected to take to verify or falsify his belief that an intruder had entered his flat. He was therefore guilty of recklessness and morally culpable ignorance.

---

11   West's Encyclopedia of American Law, edition 2. Copyright 2008 The Gale Group, Inc. All rights reserved.

12   *New Statesman*, 8 August 2011: http://www.newstatesman.com/ideas/2011/08/wilful-blindness-essay-news

13   From as far back as Aristotle, theorists have recognised that ignorance is only a legitimate excuse for causing unjustified harm when we are not responsible for our ignorance, that is, when the ignorance is non-culpable (*Nichomachean Ethics*, Bk III).

14   http://www.newstatesman.com/ideas/2011/08/wilful-blindness-essay-news

Culpable ignorance is not uncommon, sadly. It is not uncommon among Christians. All of us, as human beings, tend to be, at least initially, resistant to uncomfortable truths. The reason they are uncomfortable is that they don't sit easily with what we already believe, and our beliefs are usually important to us. We'd prefer not to hear that our beliefs are mistaken, or need to be rethought. And so we tend to look for evidence which confirms our beliefs, while neglecting to seriously consider evidence that might undermine them.

To what extent we are culpable in this is hard to judge. In this book, I have raised serious doubts about quite a number of beliefs that many of my Christian sisters and brothers hold dear. I've suggested that Adam and Eve probably didn't exist as real people, or as the original parents of the human race. That suggestion is unsettling for many. I've suggested much the same about Noah, who I understand to be mythical, as is the story of a worldwide flood. That too is unsettling for some, as are my suggestions about the desirability of ditching patriarchy or of supporting same-sex marriage. Would I suggest that those who believe the opposite of these suggestions and claims are culpably ignorant? No I wouldn't, at least not as a generalization. And one good reason for that is that these suggestions and claims are quite radical in the present setting, certainly for many Christians. It would be unreasonable for them to adopt these positions without a great deal of thought and reflection, and even then, they may come to contrary conclusions.

It may be that I am culpably ignorant in not being careful enough in considering all the available evidence. And who can do that in any case? For most of the things we believe, we have little option but to trust suitably qualified experts in the field with which we are dealing. We don't have the expertise, or the time, to investigate sufficiently. We cannot be culpably ignorant of things we are unable to know. We can trust the experts. But when the experts differ, what do we do then? My dad used to say, 'Don't trust the experts. Make up your own mind. Trust your own instincts and research.' It was good advice in some ways, but knowing my own limitations, I am not so confident that I can reliably come to good conclusions on my own, without the assistance of people I trust who know more than I do on the subject.

However, and to complicate things even further, it is still possible that, in various ways, and to some extent, I am culpably ignorant. Even taking account of my lack of expertise, and my need to depend on others, it is still possible that I have not been sufficiently careful in what I believe and keep believing. It is always possible, and not uncommon, for people to be self-deceived. The process of self-deception involves sometimes unconscious or barely conscious efforts to evade some truth we find uncomfortable. We don't want it to be true, so we find ways of convincing ourselves it isn't. Some of the tactics we are likely to use if we are self-deceiving are: (a) avoiding the subject; (b) distracting ourselves with convenient rationalizations; (c) stubbornly failing to make enquiries which would bring us into contact with relevant evidence, however unsettling; and (d) ignoring the evidence, while persisting in our original beliefs.[15]

It is not hard to think of examples of where we have become guilty of self-deception. And what makes this sad reality so insidious and challenging is that its causes are often systemic and cultural, as I began to explore in chapter 4.

On the blinding impact of ideology

F. A. Hayek wrote that 'without a theory, the facts are silent'. As humans, we require the guidance of larger narratives, including theologies, to help us make sense of our experience, but these narratives and theologies can so easily become inflexible ideologies that can blind us to inconvenient truths. It is not just individuals who can be guilty of self-deception. Groups can be as well. Groups within the grip of ideologies are especially susceptible.

An ideology is a systematized body of ideas and associated values designed to guide and give meaning to those who adopt it. An ideology can be as broad as a worldview or religion, or as narrow as an economic or political theory. Free market capitalism is an ideology, as is communism, as is individualism and feminism and evangelicalism. Ideologies supply a way of thinking about things. They can also be coercive, restrictive and exclusionary. Signing up to an ideology, such as the Gospel Coalition or the Fellowship of Confessing Anglicans, normally means joining fellow ideologues in the promotion and protection of your new (or old) way of

---

15   See further, D. Jones, *Moral Responsibility in the Holocaust: A Study in the Ethics of Character*, Lanham, MD: Rowman & Littlefield Publishers, Inc., 1999, 82.

seeing things. You are quickly socialized into a way of thinking and being which becomes the standard of inclusion for your group. Group loyalty and conformism kick in.

It is at this point that the danger of self and group deception becomes critical. Sociologists have long been aware of the power of conformism. Way back in the 1950s, Solomon Asch of Swarthmore College, Pennsylvania, conducted studies which demonstrated that, in simple tests comparing three vertical lines, most people would rather give an obviously wrong answer that kept them in a group than a correct answer that would make them outsiders. We would rather be wrong, in other words, than alone.

Studies have also shown that the collective wisdom of a group is not more, but less wise than individuals within or without it. Once within a group, people become less likely to question or to think creatively about the beliefs that define the group, because of fears that they might become an outsider. Ideologies create tunnel vision, blinding adherents to disconfirming data, with cognitive dissonance resolved in favour of the faith.

Exacerbating the problem is that ideologies tend towards simplicity and over-generalization.[16] Reality is always more complicated than our ideologies make out. And once you add the complication of group-ism or tribalism and the need to conform, you can quickly end up with dishonesty and the abuse of power. In the hands of its gurus, an ideology can become an instrument of social control. Those with a vested interest in the ideology find themselves tasked with the need to repudiate threatening ideas, to suppress contradictory evidence, and to rewrite history to conform to what the ideology expects.[17]

What makes these dynamics even scarier is that they put people into situations where loyalty to the ideology, or to their fellow ideologues, will have them doing things which they know are wrong. They will then need to suppress this knowledge. They will need the help of rationalizations to justify their actions, and in the process they will have violated their deepest human and Christian values, especially the values of love and humility. I heard once about a minister who, on being appointed to a new church,

---

16   Which, as we noted in Chapter Four, is a frequent characteristic of defensive movements such as fundamentalism and its contemporary incarnations.

17   Described under the heading of paternalism in Chapter Four.

immediately and without consultation, changed the preaching roster to exclude a highly talented and widely respected preacher who had been preaching at that church for some years. His reason? She was a woman. He did not bother to tell her, or to explain his action. He just acted, because his ideology said women should not preach to men. He had justification: the Bible prohibits such behaviour, he believed, but there was no excuse for his behaviour, and no excuse for his lack of love or humility.

Ideologies require leaders to take decisive action, such as this man took, albeit unethically, but leadership is also freighted with risk. Sociological studies indicate a frightening tendency for people to obey leaders, even when such obedience entails violating their values and engaging in unethical acts. Yale psychologist Stanley Milgram conducted experiments into obedience in 1961 which found that most people (roughly 65 per cent) will commit unethical acts when asked to do so by someone in authority. These experiments have been repeated around the world ever since with unchanging outcomes. Milgram described this capacity for humans to abandon their humanity as the inevitable result of people merging their personalities into larger institutional structures. They don't entirely lose their moral sense. Instead, it requires a radically different focus. Their moral concern shifts to how well they conform to the expectations of those in authority over them.[18]

When the leader of an ideological movement acts unethically, justifying his actions in terms of the ideology, we begin to find ourselves in frightening waters. Khaled Abou El Fadl, an Islamic scholar,[19] coined the phrase 'salvational cause amorality' to describe the tendency of ideologues to subvert the core values of those caught up in them. He, like most of the rest of us, have looked on in horror as Islamic State militants perpetrate unspeakably cruel acts on those not willing to sign up to their particular take on Islam. As he explained:

---

18   Milgram first described his research in 1963 in an article published in the *Journal of Abnormal and Social Psychology* and later discussed his findings in greater depth in his 1974 book, *Obedience to Authority: An Experimental View*.

19   El Fadl is the Omar and Azmeralda Alfi Distinguished Professor of Law at the UCLA School of Law, and the Chair of the Islamic Studies Inter-departmental Program at UCLA. He has written a number of books, including *The Great Theft: Wrestling Islam from the Extremists*, (2007).

I [recently] put myself through the gruelling chore of watching Islamic State videos posted on YouTube. It was not long before I was beside myself with absolute disgust at the ease by which these people dispatched the wounded, indulged in executions, and pursued and killed panicked and terrified retreating soldiers.

In the same night, I watched Iraqi soldiers torturing captured Islamic State fighters by slashing their backs with knives and rubbing salt in their wounds before executing them. However, it was a comment made by one of the Iraqi soldiers that captured my attention. His comment was something to the effect that normally torturing the captives and spitting on the corpses of the dead would be *haram* (a sin or immoral), but not in the case of these people because they are no better than insects. [20]

Ideologies beget or strengthen the hand of competing ideologies which are then used to justify actions which would normally be considered immoral, such as torture. They say truth is the first casualty of warfare, and it almost always is, as propaganda is constructed to vilify and dehumanise enemies who we then think we can justifiably crush like insects.

People come to believe that their cause is of such value that it justifies them in ignoring ethical obligations. The pursuit of the cause has sufficient merit to absolve them of whatever misdeeds they might commit. Normal ethical imperatives, such as the imperative to love or to be humble, are made subservient to the cause; with love and humility needing to be reinterpreted. Almost any means are justified, given the unsurpassed importance of the ends.

All of the above suggests that there are major challenges facing those who find themselves signed up to any ideology, to any idealised vision of how life is and ought to be, and that includes Christians. That includes me as an idealistic Christian. Ideologies have been a big part of my life. I grew up a fundamentalist, with encouragement to consider liberal Christians the 'enemy.' I was also, from my earliest days, an evangelical, and, in time, a Reformed evangelical. In my early adulthood, I shed Arminianism for Calvinism, under the influence of Anglican evangelicalism of the Sydney variety. I have forever been immersed in 'isms.'

20 *Khaled Abou El Fadl,* 'All for a Good Cause? Islamic State and the Delusions of 'Salvational Cause Amorality', *ABC Religion and Ethics, 17 Oct 2014.* http://www.abc.net.au/reslib/201408/r1321974_18309654.jpg

The truth is: we cannot avoid 'isms' and ideologies, despite their provisional and imperfect nature. We cannot escape them, nor should we try. Ideologies, understood positively, are simply our best efforts to understand complex reality, and to plot a course for our lives. Although they can be inflexible, abusive, exclusive and violent, they can also guide us towards better ways of thinking and living. And, to again return to the theme of this chapter, this is where love comes into its own as one of the most reliable guides.

In assessing the strengths and weaknesses of competing ideologies and practices, we can, and should, weigh them up according to how well they promote or are consistent with love; love for God and love of neighbour. Uncertainty, or humility in believing, need not paralyse us from love-guided action. It need not prevent us from joining what we consider are good causes. Love should motivate us to courageous and costly action.

I will finish this chapter with two examples of people who have endeavoured to be guided by love in their thinking and actions. The first person is John G. Stackhouse, the Chair of Theology and Culture at Regent College in Vancouver, Canada. Stackhouse, for many years, had a patriarchal understanding of the relative roles of men and women, but was 'converted' to egalitarianism, and tells the story of this conversion in a book of similar stories, entitled, *How I changed my mind about women in leadership* (2010). Crucial to Stackhouse's change of mind was the sorry impact of efforts to reimpose patriarchy. In his words:

> I needed to *feel* something of the pain of patriarchy: of being interrupted or ignored in conversation, of being passed over for recognition and promotion, of receiving condescension or suspicion instead of welcome partnership. And I needed to be confronted with [the anger of those so treated], with their refusal to be treated this way anymore.
>
> Women have entrusted me with great gifts: their stories and their feelings about what they have been through and continue to encounter. My wife has told me of how people ignore her or interrupt her. Female friends, colleagues, and students have testified to the suffering they have endured – from conversational condescension to professional marginalization to marital oppression to actual sexual or physical abuse.[21]

---

21   J. G. Stackhouse, 'How to Produce an Egalitarian Man' in *How I changed my mind about women in leadership*, Alan F. Johnson (gen. ed.), Grand Rapids: Zondervan, 2010, 241.

Stackhouse began to listen in ways he hadn't before, and what he heard and saw persuaded him that the most loving thing to do was to ditch patriarchy in all of its damaging forms.

A second person who was guided by love in his thinking and actions was David P. Gushee, known to many as the leading evangelical ethicist in the United States. Gushee followed a similar path of listening, and, in his case, his listening reached all the way back to the beginnings of Christianity, and what he 'heard' disturbed him:

> I believe that the Church has inflicted a damaging and ultimately *unchristlike body of Christian tradition, amounting to what can fairly be described as a teaching of contempt*, against sexual minorities – today called lesbian, gay, bisexual, and transgender persons. This teaching of contempt has been grounded in what is actually a relatively small number of biblical texts, as they have been interpreted by Christian leaders and reinforced by centuries of Christian tradition. It is hard to find many dissenters to this tradition, as it has been grounded in knowledge sources at the very centre of Christianity: scripture, tradition, and the leaders of the church, generation after generation. Everyone just knew that gay, lesbian, bisexual, and transgender people were well worthy of the church's rejection and disdain – not just in their sexual desires and practices, but in their persons. For some Christians, even today, being anti-gay became woven into the heart of Christian identity and even piety.
>
> The church's anti-gay teaching is comprehensive. The Church taught a disdain for LGBT people as a whole and all individuals in the group. The Church sometimes taught that LGBT people are morally inferior. The Church sometimes taught that LGBT people are evil. Certainly it taught and sometimes still teaches that LGBT people are by definition excluded from heaven. The Church warned its adherents about associating with LGBT people. The Church, at various times, ascribed particular vices to LGBT people, including sexual degeneracy, especially against children.
>
> While the leaders of the Church almost never explicitly taught that its members should perpetrate violence on LGBT people, they were, and sometimes still are, victimized by outbreaks of violence. When LGBT people were excluded or targeted by the state, few Christians could be found to stand up for LGBT people.[22]

---

22   Gushee, *Changing our Mind*, 133, 134.

As Gushee reflected on this long history of misunderstanding and abuse, he was prompted to rethink his inherited beliefs, with an experience much closer to home influential in this rethink. He explains:

> My beloved baby sister, Katey, a single mother and a Christian, who had been periodically hospitalised with depression and anxiety, including one suicide attempt, came out as a lesbian in 2008. Her testimony is that her depression was largely caused by her inability to even acknowledge her sexuality, let alone integrate it with her faith – and this was largely caused by the Christian teaching she had received.
>
> The fact that traditional Christian teaching produces despair in just about every gay or lesbian person who must endure it is surely very relevant information for the LGBT debate. It is certainly shattering news when it comes home to your family.
>
> Since Katey's decision to come out, she has been much healthier and happier, though she has struggled to find accepting Christian communities … I love my sister. Her coming out, and my conservative family's transformative experience of relating to her and now her partner, Karen, have been transformative for me.[23]

This, and other 'transformative encounters'[24] not only led to Gushee's change of mind, they inspired him to love-driven action in the pursuit of justice and greater understanding. In the final chapter of *Changing our Mind*, Gushee laments the vilification of courageous gay Christians such as Matthew Vines, who have taken the lead, in Vines' case as an evangelical Christian, in helping to bring about changes of heart and mind. In his words:

> Matthew Vines and friends, you impress and inspire me.[25] You are a youth-led movement in the Church demanding a better future for the whole Church. You are a movement for the liberation of the oppressed, like many of the most important movements for human dignity in history. You are a movement of high energy and distinctively evangelical hopefulness based on the power of

---

23   *Changing our Mind*, 118, 119.

24   As Gushee describes them in *Changing our Mind*, 110.

25   Matthew Vines is a gay, evangelical Christian who is in the vanguard of a small, but growing movement of evangelical Christians who are questioning historic understandings of homosexuality. His book, *God and the Gay Christian: The Biblical Case in Support of Same-Sex Relationships*, New York: Convergent Books, 2014, has been widely influential.

God to advance God's kingdom. You are a movement whose time has come.

I henceforth oppose any form of discrimination against you. I will *seek to stand in solidarity with you who have suffered the lashes of countless Christian rejections.* I will be your ally in every way I know how to be.[26]

It is hard to find fault with such a loving and courageous approach, regardless of what conclusions we have come to thus far on this and on other issues currently exercising the minds of Christians.

When we do finally make up our minds, we need to have the courage to speak up and to act, reliably guided by love.

---

26 *Changing our Mind*, 144.

CHAPTER TEN

The Resilience of Hope

Not all Christians are pleased by efforts to change the Church's mind about homosexuality. Many fear that any weakening of resolve on this issue will emasculate the Church and reduce its witness to irrelevance. Worse than that, it will undermine the gospel. Former Archbishop Peter Jensen, speaking at an event in Ireland in June 2015, when the Scottish Episcopal Church was moving in the direction of recognizing same-sex marriage, warned that any such move would involve 'a choice to rewrite the Bible and so the Christian faith.'[1] Many Christians, and many Christian movements, including the Gospel Coalition and the Fellowship of Confessing Anglicans, agree, and this helps to explain the fear that many feel when they encounter secular and Christian efforts to re-define marriage, and to set aside what they consider to be the clear teaching of the Bible.

And, of course, it is not just gay marriage. That is simply the latest in a succession of challenges to long-held Christian beliefs and practices, many of them two and three millennia old. Almost everything appears under threat. It is not just beliefs, but the standing or reputation of the Church which has received a battering. Increasingly, people are embarrassed to describe themselves as Christian. For the first time in a long time, a new rhetoric has begun to be heard, the rhetoric of persecution. Christians feel under attack, exacerbating the fear, fuelling the insecurity, making it

---

1   The Archbishop was reported as arguing that the Bible's teaching on homosexuality is 'crystal clear' and that '[when] the testimony of the Bible is rendered so murky, the authority of the Bible is fatally compromised.' http://www.christian.org.uk/news/backing-gay-marriage-rewrites-bible-warns-senior-anglican

more likely that Christians will feel the need to gather behind barricades of protection against enemies coming from every direction.

The fear being felt by Christians is well-founded, I think. As one looks out from those barricades of protection, what one sees is a world that has stopped believing in the literal truth of the Bible's stories and prescriptions; has stopped believing in the legitimacy of patriarchy; has stopped believing that a full-bodied expression of homosexuality is evil. And because Christianity has been so closely associated with these beliefs, many are concluding that Christianity itself is gone, at least as an intellectually and morally viable option, with the often frantic rear-guard efforts of fundamentalists simply reinforcing the conviction that it ought to go.

It is understandable that Christians are fearful. Is there an alternative to fear? Could there be a fearless faith? I think there can and should be. But it won't come easily.

How can one cultivate a fearless faith? The answer is simple: trust God. Biblical faith is a trusting faith: a faith that trusts even when everything around appears to be crumbling. It is trusting even unto and through death, which is the way of Christ. Dietrich Bonhoeffer, writing from a Nazi prison camp, speculated that Christianity itself might be dying.[2] It hasn't, but it is on its knees and struggling, especially in many of its more dominant forms, and certainly in Western countries like Australia.

Is there hope? I think there is, but only if Christians have the courage to own up to Christianity's present weaknesses and blind spots. In Biblical terms, true and lasting reformation requires genuine and costly repentance.

Getting our houses in order

Failings of the intellect

The first hopeful step towards a fearless faith is an honest admission that the Scriptures are not perfect, as early interpreters of the Bible believed, and as Christians have generally assumed ever since. Not only does the Bible contain errors of fact and understanding, it also expresses attitudes and beliefs which we now rightly believe can no longer guide us. It is a

---

2   At least, as a religion. He understood religions to be historical and temporary forms of human expression. In *Letters and Papers from Prison*, London: Fontana Books, 1959, he raised the question of what a religion-less Christianity might be like.

fully human book, which not only self-critiques, but can be critiqued. Within its pages, we encounter expressions of hatred towards enemies, and prayers that God would destroy them and their families. These prayers are embedded within some of the most devotional parts of the Bible, including the Psalms. Abusive human customs such as slavery are tolerated, with their abusiveness barely moderated by way of inadequate legislation.

Although it can be acknowledged that throughout the unfolding pages of the Bible there is noticeable progress in thinking and acting, even this acknowledgement implies previous imperfection. Moreover, more progress is required. Slavery was put to the sword only after the Bible was written. Patriarchy has taken longer to dislodge. Less than adequate understandings on gender have inadvertently caused enormous suffering to millions of our sisters and brothers. The Bible is not innocent in its very obvious humanity. This must be acknowledged.

Just as the Church has had to open doors to reveal skeletons of sexual misconduct and cover-up, it must also open doors to skeletons lying within the pages of its Scriptures. There is every good indication that there has been dishonesty about who wrote some of the books of the Bible.[3] Christians have not been upfront about this. We have thereby been dishonest.

Christians also need to stop relying on poor scholarship to prop up unsustainable positions. We need to have the courage to admit that we have given weight to scholarship which isn't up to scratch, or borders on, or even is, out-rightly dishonest. St Augustine was embarrassed in his day by Christians spouting forth on things they knew little or nothing about. In his words:

> Usually, even a non-Christian knows something about the earth, the heavens, the other elements of this world, about the motion and orbit of the stars and even their size and relative positions ... about the kinds of animals, shrubs, stones, and so forth, and this knowledge he holds to as certain from reason and experience. Now it is a disgraceful and dangerous thing for an infidel to hear a Christian, presumably giving the meaning of Holy Scripture, talking nonsense on these topics; and we should take all means to prevent such an embarrassing situation, in which people show up vast ignorance in a Christian and laugh it to scorn ... Reckless and incompetent expounders of Holy Scripture bring untold trouble and sorrow on their wiser brethren when they

---

3   As discussed in Chapter 3.

are caught in one of their mischievous false opinions and are taken to task by those who are not bound by the authority of our sacred books. For then, to defend their utterly foolish and obviously untrue statements, they will try to call upon Holy Scripture for proof and even recite from memory many passages which they think support their position, although they understand neither what they say nor the things about which they make false assertion.[4]

Christians have an unenviable record of backing the wrong horse intellectually. They have been in the forefront of resistance to many of the major scientific discoveries of the last two thousand years, with Copernicus, Galileo and Darwin being the most famous of combatants with whom they have losingly locked horns. And that resistance continues in the form of widespread unwillingness to face up to the implications of genetic studies, both for gender and the evolution of humankind. A major reason for this unwillingness has been persistent adherence to the idea that the Bible is without error.

While ever this thinking continues, Christians will continue to resist conclusions which fly in the face of literalistic understandings of what the Bible is saying. I came across a cartoon once in which Jesus is welcoming a keen, youthful-looking man into heaven. They are both depicted as standing above the clouds. Jesus speaks first:

> *Jesus:* Welcome to Paradise! Here you shall spend all of eternity in blissful contentment at my side.
>
> *Newly deceased:* I'm so excited! I led a very Christian life.
>
> *Jesus:* I just have a few qualifying questions, then we can get you checked in. First, did you reject all evidence that contradicts the Bible in the following fields of study: anthropology, astronomy, astrophysics, biology, botany, chemistry, cosmology, ecology, embryology, entomology, evolution, genetics, geology, herpetology, mathematics, palaeontology, plate tectonics, radiometric dating and zoology?
>
> *Newly deceased:* Yes.
>
> *Jesus:* Great! On to question #2. Based on Biblical teaching, do you accept the following as fact: Talking snakes?
>
> *Newly deceased:* Yes, Genesis 3:1

---

4   Augustine, *The Literal Meaning of Genesis*, trans. John Hammond Taylor, NY: Newman Press, 1982, 42-45.

Jesus: Talking donkeys?

Newly deceased: Numbers 22:28

The disturbing thing about the cartoon, for me at least, is that Christians are too often expected to believe things which they have every good reason not to believe. How much better if Christians were released to be in the forefront of scientific discovery? How much better if they were not so resistant to uncomfortable conclusions, but welcomed them as correctives to previously inadequate thinking? How much better if Christians had the attitude that all truth is God's truth, and that it simply cannot (legitimately) be threatening, no matter what we find? As Augustine insisted all those years ago, one must not interpret the Scriptures in such a way as to contradict the adequately credentialed conclusions of good science.[5]

It is not that Christians haven't heeded Augustine's advice. Many have. Most of the very first geologists were Christian, many of them clergymen. When the evidence contained within the rocks they studied contradicted a literal or literalistic reading of the Bible, they were quick to shed that reading, however uncomfortably. Christians were also able, some very quickly, to accept and adjust their thinking in the light of Copernicus, Galileo and Darwin. So it is by no means all Christians who are still fighting every step of the way to retain the notion of a perfect Bible. It is not all Christians who have had to be dragged, kicking and screaming, into newer ways of understanding the world and our place within it. But how good it would be if we were able to stand shoulder to shoulder with every other seeker after truth, willing to walk in whichever direction the quest leads us, regardless of the adjustments we might have to make to our treasured theological formulations. Perhaps then the way of Christ might be more winningly commended.

Perhaps the greatest of all scandals is that Christians who claim to worship Christ as the way, the truth and the life, are not known for their fidelity to the truth; are not known for being guided by truth. In an earlier chapter, I discussed Billy Graham's choice to set aside critical and scientific issues which suggested that his literal reading of the Bible was problematic. At one point during a conference he was attending with good friend Charles (Chuck) Templeton, he said to his friend:

---

5   See, for example, 'The Literal Interpretation of Genesis' 1:19-20; 2:9.

Chuck, look I haven't a good enough mind to settle these questions. I don't have the time, the inclination, or the set of mind to pursue them. I have found that if I say, 'The Bible says' and 'God says' I get results.

Templeton issued him with a sharp rebuke:

Bill, you cannot refuse to think. To do that is to die intellectually. You cannot disobey Christ's command to love God 'with all thy heart and all thy soul and all thy *mind*!' Not to think is to deny God's creativity. Not to think is to sin against your Creator. You can't stop thinking. That's intellectual suicide.[6]

I think Templeton was right, regardless of the results of Billy Graham's many evangelistic crusades.[7] The fact that something works and gets results is not a good enough reason for thinking that Billy Graham made the right decision.[8] We have already discussed how effective strong and decisive leadership can be in forging strong and controlling cultures. Militant Islam is frighteningly successful at the moment. Results tell us almost nothing about whether something is true or good, which leads naturally to a second category of failings for which Christians will need to repent.

Moral Failings

When the topic of moral failings comes up, we immediately and understandably think of sexual abuse cases which have tarnished the reputation of Christian churches around the world, the very same reputation that guided efforts by church authorities to keep the abuse secret, and to silence its many victims. This inexcusable and systemic immorality is now being exposed for the evil it is. There is no question that Christians must fully and sincerely apologise for this iniquity, and take every possible step to prevent recurrences, while fully and generously compensating and supporting all victims, even if that means that churches are thereby bankrupted. Better to be financially than morally bankrupt.

---

6   Quoted in William Martin, *A Prophet with Honour: the Billy Graham story,* New York: Quill William Merrin, 1991, 111.

7   He was right, despite the outcome of his own faith journey, which he describes in his starkly entitled apology for agnosticism: *Farewell to God: My reasons for rejecting the Christian Faith,* Toronto: McClelland and Stewart, 1996.

8   This is not to say that Billy Graham is not to be admired for many great achievements throughout his long and distinguished ministry. I myself have long been an admirer of his.

But there are other immoralities for which there needs to be wholehearted repentance, and reparations made. Christians can be guilty of being secretive and underhand in the way they enforce compliance with their particular take on Christianity. They can discourage questioning. They can suppress inconvenient truths by not 'giving them air.' They can stigmatise doubters and threaten them with exclusion. They can stoop to the use of fear, because fear most definitely 'gets results.' They can simplify complex truths, and then express them overconfidently, whilst also vilifying those who disagree, thus constructing enemies to help create and protect in-group identity. This is a strategy which definitely works. But it is immoral, and it too needs to be repented of, or, once again, the watching world will rightly be unimpressed, as will the victims of these intellectual and social sins.

A friend of mine who went through Moore College with me, way back in the early 80s, and who is now an Anglican Bishop in South Australia, recently provided a poignant example of this 'successful' policy. He was on Facebook discussing issues of abuse within the church when he bravely opened up about his own experience of abuse. He had, for years, advocated for an egalitarian reading of Biblical texts relevant to the issue of women's ordination. It got him into trouble with the powerful anti-women's-ordination culture which was dominant in Sydney. This is what he wrote:

> My wife Fiona and I have experienced significant abuse because of our advocacy of views in this area: social, spiritual and ecclesial abuse for close on three decades. We try hard to wear it with grace, and not return in kind. It is abuse that cuts deeply into our spiritual integrity, my capacities in ministry, as a leader and as a scholar, and my personal identity. We have sought to sit down and explain our experiences for many, many years, and have found no-one among our Sydney Anglican connections (other than egalitarian friends) is interested, let alone willing to allow such views ANY public expression within internal media platforms.

> What is of greater concern is that I am all-too aware of the pain, frustration and disillusionment of the next generation, including a number of my nieces. They have been told to be quiet, not to be trouble-makers, and that being submissive means you are best to avoid questioning any of the voices 'up front.' Their concern is now for their children as much as themselves. Do the Sydney Anglican internal media platforms, conferences or discussions offer them any voice whatsoever (whether to all female audiences or otherwise). No, again

they are either ignored or set aside. I know the extent to which this happens in local contexts.

The abuse I have received has been in the name of complementarianism. It is presented as undeniable 'Biblical truth,' and to question such views is characteristic of those compromising gospel fidelity.

Bishop Tim Harris has had his evangelicalism (and even his conversion) questioned simply because he came to different conclusions about the relevant texts, in context. This is entirely unacceptable. Behaviour such as this brings the gospel into disrepute.

Failures to love

Love was to be the hallmark of disciples of Jesus, the chief means by which they would be known in the world. At times, that was how Christians could be identified. In the early years of the movement, Christians were known for their amazing capacity to care not only for their own, but for pagans, widows and prisoners as well. Their high valuation of women, children and slaves marked Christians out as a very odd, but special people. Many Christians today are known for their love. However, in the public mind, increasingly, Christians are better known for being exclusive, intolerant and hard-hearted.

Here in Australia, we have failed the test of love for not sufficiently taking the side of, and arguing the case for, those who are marginalized and victimized in our midst. This includes our LGBTI sons and daughters, and it includes those who are seeking asylum after fleeing the world's trouble spots, while politicians dishonestly describe them as 'illegal' immigrants. We have not done enough to undo the damage of our terrible mistreatment of our nation's first peoples. We have not spoken up and done much at all to stem the hatred and violence currently being directed towards Islamic people peacefully living in our midst, who are suffering and being abused in angry reaction to atrocities committed in the name of Islam elsewhere in the world. The absence of Christian leaders taking a stand against this violence is embarrassing and deeply disappointing. The absence of Samaritan-like efforts to stand with and beside these hurting and frightened people is yet more proof that Christians have more repenting to do – in this part of the world, anyway.[9]

---

9   There are, of course, any number of admirable exceptions to the generalisations

Theological fine-tunings

Repentance doesn't come easily. Nor does making adjustments to our theologies. But I suggest we have no choice, that is, if we would like to see Christianity rightly win the hearts and minds of those currently walking away from it. We need to get our theological houses in order. To do this, we will need to make some necessary modifications to the following doctrines:

Biblical authority: I am constantly in conversations with people who ask me, 'But what about the authority of the Bible? Isn't it undermined by what you are saying?' The simple answer is: yes. Or, at least, some earlier understandings of Biblical authority are undermined, including inerrancy. Others ask, 'Do you believe the Bible is inspired by God?' I do, although the exact nature and extent of this inspiration is an open question.[10] In thinking about this topic, I have been greatly helped by the German Reformed theologian Jürgen Moltmann. Moltmann differentiated between two types of hermeneutic. The first, a 'hermeneutics from above,' locates the authority of the Bible in God's direct communication with humans through the Scriptures, understood to be God's written Word. The authority of the Bible lies in the God who speaks. This was the view of another great German theologian, Karl Barth. A 'hermeneutic from below,' by contrast, highlights the humanity of the Scriptures, viewing them as time and culture bound testimonies of faith. Moltmann proposes an understanding of hermeneutics in Trinitarian terms. He suggests that we can view the testimonies of faith as expressions of the life and testimony of the Spirit, who is the giver of life. As he puts it:

> It is a movement of thanksgiving and praise, but a movement too of lament and doubt, which proceeds from the indwelling Spirit, through the Son/Eternal Word/the eternal Wisdom, to the Father.[11]

---

contained within this paragraph, but the point is that we've not done or said enough. I long for a day when these exceptions become the norm.

10   2 Timothy 3:16 asserts: 'All Scripture is inspired by God, and is useful for teaching, for reproof, for correction, and for training in righteousness, so that everyone who belongs to God may be proficient, equipped for every good work.' Inspiration is here decisively linked to good works. The Scriptures are inspired for a purpose, that purpose being practical. Further implications, including inerrancy, are more tenuously inferred from this verse.

11   Jürgen Moltmann, *Experiences in Theology: Ways and Forms of Christian Theology,* 2000, 143.

Some such understanding of the Bible's nature and authority makes good sense to me. It certainly allows for the possibility of human error and limitation within and throughout the long process of Biblical composition. It can also help in the process of rethinking or re-appropriating key Christian themes.

Creation: For some time now, it has been obvious that Biblical descriptions of God's creation of the universe and of humankind cannot reasonably be taken literally. That God is, in some sense, and by some means, the creator of the world is certainly the conviction of the Bible's authors and characters. Christianity, and its parent, Judaism, is monotheistic. But questions about the relationship between God and the universe are large and challenging, especially as we gain deeper and greater understandings of natural processes which don't appear to require or invite intervention by a deity.

Fall: In what sense can we now describe human beings as 'fallen'? Genesis 2 and 3 describe a 'fall' into sin and out of intimate relationship with God. It is a provocative and evocative story, which, in its depiction of human frailty, is certainly true to who we are, and can so easily become. But how do we now read and appropriate this story, given our growing understanding of evolutionary processes, some of which are likely to have important things to say about our human nature and propensities. Here is another job for the theologians among us.

Incarnation: Christian theology has been profoundly shaped by the conviction that 'God was in Christ reconciling the world to himself,' 2 Corinthians 5:19. God was 'in' Christ. The author of John's Gospel wrote in his prologue, 'In the beginning was the Word, and the Word was with God, and the Word was God,' John 1:1. Jesus was God in some profound and transformative way, according to the authors of the New Testament. It was this conviction which was the impetus for the development of a theology of the Trinity. Monotheism suddenly got complicated.

Relevant to a doctrine of the incarnation is the question of the extent of Jesus's knowledge. We have noted that Jesus appeared to believe in Adam and Eve, Noah and Abraham, Moses and Jonah. He appeared to accept these Biblical characters and stories as actual and factual. This suggests limitations of understanding and knowledge; limitations one would expect of a first century Jew, but which don't sit so easily with idea that Jesus was

God. It also has implications for our acceptance (or otherwise) of what Jesus said. As a theological lecturer once said to me, 'If Jesus was wrong in some of his beliefs, how can we trust him on other things he said?' That is a fair question, and needs to be thought through.

Salvation: Two of the Bible's major themes are (1) that human beings have a history-long tendency of stuffing up, and of thereby creating havoc for themselves, their neighbours and the created order. Human beings certainly do make a mess of things, and always have. It is hard to argue with the accuracy of this observation. (2) The second major theme is that God, though he could have left human beings to reap the inevitable harvest of their foolish choices and destructive behaviour, set in train a plan to address and overcome this seemingly intractable problem, for the good of humankind, and, ultimately, for the glory of God.

Frederick Beuchner suggests that these pervasive themes can be used to sum up the Bible's central plot:

> I think it is possible to say that in spite of all its extraordinary variety, the Bible is held together by having a single plot. It is one that can be simply stated: God creates the world; the world gets lost; God seeks to restore the world to the glory for which God created it.[12]

These two themes, of human failure and of God's saving intervention, weave their way throughout the pages of the Bible, climaxing with the image of a new heaven and a new earth, its arrival proclaimed in the following terms:

> See, the home of God is among mortals. He will dwell with them; they will be his people, and God himself will wipe every tear from their eyes. Death will be no more; mourning and crying and pain will be no more, for the first things have passed away. Revelation 21:3-4.

It is an inspiring storyline which has nurtured the hopes of countless Christians. However, it is not without its problems. We recognize lostness, and long to be found. We recognise moral failure, and crave forgiveness, and Judaeo-Christianity offers both. However, there is a catch. There is some fine print often added in, with Biblical warrant, and that is that the only way to be forgiven and found is to accept Jesus as your personal Saviour and Lord. Raising the stakes, and putting additional pressure on anyone

---

12   Frederick Beuchner, 'The Good Book as a Good Book,' in *The Clown in the Belfry: Writings on Faith and Fiction,* San Francisco: HarperSanFrancisco, 1992, 44.

considering such acceptance, is that the alternative to being forgiven and found is to be eternally lost, is to suffer the deserved punishment of hell, considered by many to consist of eternal conscious torment.

The Bible is consistent in its message. Evil will be punished. Redemption is possible. But this story, which mostly makes good sense within the pages of the Bible, accumulates problems along the way, especially when set within a wider context. The first problem, overcome within the Bible, is that evil is often unpunished in this life, just as goodness is frequently unrewarded. The idea of justice being done after this life comes to full flowering in the Inter-Testament period and into the New Testament, and it is a welcome idea. However, as people have sought to understand and make sense of the Biblical data, they have become aware of new problems and puzzles, some of them created by the notion of a judgement and afterlife. These have included fair questions about who and how many will be saved and lost? What about people from other religions or convictional bases? What about those who have been disillusioned or hurt by people of faith, or who are not willing, understandably, to sign up to beliefs for which there is so little evidence? Is not eternal conscious torment a somewhat excessive penalty for human sinfulness? None of these questions has an easy answer, and all of them suggest that it would be good for Christians to think long and hard about how they understand Biblical descriptions of hell.

Such rethinking, of course, has been going on for some time. Roman Catholic thinkers, for example, have proposed the notion of purgatory, conceived of as a place where residual unrighteousness can be painfully removed, but in a process that won't last forever. Protestant theologians have proposed annihilation as the destiny of all or most of those who don't end up being saved. Others have argued that all will be saved ultimately.[13] But maybe the best way to approach this topic is to tap into the impulses that led to the emergence and development of ideas about heaven and hell. As I understand it, belief in heaven and hell arose out of the conviction and hope that God's justice and graciousness will one day find lasting expression in worlds beyond this world. The developing doctrines, which have always

---

13   For some carefully argued examples of arguments in this direction, see Eric Reitan & John Kronen, *God's Final Victory: A Comparative Philosophical Case for Universalism*, Bloomsbury Academic, 2011; Gregory MacDonald, *The Evangelical Universalist*, (second ed.), London: Cascade Books, 2012; Thomas Talbott, *The Inescapable Love of God* (second ed.), Eugene: Wipf and Stock Publishers, 2014.

been expressed in metaphorical and this-worldly terms, were the trusting products of hopeful hearts. And, as such, they retain relevance.

Much more could be said about this broad topic of salvation. The task of understanding and appropriating Biblical descriptions of who will be 'saved' and who will be 'lost,' especially when those descriptions are embedded within apocalyptic understandings of the imminent end of the world, is a complex and demanding task.

I have become increasingly aware that the authors of the New Testament believed themselves to be living on the edge of the end of time, with this conviction profoundly affecting their priorities and expectations. In today's world, that expectation has translated into forms of Christianity which are so fixated on end times, and on life after death, that they have all but abandoned concern for this world. Christianity has been reduced to standing on street corners and lifting banners to proclaim, 'The end is near. Repent and be saved.' Somehow, Christianity must rediscover its place within the mucky reality of the here and now, trustingly leaving the future with God. Martin Luther, who believed the end was about to come in his day, once famously said, 'If I knew Jesus was coming back tomorrow, I would go out and plant a tree.' He had his priorities right. Do we?

Risking ruin

The greatest fear, harboured by many Christians, is that if they start to tinker with their theology, even a little, the whole super-structure of their faith will come crashing down. The suggestions made in this book, however plausible or sensible they may sound, are, for many, a recipe for ruin. Far from healing or improving Christianity, they will destroy it, which is the conviction of Peter Jensen, mentioned at the beginning of this chapter. I don't believe he is right, and even if he is, Christianity has no choice but to reconfigure itself if it wants to remain an intellectually viable option for contemporary humans.

A radical rewrite is required, but will it stop the currently rapid demise of Christianity in places like Australia? Will it bring people back into our churches? It might. And then again, it might not. As some evidence that a more liberal or progressive understanding and appropriation of the Christian faith might not succeed in reversing the current exodus from Christian churches is the fact that churches who do adopt something like the approach recommended in this book are bleeding numbers just as seriously, and, in some cases, more seriously than their more conservative neighbours. In the US, for example, the Episcopalian denomination is known for its radical acceptance of same-sex unions. One of its best known clerics, Bishop Gene Robinson, was the first openly gay bishop in the world. Strangely perhaps, in a setting where increasing numbers of Americans are similarly accepting of same-sex unions, numbers attending Episcopalian churches have, for some time now, been in steep decline,[14] as is also the case, to varying degrees of steepness, in other of the more liberal Protestant denominations, including the Presbyterian, Methodist and some Lutheran churches.

Some attribute this decline to the unfaithful jettisoning of conservative doctrines. I've heard it argued that liberal Christians such as Gene Robinson, or the equally famous, or infamous, Bishop 'Jack' Spong, have capitulated to fashionable trends, and are reaping the rewards of their cowardly compromise. But before rushing too quickly to say 'amen' to such a conclusion, it might be worth reflecting a little more carefully. On closer inspection, such claims are unhelpful and likely to backfire.

If growth, or the lack of growth, is any indication of the rightness or wrongness of a cause or movement, then the 'rightness' of Christianity itself is questionable. Thinking in worldwide terms, the fastest growing religious movements, in order, are: atheism, agnosticism, Bahá'í, Spiritualism, Daoism, Confucianism, Sikhism, Islam and Christianity.[15] To the extent that these comparative growth rates tell us anything, one could argue that they strengthen the case for atheism or agnosticism, particularly when one takes into account that these belief systems are likely to have grown most strongly in secularised and Western countries where there is low to negative population growth. Increasing numbers of atheists and agnostics cannot therefore be accounted for in terms of population growth or big families.

It is not sensible, I think, for any brand or sub-grouping of religion to link the rightness of their cause to a growth in numbers. As a perhaps telling

---

14   Since 2000, the Episcopal Church has lost more than 16 percent of its membership, and this on top of decades-long decline.

15   These comparisons are drawn from The World Religion Database (WRD), a database of international religious statistics based on research conducted at the Institute on Culture, Religion and World Affairs at Boston University.

illustration, according to the 2011 Yearbook of American and Canadian Churches, the fastest growing religious movement in North America is the Jehovah's Witnesses. Not far behind is the Church of Jesus Christ of Latter-day Saints, and behind them, the Assemblies of God and the Roman Catholic Church. Evangelicalism, as a pan-denominational movement, is in decline in the US.[16]

Equally fraught is the accusation that more liberal churches are compromising or selling out on the gospel and that that is why their numbers are declining. To again mention the US, a very good case can be made that evangelicals, by and large, but with notable and increasing exceptions, have been far too closely aligned with free enterprise economics and uncritical nationalism, to the serious neglect of issues of justice and stewardship. Evangelicals have been culpably blind to the plight of the underprivileged in their midst, rationalizing their neglect in terms of a preachy individualism that one could argue is a serious betrayal of the Christian gospel. They have appeared blind to the impact of their extravagant materialism on their and the world's environment. They appear to have swallowed, 'hook, line and sinker,' the propaganda of powerful and often rapacious economic interests. Evangelicals need to be careful about throwing stones of accusation from the glass houses they comfortably live within, especially when their numbers are also declining.[17] There is similar neglect and self-serving blindness amongst evangelicals here in Australia.

---

16   According to various sources, including the Pew Research, Religious and Public Life Project, and American Values Atlas, the percentage of evangelical Protestants in the US has declined from 26.3% to 18% between 2007 and 2013; with a much greater decline amongst those in younger age groups.

17   Just days after the US Supreme Court brought down its historic ruling granting the right of LGBTI people to marry, Benjamin L. Corey posted an article suggesting that if God was going to bring judgement upon the United States, there would have already been any number of good reasons to do so, including the genocide of its native inhabitants, the enslavement of black Africans, the maintenance of its power by war after war after war, its poor track record on civil rights, the denying of legal protection and the torturing of terror suspects, resistance to gun law reform continuously costing the lives of thousands, failure to solve the world's food crisis which would cost $30 billion a year, when the US's military budget is over $664 billion, and putting up with the correctable fact that almost half of Americans live in areas where air pollution has reached dangerous levels. http://www.patheos.com/blogs/formerlyfundie/gay-marriage-is-the-law-of-the-land-and-god-isnt-going-to-freak-out-about-it/

The situation is always more complicated than ideologues make out. Even the relative success of Christianity, which is still growing around the world, needs to be carefully understood. In Africa, for example, Christianity has grown, as has Islam. In 1900, Muslims and Christians were relatively small minorities within the religious landscape of sub-Saharan Africa, with the vast majority of people practicing African traditional religions. However, since then, the number of Muslims living between the Sahara Desert and the Cape of Good Hope has increased more than twentyfold, rising from an estimated 11 million in 1900 to approximately 234 million in 2010. The number of Christians has grown even faster, soaring almost seventyfold from about 7 million to 470 million. Sub-Saharan Africa is now home to about one-fifth of all Christians in the world (21%) and more than one-in-seven of the world's Muslims (15%).

Leaving Islam aside, there are obviously many reasons for the spectacular growth of Christianity in Africa, as well as in other regions of the so-called 'Global South.' One might ask: is this growth the result of Africans embracing traditional and conservative Christian beliefs? Is that why God is blessing the growth of Christianity in these areas of the world at the expense of the compromised West? Once again, the situation is more complicated than that. Much of the growth in Christian numbers in the Global South, including Africa, has been generated by neo-Pentecostalism, a movement with historic roots in early twentieth century Pentecostalism and the charismatic revivals of the 1960s and 1970s.

Neo-Pentecostal churches are notable for Biblical literalism, strong charismatic leadership, the claimed witnessing of miraculous signs, and for strong versions of the 'prosperity gospel' - the belief that financial and other success is the result of divine blessing. Sociologists who study the movement, pre-eminently David Martin, suggest that the popularity of these churches is related to the way in which Christianity is linked to access to power.[18] People are drawn to the neo-Pentecostal movement because of the expectation that they will receive tangible benefits, including health, wealth and good marriages. It is not therefore surprising that Neo-Pentecostal versions of Christianity are attracting adherents, especially in less developed regions of

---

18   See further, Christopher Brittain, 'Plague on both their houses: the real story of growth and decline in liberal and conservative churches,' ABC Religion and Ethics, May 2013, http://www.abc.net.au/religion/articles/2013/05/08/3754700.htm

the world. It is also not surprising that conservative versions of Christianity have found a ready home in societies already deeply patriarchal and hostile to any liberalisation of attitude towards homosexuality.

Ironically, perhaps, the characteristics which make Christianity attractive to people in the Global South are simultaneously alienating people in other parts of the world, including Australia, the US and Europe. Two hundred years and more of Enlightenment-generated thought and research has put paid to Biblical literalism, while opening the door to a more ready acceptance of what scientific discovery can teach us about all manner of things, including human origins and gender. As a result, many are mystified by what appear to be archaic and needlessly discriminatory attitudes towards LGBTI people. Christianity and its claims are making less and less sense, especially to younger generations, hence the growth of agnosticism and atheism.

It is revealing, and somewhat alarming, to see how far this trend has gone in the former heartland of Christianity, certainly of Protestant Christianity. Following is a list of European countries ranked according to their belief (or otherwise) in God. The results are from the Eurobarometer Poll conducted in 2010. People were asked to choose one of the three statements at the head of each column.

Country	'I believe there is a God'	'I believe there is some sort of spirit or life force'	'I don't believe there is any sort of spirit, God or life force'
Malta	94%	4%	2%
Romania	92%	7%	1%
Cyprus	88%	8%	3%
Greece	79%	16%	4%
Poland	79%	14%	5%
Italy	74%	20%	6%
Republic of Ireland	70%	20%	7%
Croatia	69%	22%	7%
Switzerland	44%	39%	11%
United Kingdom	37%	33%	25%
Belgium	37%	31%	27%

Country	'I believe there is a God'	'I believe there is some sort of spirit or life force'	'I don't believe there is any sort of spirit, God or life force'
Bulgaria	36%	43%	15%
Finland	33%	42%	22%
Slovenia	32%	36%	26%
Iceland	31%	49%	18%
Netherlands	28%	39%	30%
France	27%	27%	40%
Norway	22%	44%	29%
Sweden	18%	45%	34%
Czech Republic	16%	44%	37%
European Union	**51%**	**26%**	**20%**

Belief in God remains strong in some, mostly Roman Catholic, countries, but in the United Kingdom, France, Germany and the Scandinavian countries, decidedly less than 50% of people profess belief in God. Far fewer attend church. Church going simply does not appeal.

This, for many, is a grim situation. What should Christians do? Broadly speaking, we are faced with two, I think invidious, options. We could choose to remain conservative, following in the footsteps of our predecessors, and inspired by the success of Neo-Pentecostalism. We could simply dig in on matters of doctrine and belief. We'd certainly have a ready-made ally in the second largest religion in the world, Islam, in resisting any liberalisation of views on homosexuality. We'd retain their respect. But if we do so choose, we will continue, certainly here in Australia, to go the way of ageing and dwindling congregations. Australia appears headed in the direction of post-Christian Europe, and I don't see that trend reversing any time soon. Conservative Christianity won't win back those who have left it.

But nor will liberal Christianity, it seems, although a tendency has long been observed that many who come in the front door of liberal churches have walked out the back doors of conservative churches. Nevertheless, the question is: will liberal Christianity win new converts who weren't previously going to church? If not, then the dwindling numbers will continue, with some people simply delaying their exodus by taking one or two detours on the way out.

Given such a disheartening situation, what should we Christians do, regardless of whether we are liberal or conservative. I have three suggestions. The first is:

Do what integrity demands

Integrity is a great word. It denotes wholeness and honesty. It often requires courage. It means being willing to readjust our thinking, if necessary, and to bravely face the consequences. Integrity demands of us that we are honest about what we don't know, and that we pursue even uncomfortable truths. When we suspect that something which is very dear to us might not be true, or might not be true in the way we once thought, we have an intellectual and moral duty to attempt to find out what is true, or, at least, to listen to those who might reliably guide us towards the truth. We will need to be especially vigilant when our prejudices are tugging us away from such an investigation, or nervously urging us not to disturb sacred cows. The danger of becoming culpably ignorant is ever present. And, to avoid it, we simply must remain open to even the most uncomfortable of conclusions. We cannot, reasonably or ethically, discourage discussion or research, or the honest tabling of alternative ideas, even if such ideas threaten to undermine our life's work, or career-long preoccupations. Integrity demands openness and honesty, regardless of the cost.

Integrity demands of us that we don't procrastinate in acting upon our evolving understandings. We need to have the courage to speak up, even when we are in the minority, even when the tide is moving against us, even when the cost of being honest is likely to be great. We need to be willing to be counter-cultural, whether that be with respect to our secularised surrounding cultures or within our own Christian cultures. We need to have the courage to speak out against the prosperity gospel with its compromised and seductive promise of health and wealth. We need to have courage to point out to our governments that their single-minded preoccupation with economic development is not delivering their citizens into a Promised Land flowing with milk and honey for all, but instead is widening the gap between the rich and the poor. It is despoiling the earth and leaving those seduced by its promises spiritually and even financially impoverished, as has been so courageously and insightfully articulated by Pope Francis in his encyclical on the environment - *Laudato Si* (Praise Be): On the Care of Our Common Home - made public in June 2015.

We need to act quickly to tend to wounds caused by centuries, in fact millennia, of loathing and violence directed at those whose gender doesn't fall neatly into the categories of male and female. We need to act quickly, because every day we procrastinate more of our sons and daughters, brothers and sisters are harming themselves and taking their lives, and rejecting the faiths which have treated them so callously.

Integrity demands that when we have done all the thinking and researching and listening and praying that is often needed to come to an informed mind on complex issues such as patriarchy or homosexuality, we act and act quickly. To not act is to be guilty of negligence, and our integrity is lost. Martin Luther King was once questioned about the wisdom of taking time to implement the teachings of Christ. In his Letter from Birmingham Jail, written in 1963, he wrote:

> [Time] is neutral; it can be used either destructively or constructively. More and more I feel that the people of ill will have used time much more effec-tively than have the people of good will. We will have to repent in this gener-ation not merely for the hateful words and actions of the bad people, but for the appalling silence of the good people. Human progress never rolls in on wheels of inevitability; it comes through the tireless efforts of men willing to be co-workers with God, and without this hard work, time itself becomes an ally of the forces of social stagnation.

My strong suspicion, often confirmed by quiet conversations with Christians in Sydney, is that many people are willing to rethink issues of patriarchy and homosexuality. They keep seeing the casualties of hard-line attitudes and behaviour. But fear prevents them from speaking up. They need, we need, a fearless faith, a faith that renounces fear, and embraces integrity and courage. We need, in fact, to be like Jesus, which is my second suggestion:

Be Christ-like

Jesus is our model of fearless faith. He certainly had faith, faith enough to entrust himself to his reliable Father, faith enough to be willing to confront prejudice and self-serving resistance to change. And he was all about change; radical change that threatened to splinter previous understandings and practices. He rattled the cages of virtually every sub-grouping of his society, especially the religiously and politically powerful.

His was a fearless faith, and because of that it was a faith that was willing to be unpopular. The Gospels of Matthew and Luke both contain an account of the temptations of Jesus. In Matthew, Jesus is first tempted by the devil to use his powers to meet his physical need for food, a superficially reasonable suggestion in the context. The devil then takes Jesus to the pinnacle of the temple, quoting Scripture to the effect that if he jumps off the pinnacle, in a very public and spectacular display of trust, God will command his angels to protect him from harm. And then finally, the devil tempts him with the offer of being given all the kingdoms of the earth; the promise of unlimited political power.

As I understand the temptations, which clearly continued throughout his public ministry, the devil was attempting to seduce Jesus by the lure of popularity and power. He was being tempted to use his powers to win at least superficial acceptance for his cause. How tempting to give people bread to win them over. How tempting to woo them with spectacular display, or to enforce compliance through the use of fearsome force? These were real temptations, especially when the demanding crowds began to surge around him, turning him into an instant sensation.

But what did Jesus do? He said no, and instead of succumbing to temptation, he confronted and scandalised, prodded and pushed, irritated and criticised – criticising especially those who may have supported him had he kept them onside. I've often noticed, as I have read the Gospels, that Jesus appeared to be most provocative precisely when he was in danger of becoming popular. He'd say things that resulted in people turning their backs on him and walking away in anger or bemusement. He did everything he could, it seems, to make his cause unpopular. He even told potential disciples that if they wanted to join his cause, they'd need to take up their cross and follow him, presumably to crucifixion and death. His was not the promise of health and wealth and upward mobility, but of suffering, death and downward mobility. His way was narrow, he said, and few would find it.

Looking at the state of contemporary Christianity, it seems he was right. The fact that we Christians worry about numbers, or judge the success of our movements by how many people we can persuade into our churches, is evidence that we ourselves have been seduced by the god of success, and that we have not succeeded, as Jesus did, in resisting the twin lures of popularity and power.

It may be that Christianity itself will need to walk a similar path of eschewing privilege, power and popularity, while simultaneously challenging the values that make these things attractive. This could mean that Christianity as we know it dies some form of death, that, in having this sort of integrity of heart, mind and action, it follows the path of Jesus all the way to its own death. Perhaps that is the only way for it to rise again to become the transformative and life-giving reality it was always meant to be.

Be content to live with uncertainty

A third suggestion about what Christians might do in the face of the alarming realities currently afflicting contemporary Christianity is that we learn to be content with uncertainty. The fact is: there is much we don't know. There are numerous things about which we are quite reasonably uncertain. We don't know for sure that even the most central of our Christian beliefs are true. There is reasonable doubt. We cannot know for sure that our pet theological systems, such as Calvinism or evangelicalism or liberalism or Catholicism are enlightening or misleading. Probably they are a mixture of both. And there is every good reason to think that our interpretations of individual Biblical passages are not the only valid interpretations. If we think they are, then we are almost certainly fooling ourselves.

To be anything other than humble is to be out of touch with reality; and if that out-of-touch-ness translates into ecclesiastical power and control, we end up with forms of Christianity that ought to die.

Richard Holloway in his stimulating and moving autobiography, *Leaving Alexandria: A memoir of faith and doubt*, 2012, includes a poem written by a friend of his, who he describes as the greatest Israeli poet of the twentieth century, Yehuda Amichai:

> From the place where we are right
> flowers will never grow
> in the spring.
>
> The place where we are right

is hard and trampled
like a yard.

But doubts and loves
dig up the world
like a mole, a plough.

And a whisper will be heard in the place
where the ruined
house once stood.[19]

Holloway describes himself as still tugged by the possibility of the transcendent, but in his words:

> But only whispers and tugs; nothing louder or more violent. Religion's insecurity makes it shout not whisper, strike with the fist in the face not tug gently with the fingers on the sleeve. Yet, beneath the shouting and the striking, the whisper can sometimes be heard. And from a great way off the tiny figure of Jesus can be seen on the shoreline, kindling a fire.

> I don't any longer *believe* in religion, but I want it around: weakened bruised and bemused, less sure of itself and purged of everything except pity.[20]

Holloway speaks for many of us who would like to see the emergence of a humbler Christianity. Humility is an attractive quality. Not only is it realistic, it also opens doors to deeper and more honest conversations with each other. When we unreasonably and arrogantly give the impression that our views, or our religion, or our particular take on our religion, is the only acceptable take, and that others simply have to fall into line with what we think, we alienate people, and understandably so. They ought to be alienated. This is not to say that we are not right in some of our views, even some of our more important views, but when we admit that even these beliefs are not all sewn up, when we are honestly up-front about our own unresolved struggles, we give permission to others to similarly be honest, even to join us on our still active quest of faith seeking understanding.

---

19   *The Selected Poetry of Yehuda Amichai,* translated by Chana Bloch and Stephen Mitchell, University of California Press, 1996, 34; quoted in Richard Holloway, *Leaving Alexandria: A memoir of faith and doubt,* Melbourne, The Text Publishing Company, 2012, 348.

20   *Leaving Alexandria,* 348, 349.

One of the things I have noticed over the years, in each of my five careers, as a high school teacher, a pastor, an academic, a chaplain and a parole officer, is how easy it is to talk with people about issues of faith and belief. I keep being surprised by how many people are willing to acknowledge a faith, even if at times it is no larger than a mustard seed. And the doorway to conversation is always opened wider when I admit that my faith is sometimes similarly-sized.

It is hard, I think, for many Christians to admit uncertainty when it comes to their relationship with God. They would like to be certain. Some believe they are certain. Some believe that any admission of uncertainty equates to a lack of faith. Others are likely to point to a verse at the beginning of Hebrews 11, a verse which introduces a long list of heroes of faith. Some English translations suggest we can be certain about our faith:

> To have faith is to be sure of the things we hope for, to be certain of the things we cannot see. *Good News Translation*

> Faith means being sure of the things we hope for and knowing that something is real even if we do not see it. *New Century Version*

> Now faith is being sure of what we hope for and certain of what we do not see. *New International Version*

These translations certainly give the impression that faith can be certain, but, in context, almost the opposite is implied. As F. F. Bruce notes in his commentary on Hebrews:

> In Old Testament times, he [that is, the writer of Hebrews] points out, there were many men and women who had nothing but the promises of God to rest upon, without any visible evidence that these promises would ever be fulfilled; yet so much did these promises mean to them that they regulated the whole of their lives in their light.[21]

Bruce, taking account of various interpretive possibilities, and bearing in mind the context, translates Hebrews 11:1 thus:

> Now faith is the assurance of things hoped for, a conviction of things not seen.

This lines up with a number of other English translations, including the following elaborated translation by *The Message*:

---

21   F. F. Bruce, *The Epistle to the Hebrews,* Grand Rapids: Wm. B. Eerdmans, 1964, 277.

248

The fundamental fact of existence is that this trust in God, this faith, is the firm foundation under everything that makes life worth living. It's our handle on what we can't see.

In other words, faith is akin to hope. It is believing in spite of a lack of firm evidence, in spite of not being able to see. It comes close to the great Danish philosopher, Søren Kierkegaard's understanding of faith. Kierkegaard's model of faith is the Old Testament patriarch Abraham. Although plagued by doubt and lacking proof that everything would work out, Abraham believed in God. He took the risk of faith, and it determined his life's journey.

A Uniting Church of Australia minister, Stephen Reid, once wrote an article telling the story of his pilgrimage within, and, in some senses, out of evangelicalism. In it, he helpfully differentiates between certainty and assurance:

Certainty is an expression of confidence in my own cognitive powers. Assurance is an expression of confidence in God. I have changed my mind enough times, and have forgotten so much of what I have ever learnt, that I have little confidence in my own brain. But I do have confidence in God. I am confident of the creative power that gives me life. I am confident of the grace that draws me into the presence of eternity. I am confident of being cradled in a mysterious spirit of compassion, and, cradled there, have a sense of being incorporated into God's loving purpose. If you ask me: Am I certain of these things, then I would say that I am not. But deep in my bones, I feel them as a reality, and though I have no certainty, I choose to live as though they are true.[22]

Reid is honestly expressing the uncertainty that lies at the heart of many people's faith. Like Kierkegaard and Abraham before him, Reid's faith exists and persists despite uncertainty, and maybe also because of uncertainty. That is why we call it faith. We don't know for sure. Sometimes we believe in spite of evidence that suggests we shouldn't.

Some would say that is irrational. They might reasonably ask, 'Isn't that the problem with fundamentalism? Fundamentalists keep on believing what they understand the Bible to be saying even when there is no independent evidence for these beliefs; and even when independent evidence suggests otherwise. Isn't that unreasonable?' That is a fair question.

---

22   Stephen Reid, 'Coming Home: An Intellectual Pilgrimage in Evangelicalism', unpublished article, 3.

As I have argued in this book, it isn't good to keep believing when evidence against one's beliefs is strong, or strong enough to suggest we should jettison those beliefs, or, at the very least, suspend belief. It is possible to become irrational and even immoral in one's believing. It is frighteningly easy to become culpably blind, when we self-servingly persist in beliefs that ought to be surrendered. But that, I think, is the point. The sorts of beliefs that Stephen Reid believes, but about which he isn't certain, are not in the category of beliefs we should jettison because there is no evidence for them or decisive evidence against them.

Belief in God, for example, has neither decisive evidence for nor against it. Perhaps that is why there is uncertainty at the heart of theism, but also of atheism. God, if God exists, appears hidden, out of sight. We might, at times, think we have caught sight of God, the vaguest of outlines of what appears to be a gardener quietly walking by in the cool of the evening. And so we believe, but no sooner do we see or sense this reality called God than we are again in doubt and wonder whether what we saw was simply the inanimate shadow cast by the trees of the garden; a garden whose existence has no ultimate rhyme or reason.

Faith exists in the sometimes scary and uncertain no-man's land that lies between the cut-and-dried certainties of ideologies on either side. What I find fascinating is how many people feel uncomfortable about staying in so uncertain a place. Theists who become atheists too often trade the certainty they once felt as theists for a similar and unwarranted certainty about their newly acquired atheism. But such overconfidence is neither warranted nor attractive. Atheists who become theists are less likely, I think, to be so overconfident.

Nevertheless, faith can flower even within an environment of uncertainty. Francis Spufford, an acclaimed British writer, describes his jettisoning of atheism in favour of theism in a wonderfully written little book with the large title, *Unapologetic: why, despite everything, Christianity can still make surprising emotional sense.*[23] Spufford is refreshingly honest in his acknowledgement that he does not know for sure pretty much everything he had earlier come to believe as a Christian, prior to becoming an atheist. He articulates what he does believe, or think, in the following terms:

---

23   London: Faber and Faber, 2012.

I think that the reason that reality ... is in some ultimate sense merciful, as well as being a set of physical processes all running along on their own without hope of appeal, all the way up from quantum mechanics to the relative velocity of galaxies by way of 'blundering, low and horribly cruel' biology (Darwin), is that the universe is sustained by a continual and infinitely patient act of love.[24]

As for any certainty about this belief, Spufford is honest:

That's what I *think* ... No I can't prove it. I don't know that any of it is true. I don't know if there's a God. (And neither do you, and neither does Professor Dawkins, and neither does anyone).[25]

But, as he goes on to point out, his belief or feeling that there is a source of meaning standing behind the observable and experienced universe is not invalid for being unprovable:

[Like] every human being, I am not in the habit of entertaining only the emotions I can prove. I'd be an unrecognizable oddity if I did. Emotions can certainly be misleading ... But emotions are also an indispensable tool for navigating, for feeling our way through the much larger domain of stuff that isn't susceptible to proof or disproof ... We dream, hope, wonder, sorrow, rage, grieve, delight, surmise, joke, detest; we form such unprovable conjectures as novels or clarinet concertos; we *imagine*. And religion is just a part of that, in one sense. It's just one form of imagining, absolutely functional, absolutely human-normal.[26]

And maybe that is why religions of all kinds continue to thrive; even those that appear to be based on conjecture or on unlikely sounding stories. Human beings employ stories to help them make sense of life, and to supply them with beliefs and values by which they can most successfully negotiate life. And that I think is one of the reasons why people sometimes switch sides, from theism to atheism, or from atheism to theism. A. N. Wilson, for example, a high profile atheist, switched twice during his life. In a *New Statesman* article dated 2 April 2009, he tells the story of his conversion to atheism about twenty years earlier. It was, for him, a Damascus Road experience, propelling him into a similar, but opposite-to-Paul evangelistic zeal for atheism, with ample encouragement from other high profile atheists

---

24   *Unapologetic*, 19, 20.

25   *Unapologetic*, 20, 21.

26   *Unapologetic*, 21.

including Richard Dawkins and Christopher Hitchens. But having been a 'doubting Thomas' for all of his life, Wilson began to doubt the unwarranted certainties of atheism, and by degrees returned to theism, his opinion being turned by observations about the apparent dignity of humankind, language, music, and morality:

> [The] existence of language is one of the many phenomena – of which love and music are the two strongest – which suggest that human beings are very much more than collections of meat. They convince me that we are spiritual beings, and that the religion of the incarnation, asserting that God made humanity in His image, and continually restores humanity in His image, is simply true. As a working blueprint for life, as a template against which to measure experience, it fits.[27]

Even Richard Dawkins admits to being religious according to a broad definition of that term. In his book, *The God Delusion*, he notes that it is possible to be religious without belief in the supernatural, while observing that 'a quasi-mystical response to nature and the universe is common among scientists and rationalists.'[28] He quotes with approval Einstein's thought on what religion meant to him:

> To sense that behind anything that can be experienced there is something that our mind cannot grasp and whose beauty and sublimity reaches us only indirectly and as a feeble reflection, this is religiousness. In this sense I am religious.[29]

This sense of something that lies behind is a powerful one, I think. It is exactly this sense that keeps drawing me to the Christ, which keeps me trustingly content within my lifelong Christian faith. The enigma of Jesus is the same as the enigma of nature. What is so patently obvious to all about Jesus is his humanity. Christian theology has always insisted on the full humanity of Jesus. The fully human Jesus comes to us fully clothed in the thoroughly human Scriptures. We don't doubt his humanity, nor the humanity of the Scriptures, but we also sense (that word again), we sense that in Jesus, in some profound sense, a sublime beauty from behind everything has materialised to draw us beyond our lesser selves towards a

---

27   'Why I believe again' *New Statesman*, 2 April 2009.

28   Richard Dawkins, *The God Delusion*, London: Bantam, 2006, 11.

29   *The God Delusion*, 21.

way of being which will have us sharing in that beauty, as we find our true selves in God.

None of this we know for sure. This might just be wishful thinking. But I am living my life as if it were true. It makes good sense to me. And I don't know anyone more worthy of imitation than Jesus. I don't know anyone more able to inspire people and nations and religions along the path to a better world than Jesus, described in our tradition as the Prince of Peace.

Let nothing disturb you.
Let nothing frighten you.
All things pass. God does not change.

Christ has no body now on earth but yours;
No hands but yours; no feet but yours.
Yours are the eyes through which the compassion of Christ
must look out on the world.

Yours are the feet with which he is to go about doing good.
Yours are the hands with which he is to bless his people.

Teresa of Ávila

On that day, when evening had come, Jesus said to them, 'Let us go across to the other side.' And leaving the crowd behind, they took him with them in the boat, just as he was. Other boats were with him. A great windstorm arose, and the waves beat into the boat, so that the boat was already being swamped. But he was in the stern, asleep on the cushion; and they woke him up and said to him, 'Teacher, do you not care that we are perishing?' He woke up and rebuked the wind, and said to the sea, 'Peace! Be still!' Then the wind ceased, and there was a dead calm. He said to them, 'Why are you afraid? Have you still no faith?' And they were filled with great awe and said to one another, 'Who then is this, that even the wind and the sea obey him?'

Mark 4:35-41

Acknowledgements

The bringing to birth of a book like this involves a life-time of learning, reaching back into childhood, with all of those foundational influences. I am profoundly indebted to my father, the ever-restless questioner, and to my mother, who exemplified the gentle art of listening. Their influence, and therefore contribution to this book, is huge, but even more influential, certainly in the long process of editing and getting the book ready for publishing, has been the perceptive and ever generous influence of my wife, Judy.

I am also hugely grateful to the following people who have read, critiqued and edited the evolving manuscript of *Faith Without Fear*: Jan McIntyre, Derek Brookes, Ruth McCall, Dave Smith, Robert Lincoln, Natalie Cooper, Vic Branson and Lindsay Stoddart. A big thank you also to the members of our Wednesday night Bible Study group who read through an early form of the manuscript, and whose many comments and suggestions were invaluable.

Finally, I am immensely grateful to the father and mother and son whose stories are told within the pages of this book, bringing powerful, poignant and personal reality to the issues discussed within it.

Index